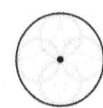

Quest for Presence: Experience and Praise

I have just finished reading *Quest for Presence: Book 4—The Trajectories* and found it to be both substantively and stylistically brilliant. Dr. Bennett clearly has been engaged in process philosophy in addition to wellness seminars and writings. Seldom have I seen such a scientifically sound and philosophically coherent book that is so clearly and engagingly written, with so many useful, practical exercises to guide readers to enhance their daily planning to increase time awareness and enrich meaning in their lives. Bravo!

—Raymond C. Hawkins II, Ph.D., ABPP (Clinical Psychology), Associate Faculty, Clinical Psychology, Fielding Graduate University

As a fellow traveler in the integration of consciousness and spiritual intelligence, I have witnessed firsthand—Dr. Joel Bennett's *Quest for Presence: Book 4—The Trajectories*. Building upon the wisdom of Books 1 through 3, this volume deepens the sacred journey toward conscious living with clarity and grace. Dr. Bennett's work is a tapestry of science, soul, and spiritual presence—an offering that speaks to the healer, seeker, and leader within us all. His commitment to integrating presence, purpose, and transformation resonates deeply with my own work in whole-person care for emotional and spiritual intelligence. This book is a luminous guide for those walking the path of awakening to their soul's purpose.

—Keyaunoosh Kassauei M.D., Founder/Leader My Conscious Coaching Group a 501C3 coaching nonprofit (http://www.myconscious.org)

Quest for Presence: Book 4—The Trajectories is a luminous invitation to explore the unfolding rhythms of your life. With poetic clarity and scholarly depth, Dr. Joel Bennett weaves together spiritual wisdom, neuroscience, philosophy, and contemplative practice to help readers reimagine time as a living force—one that pulses with Rhythm, Transition, Interruption, and Transcendence. Rather than offering yet another take on time management, this book asks a deeper question: **How do we make life meaningful—especially in the fleeting and fragile moments of transition?** Bennett shows how we are not passive recipients of time's passing, but active participants in the dance between the temporal and the eternal. Whether you are a coach, therapist, pastor, or simply a seeker, this book is a companion for making sense of time—its fleetingness, its fullness, and its quiet call to live meaningfully

—Etta Hornsteiner, Board-Certified Health & Wellness Coach-Practitioner; Creator of Time ReDesign and Seven Thresholds to Transformational Living

In a world pulling us in a million directions, Joel Bennett's latest book on the 'Trajectories' from his Quest for Presence collection is a revelation. I often felt my life was self-imposed chaos, without truly understanding why. This book offered unprecedented clarity, providing a genuinely unique and actionable map—not just abstract ideas—to navigate the whirlwind. Concepts like Transcendence, Rhythm, and Timing are not just theories; they are practical keys that have fundamentally shifted how I view my day and my relationship with time. This is not another self-help book; it is a profoundly real guide for embracing a more intentional, present, and fulfilling life.

—Dila Dzhuraeva, MBA, Customer Success Leader

The QUEST FOR PRESENCE collection (including *Book 4, The Trajectories*) contains many new, deep, and dense topics that are difficult to grasp. While I wrestle with the writing, I often find many revealing nuggets that tie into other vital ideas, guiding me in my life. There is always something to chew on. For example, in this book, Bennett writes "One of the greatest ironies of our modern society is that our obsession with the present (all that matters is now) ultimately leads us to have less presence." Well...that pretty much hits the mark for me and—as with other books—often synchronistically connects with other spiritual readings I find valuable at the time. Many of us are obsessed with the present and don't take the time to notice the synchronicities that adorn our lives. If you can take a moment to browse through Quest for Presence, it might loosen your obsession, if only for a fleeting moment.

—Art Wimberly, aspiring anam cara

People crave a deeper rhythm and connection in their lives. *Quest for Presence: Book 4—The Trajectories* offers that rhythm. Reading helped us slow down long enough to hear ourselves again. Many of our clients, colleagues, and friends, live on the edge of overwhelm, feeling incongruent in the world. The Trajectories offers a language for a way through that does not involve abandoning who we are or escaping our lives. It brought to our awareness again the small, quiet knowing we've all learned to ignore in a culture that values speed over depth. What we appreciate most is that this book does not just talk about presence or mindfulness, it offers that experience while you are reading. The journey of the meandering Pooh and the wise Owl brought a level of connection and emotion often not found in works about presence.

—Theresa Hubbard and Walker Bird, My Inner Knowing Podcast

In *Quest for Presence: Book 4—The Trajectories,* Joel Bennett has cracked open the inner workings of the universe and laid it bare for all to study and experience! Deeply layered, amazingly creative, and always immediately helpful and profound throughout. Bennett has deconstructed time and its use and misuse in a more complete way than anything I have ever seen. He will guide you with the most heart- and mind-opening insights to the most practical applications. It is more than a book, it's a path to carry throughout your life and help you elevate whatever you are facing today.

—Jonathan Ellerby, PhD, Bestselling author of
The Seven Gateways of Spiritual Experience

Quest for Presence

BOOK 4

THE TRAJECTORIES

Joel B. Bennett, PhD
Foreword by Robert Cummings Neville

ORGANIZATIONAL WELLNESS AND LEARNING SYSTEMS

QUEST FOR PRESENCE MANDALA

The Radiant Forces

Form — Chaos — Nurturing Conditions — Time Shaping

The Soulful Capacities

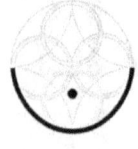 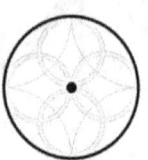  

Acceptance — Presence — Flow — Synchronicity

The Attractions

Crafting — Potentiating — Discerning — Centering — Synthesizing — Coordinating — Intending — Catalyzing — Opening

The Trajectories

Transcendence — Interruption
Rhythm — Pacing
Timing — Routine
Transition — Scheduling

The Treasures

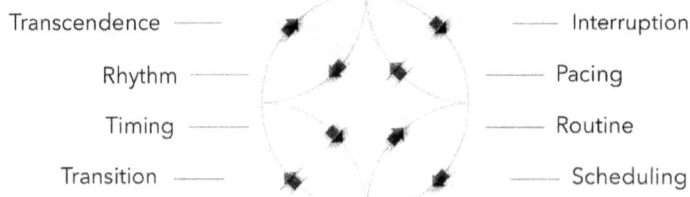

Start here and flow clockwise

← Spontaneity → Momentousness → Fulfillment → Clutch →
Optimism → Effortlessness → Ordinariness → Coherence →
Adoration → Resonance → Patience → Preciousness →
Savoring → Poignance → Release → Awe → Spontaneity →

Published by
Organizational Wellness and Learning Systems
FLOWER MOUND, TX

© 2025 by Joel B. Bennett, PhD

ISBN: 978-0-9915102-9-0 (Paperback) • 979-8-9899095-3-7 (hardback) 979-8-9899095-4-4(Ebook)

All Rights Reserved. No part of this book may be reproduced or transmitted in any form or by any means, electronic or mechanical, including photocopying, or by any information storage and retrieval system, except for the purpose of brief excerpts for articles, books, or reviews, without the written permission of the author.

This book is not intended as medical or psychological advice. Please consult with a licensed professional if you have questions or concerns. This book represents my own opinions.

Scripture quotations marked (NIV) are taken from the Holy Bible, New International Version®, NIV®. Copyright © 1973, 1978, 1984, 2011 by Biblica, Inc.™ Used by permission of Zondervan. All rights reserved worldwide. www.zondervan.com. The "NIV" and "New International Version" are trademarks registered in the United States Patent and Trademark Office by Biblica, Inc.™

Quotation from Geneva Bible accessed from https://www.biblegateway.com.

Unless noted, other quotations were found from the "Spirituality and Practice" website (https://www.spiritualityandpractice.com), "Spirituality & Health" magazine, or from quotations resources on the internet, including "The Quotations Page," "Brainy Quote," or "Good Reads."

Editing by Candace Johnson, Change It Up Editing, Inc.; Mary Anne Shepard; and Sue Hansen, Duck Sauce Life, Inc.

Cover and interior by Gary A. Rosenberg

Diagrams and pictures by author; images by Jeffrey McQuirk

The intrinsic quantum indeterminacy of things produces a blurring... which ensures that the unpredictability of the world is maintained, even if it were possible to measure everything that is measurable.

Both the sources of blurring—quantum indeterminacy, and the fact that physical systems are composed of zillions of molecules—are at the heart of time. Temporality is profoundly linked to blurring... The time of physics is, ultimately, the expression of our ignorance of the world.
TIME IS IGNORANCE. (p. 148)

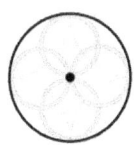

What causes us to suffer is not in the past or the future: it is here, now, in our memory, in our expectations. We long for timelessness, we endure the passing of time: we suffer time.
TIME IS SUFFERING. (p. 190)

~CARLO ROVELLI, ITALIAN THEORETICAL PHYSICIST,
FROM THE ORDER OF TIME (L'ORDINE DEL TEMPO)
(2018, PENGUIN BOOKS)

Note: Quotations above are from original source but formatting is changed for emphasis.

Quest for Presence Collection

The Connoisseur of Time: An Invitation to Presence

BOOK 1. *The Map and Radiant Forces*

BOOK 2. *The Soulful Capacities*

BOOK 3. *The Attractions*

BOOK 4. *The Trajectories*

BOOK 5. *The Treasures and Destiny*

Quest for Presence: Contemplations Workbook

So that we may meet:
Through this blur
That again is what was when
We were now
Here.

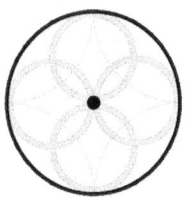

Contents

Foreword	xv
Preface for Book 4	xix
Author Note	xxxiii
Introduction to All Books	1
Introduction to Book 4: *The Trajectories*	3

PART ONE. Wise Old Owl and Pooh

Chapter 1. Your Day and This Happening Life	11
Contemplation (QfP 4-1): The Trajectories	15
Chapter 2. Contemplating the Eight Trajectories	19

PART TWO. The Trajectories—Pallet, Picture, Poem, Portrait

Chapter 3. Contemplating Routine	33
Contemplation (QfP 4-2): Routine	44
Chapter 4. Contemplating Timing	47
Contemplation (QfP 4-3): Timing	65
Chapter 5. Contemplating Rhythm	69
Contemplation (QfP 4-4): Rhythm (Entrainment, Being Synchronized)	80

Chapter 6. Contemplating Transition	83
Contemplation (QfP 4-5): Transition	*97*
Chapter 7. Contemplating Transcendence (Timelessness, Time Transcendence)	99
Contemplation (QfP 4-6): Time Transcendence (Timelessness)	*110*
Chapter 8. Contemplating Scheduling	113
Contemplation (QfP 4-7): Scheduling	*125*
Chapter 9. Contemplating Pacing	129
Contemplation (QfP 4-8): Pacing	*140*
Chapter 10. Contemplating Interruption	143
Contemplation (QfP 4-9): Interruption	*154*
Chapter 11. Dynamics and Origins of the Trajectories	157
Contemplation (QfP 4-10): The Mandala of the Trajectories, A Guided Visualization	*172*
Appendix 1. Day Crafting Tool (Embracing the Trajectories)	175
Appendix 2. Day Crafting Tool (Sample Profiles)	179
Key Terms	199
Bibliographic References for the Essays	203
Research Notes	221
Acknowledgments	239
About the Author	245

Foreword

There can be many visions of eternity, depending on the things that make connections. An object of experience can be grasped in different ways, interpreted with different categories, and related to different things. Our views of eternity all focus on certain aspects, and these aspects can overlap or be so diverse that it is unclear whether they are about the same object. Joel Bennett and I have different, yet overlapping, visions of eternity.

My own is metaphysical. That is, I am an academic thinker who looks for principles of ultimacy, of which eternity is one. For me, whatever is ultimate must cause or give rise to all the things that are in time. Thus, to be truly ultimate, the ultimate cannot itself be in time. The ultimate, in fact, causes all temporal things, and that also includes time's flow. Therefore, the ultimate is eternal, that is, non-temporal. It is as close to the future and past as it is to the present. These three modes of time are all equally real. The flow of time is a dynamic transition from future to present to past.

The present is a dynamic change, but so are the structures of the future and additions to the past. In one sense, the present is contingent on the past and future, but this is a temporal contingency. From the metaphysical view, the whole array of changes is contingent on the ultimate. Everything that is determinate, having a specific terminal point, is future through many changes, has a present moment when it becomes fully actual, and then becomes a past reality that does not change but does have different results as present time moves on.

The metaphysical question then is how the ultimate can be together with all things in time, through all times, and through all time's changes. All the temporal answers to this question need to be rejected. The ultimate cannot be a first mover, as Thomas Aquinas thought. It cannot be a future attractor as Aristotle and Plato seem at times to have thought. It cannot be a supervenient present in which a God perceives all things in all times at once, for this denies the reality of the past and future; this is the most common way we conceive of God. So, I say that the ultimate relates to all things eternally. Eternality is part of the relation of the ultimate to the things it creates.

This metaphysics is pretty heady stuff, not for everyone. Joel Bennett approaches eternity more directly, through how it registers or manifests in human experience. Instead of asking, as I do, how the ultimate relates to all things, he asks how eternity shows up in our thoughts, feelings, behaviors, and the times we spend alone and with others. He does not fudge on the true nature of eternity. He rejects all the temporalizations of eternity. Instead, he marks out how eternity appears in our personal experience. He is a true psychologist in the transpersonal sense. I am excited to write a foreword to this book that expands on this transpersonal research.

I said at the beginning that there are different approaches to eternity, and I contrasted Joel's psychological approach to my metaphysical one. As a psychologist, he integrates different disciplines to discover and guide us on how experienced moments of time testify to something more than temporality. As a metaphysician, I track eternity through the problem of the search for the ultimate. What other integrative approaches are there? One major approach is sociological, both in practice and in theory. Peter Berger, a sociologist, wrote *A Far Glory: The Quest for Faith in an Age of Credulity* (1992), marking out many of the ways eternity shows up in societies. Robert Bellah's *Religion in Human Evolution: From the Paleolithic to the Axial Age* (2011), combines cognitive and evolutionary approaches to a history of religion and our experience of transcendence.

All of these and many more are legitimate approaches to eternity. Bellah, Berger, and Bennett all write with an ear open to eternity in other extant fields. They may represent wider to narrower apertures, from the evolutionary to the societal and the personal. I suppose it would be helpful to propose an integration into a single work. But perhaps current or further integration would be premature: Who knows what other approaches might be found?

For now, it is right and appropriate for me, from one approach, to write a Foreword for Bennett's *Trajectories* from a different field. Bennett's book is a vignette for appreciating the ways eternity shows up in the moments of our lived time, particularly in the blur of our modern day-to-day lives.

—Robert Cummings Neville

Preface for Book 4

Between the darkness of the womb and that of the tomb, our life arcs through the light, and we exercise our mysterious capacity to shape, define, and enact ourselves, as beings both inside and outside of time. (Raymond Tallis, *Of Time and Lamentation*, p.617)

Today is *the* day, *a* day, and *yet another* day. It can be all three: momentous, a tick mark on our calendar, and also rote or ordinary. How we craft the arc of our day need not be so mysterious. It depends on a different and deeper type of time "management"; it depends upon the interplay between creative cosmic forces that birthed this day, our personal presence, and the ability to discern our destiny.* These cosmic forces create multiple and noticeable trajectories of energy every day of our lives. We can, each of us, find and create amazing opportunities within the flow and fleeting nature of time.

Yet, we may only fully discover the gift of this day when our future self reflects on our whole-time here. We see the paths we have traveled through the larger arc of our life journey. We then receive insight, notice how events unfolded, and grasp the context—where today situates—within the past-to-future transition point that is now our life. Today is: momentous because it is a culmination that shapes a future and important decision; a calendar reminder because of past

---

* These three aspects are developed in depth in previous books in this collection. Cosmic forces that birthed this day (Book 1), our presence (Book 2), and the ability to discern our destiny (Book 3).

scheduling; or simply ordinary, as we relax into the fleeting presence of morning light.

The three temporal modes (our experience of "tensed" time)—the past, the present, and the future—continuously influence each other and infuse meaning into our day and our life. Their togetherness is an eternal dance, which we experience as flow. Throughout the history of religion, the temporal is always contained within and infused with the eternal. In *Eternity and Time's Flow* (1993), Robert Neville reviews three religious and metaphoric visions of how time and eternity interact.

In India, Brahman, the underlying consciousness and eternal source of all things, intertwines with Shiva, the dancer responsible for temporality: the creation, destruction, transformation, and the cyclical nature of the cosmos. In China, the Tao (the great watercourse way) that cannot be named is the mother of the Tao that can be named. The unnamed Tao is eternal; the named Tao is temporal. Neville writes that "the symbol in the West for time within eternity is life" and develops the idea of the "divine life" where persons know a responsive God as the "great living eternal creator within which 'we live and move and have our being' (Acts 17:28)." (Neville, 1983, p. 180).

This interplay between eternity and temporality is also found in Native American traditions. For example, Navajo culture acknowledges a linear, worldly time where humans live (the Third World), and they believe all beings also exist in eternity (the Fourth World). The universal, cross-cultural distinction between the temporal world (past, present, future) and the foreverness of eternity speaks to humanity's multilevel awareness of time. However, in the modern world, with an overemphasis on consumerism, technology, and clock-time, many cultures are now obsessed only with the present moment.

> As soon as a society's economy appears to guarantee by routine a modicum of luxury, and the desperate future orientation of the "work ethic" is relaxed, its people become the "now generation." ... Yet modern society turns on consumerism ... A significant part

of being human in modern culture is the right, even the obligation, to feel good in the present. There is a truth to this: self-reflexive pleasure, pleasure at feeling pleasure, is a good. But the price of the present pleasure includes making good on real connections with past and future, and these a consumer society neglects almost pathologically. (Neville, 1993, pp. 26–27)*

One of the greatest ironies of our modern society is that our obsession with the present (all that matters is now) ultimately leads us to have less presence. We are distracted (fragmented) so much that we miss the happening (wholeness) of our life, from the momentous to the ordinary.

This book is about the temporal and the eternal or how we might, by appreciating the whole-time of our life here, see it in the context of eternity. I provide a language to help us view our daily life as an unfolding dance of the past, present, and future—all together in mutual affinity. By doing so, we can still have the good of pleasure—enjoying the treasures and grace of life—while also embracing the past and the future. In this way, we may capture or at least glimpse more of the Eternal, witness Shiva, follow the Tao, enter the divine life, and witness the eternal in *the* day, *a* day, or *yet another* day.

The Dance of Past, Present, and Future

There are at least three ways to view the interplay of the temporal modes. The first is our psychological or cognitive orientation toward

---

* From Neville, R. (1993). *Eternity and Time's Flow.* State University of New York (Albany). Neville's book is a reminder of how any deep study of time and temporality must consider all three temporal modes—past, present, and future—as not only a contrast with but as part of eternity. We are not spending this life "passing through time" to find the eternal (transcendence), but rather this life includes the eternal within it (immanence). Time exists within things, including us. Time has a primitive, innate, ontological status. It simply exists in and of itself. And we exist with it. This book, a delineation of the Trajectories, is an attempt to help us come back to a sense of the eternal (unfolding cosmic Radiant Forces) as it works its way into our very being in this, our daily life.

time. Research on *psychological time perspective* shows that individuals vary in how much weight they give to the past, present, and future. (This is noted in Chapter 8, "Contemplating Scheduling".) Alternatively, we can have a deep sense of the past and the future, one more transcendental than merely cognitive. Our imagination and our faith can bring a sense of mystery, awe, and even a "closeness to God." (This is noted in Chapter 7, "Contemplating Transcendence".)

The third way, to be fully developed here, includes and integrates these two views within a dynamic framework of our experience of daily well-being. This framework looks more carefully at the shifting, even playful, roles of past, present, and future, and is intended to guide our appreciation of the fact that the day is a gift from eternity. It includes the momentous, the date, and the ordinary as well as the schedule, the transcendent, and more. Sometimes the present takes center stage in the dance. More often, the three actively take turns.

With this idea of turn-taking, and in what follows, it may seem that each of the temporal modes is endowed with its own character, intelligence, and intentionality. In fact, in ancient Indian Vedic philosophy, time is a creative force endowed with such qualities. You are invited to consider this view as an alternative to the clock-world of a consumer-driven, mechanical, technological society. We will return to the idea of force, or cosmic force, later. For this introduction, consider the three modes through the metaphoric lens of the dance. Imagine that they move along an arc or Trajectory—across the stage that is our day.

The Eight Trajectories

Imagine that the three line up to dance. As a preview, eight different dances will unfold. We watch as our attention is drawn to one or more of the three for different moments and durations. Recall from above in the first paragraph the sentence that notes *finding*, *flow*, and *fleeting*: "It is all about what we find in the flow and fleeting nature of time." By *finding*, certain temporal modes become more noticeable or salient. By *flow*, we appreciate their wholeness: how all three depend on each other in a seamless orchestration. By *fleeting*, we sense how their configuration continually coalesces, dissipates, and somehow reorganizes like clouds in the sky or swirls in a stream.

Let's return to the stage and watch as eight scenes unfold. In the first scene, titled "Routine," the present steps forward to honor the past while the future steps into the background. Here we have the (past) recurring *Routine*: comfort, familiarity, habit, and tradition. Routines are often inherited from past social and cultural structures. They may also be sparked or catalyzed by *Scheduling*, wherein the three players shift. On to Scene 2. With scheduling, the present pays more attention to potential events in the future than those of the past, if only for the moment to prioritize one future place or event over another. These two—Routine and Scheduling—rarely function separately for any length of time. When we get stuck (the present does not budge), we reschedule. When our schedules overwhelm (the future overloads us), we find routine. This is the first example of how the past and future take turns in yielding to or working with the present. Other scenes follow.

But the present also honors, or rather brings together, the past and future with equal attention. This manifests as *Transition*: we recognize that the past is receding and the future is about to move in. There is, with the present swaying in the center, a dual sense: on one side, of probability and opportunity for the future, and on the other, an impermanence and letting go of the past. Unlike with Routine and Scheduling, the present is not squarely center stage; Transition requires that all three temporal modes work together. The present wobbles both ways as only a changing link point. However, as all life is in transition, the present sometimes jumps into the center and, with a certain suddenness, marries the past and future. *Timing* then becomes everything.

Timing is perhaps the most compelling type of the three-modal dance. It is all about *when* and the instantaneous action, taken in the present, to select among any number of options—to begin, to end, to delay, to resume, to speak, to be silent, to strike, to hold back. Surely, the present takes center stage, but only with a sensitive eye to the future potential. We could not say "the time is now" without more than just an awareness of the antecedents or the upcoming events. It is our knowledge of the past and foreknowledge of the future that gives the present its timeliness. The Greeks called this *kairos*.

Timing, the simultaneous honoring of past and future, stands in direct contrast to *Interruption*, where the present dominates to push the past and future aside. Interruption is the embodiment of chaos and shows the discontinuity, randomness, and uncertainty of the temporal world. Perfect timing for one can be a stark interruption for another. Imagine the predator catching its prey in that single moment of clasp, neither too soon nor too late. Just so, as Timing is the most compelling of the dances, Interruption is, almost by definition, the most disturbing. The heartless present cares nothing for the past or the future. At least for the time being.

It is important to understand that these dances can change in an instant. Someone or something interrupts us and, within moments, we resume our routine; the intrusion was a minor hassle. Alternately, the interruption may be a reminder from our smartphone scheduler. We almost forgot to call someone who was only available at a very specific time. More generally, the corrective dance to interruption lies in *Pacing*, where present, past, and future play an equal role in a move toward the future. With Pacing, we typically mitigate the negative effects of Interruption. It is as though the past and future tell the present, "Hold on, not too fast," and find a way to recalibrate afterward.

Pacing is regulatory, homeostatic, and circulatory. The system knows when to speed up or slow down, when to start or end the cycle at key points in time; that is, the present attends to the duration or frequency of what came before so that a similar duration or frequency will come next. Too hectic a pace leads to exhaustion. Too slow a pace results in lethargy. Again, past, present, and future fall into line.

The dynamic framework of the three temporal modes flows; it is not a closed, mechanical system. We are not robots that simply carry out routines, self-correct when interrupted, and then use timing mechanisms to pace ourselves through recalibrating our schedules. We are alive. We are part of nature. Other living systems also participate in the dance. Again, we are not machines. We learn, grow, and must enter into a society teeming with others. We can also enter, echoing Neville's assessment of Western religion, into the "divine life" with the eternal.

Our ability to communicate and coordinate with others depends upon the mutual entrainment of rhythms. Sometimes we coordinate well, sometimes not. But, as an open system, we continuously receive feedback on the matching of rhythms and can align or self-correct, synchronize, syncopate, and find some cadence to life. This is *Rhythm Entrainment*. Here, the past, present, and future find a tempo where each step forward and back at particular times in a sort of pas de trois. Rhythm Entrainment, the most enlivening or vitalizing of all three mode configurations, reminds us of the immense power of biological time as an awakening force.

Finally, there comes a point where all three players take a rest or merge into each other or simply disappear. This is the experience of timelessness or time *Transcendence*, which is as integral to the dance as the previous configurations and can happen at any instant. Eternity becomes real. "By virtue of the eternal dimension of temporal life, persons individually and collectively, as part of nature, participate in the eternal divine life ... which means redeeming the time" (Neville, 1993, p. 223). This redemption does not only show up as a "religious or spiritual" experience. Much of the research on the "flow state" shows that, while not particularly common, people experience the dissipation and even cessation of time when deeply absorbed in a hobby, a sport, or a passionate endeavor.

Flow, Transience, and Salience

This book is about time's flow, transience, and salience—and these within and across the eight Trajectories: Routine, Scheduling, Transition, Timing, Interruption, Pacing, Rhythm Entrainment, and time Transcendence. By flow, I mean both (1) how the past flows into the present and from the present into the future; and (2) how there is flow across the Trajectories (over the day, the week, and so on). For example, Scheduling may flow into Transition (we anticipate coming home to tidy up before dinner) and Interruption may flow into Routine (given all the distractions we seclude ourselves from so we can focus). These shifts can occur within a day or across days of the week.

Time's transience refers to its fleeting nature: how we experience time as it winks in and out of existence. Our experience of transience may be a hallmark, if not the center of, human consciousness. Machines cannot experience time as fleeting no matter how much computer programming or mathematical formulae can measure, predict, or solve problems of time. The three temporal modes have not been randomly thrown together into some conglomerated block that is just hanging in the void and nothingness of existentialism. They are also not reducible mathematical abstractions—$time^x$, $time^{x+1}$, $time^{x+2}$, $time^{x+\ldots n}$. These notations cannot capture our experience of transience.

In *Of Time and Lamentation: Reflections on Transience* (2017), Raymond Tallis eloquently argues that our human experience of time cannot be reduced to the parameters of natural science.

> Only when we rescue time from its reduced state as a parameter, a physical dimension, from being merely the successive values of a variable referenced to an axis in a coordinate system, and return it to our lives—to the place of terror, of hope, of ordinary forgetful or mindful busyness, of anticipation, joy, of ordinary days—can it be seen for what it is. (Tallis, p. 335)

To rescue time from the clock prison requires seeing, noticing, attending, or witnessing the event in the flow of time. Salience is inherent in our awareness of time.

> In the philosophy of mind, "salience" is often used to describe the way in which a thing (object, state, property, process); t

"stands-" or "jumps-out" to an agent. Salience is routinely described in comparative terms; t is considered salient relative to other things, themselves backgrounded. (PhilPapers; https://philpapers.org/browse/salience)

The present is not the only salient mode. As described in the previous section, the past and future take their turns. It is our human awareness, our presence then—our ability to attend to the moment of unfolding—that brings flow, transience, and salience together. This togetherness is the purpose of the entire Quest for Presence collection and the many exercises and contemplations within. Beginning with *The Connoisseur of Time*, where the reader is asked to contemplate seven readings—from atheism, the New and Old Testaments, Buddhism, Islam, and others—I encourage us to quest into this togetherness.

"Day Crafting," the primary tool offered in this book, offers another method for cultivating Presence. While one can simply start using that tool (located in Appendix 1), day crafting is optimized if used after reading the chapters on the Trajectories. It is best to use a tool when its "use contexts" have been studied beforehand. We want the surgeon to know more than just about the scalpel. Time is not just a slice, as the quantum physicists often indicate. This parallels the idea of rescuing time from reductionist science that focuses on only the now of the material, sensate world. Our human experience of time extends bidirectionally from the now; it is crafted from our memory, our anticipations, and the meaning these give to the present. Both Neville and Tallis refer to the "thickness" or "fatness" of time.

For Tallis, time has its roots in human consciousness that lies beyond, and includes, the present as well as continuity and public discourse. "The very fact that that which fattens 'now'—except for its immediate surrounds—are not experiences but memories and anticipations, and their proxies in our discourse, reaches to the heart of the human present tense"(p. 299). For Neville, time's thickness is tied together with personal identity or that which offers the continuity and *ongoing-ness* that we experience: "It is essential to a person, being temporally thick, that past and future be involved in the present" (p. 48).

Neville describes three levels of personal temporal thickness: like Tallis, the present gets its meaning from memory (past) and anticipations (future); but, also, the past and future have their own reality; and one's personal identity occurs in eternity: through a developing sense of moral responsibility our actions now have consequences that extend beyond our own life.

> Within eternity, the person is never only at a present moment, never only faced with a future, never only a finished story but eternally all three. Within eternity, the person is responsible as an innocent, responsible as a chooser, and responsible as a finished life … Without the fullness of our time, we are incomplete as temporal beings, and our eternal identity is only as temporal beings. (Neville, pp. 188–189)

It is, then, our responsibility to discern the meaning of this whole project of our happening life. The importance of discernment was introduced in Book 1 of QfP (Chapter 10), and it requires both attention and intention. Quest is a verb; we move into the adventure of what is unfolding. We must make the effort. We pierce the veil of the illusory temporal world. Most of Book 3 is devoted to discerning our own destiny—how our personality and soul interact to draw us toward the future unfolding of our own personhood.

> The discernment of one's destiny is perhaps the most important preparatory part of education. It cannot begin too soon; but for most of us the question is raised only relatively late in life … Destiny is the occasion or path to which our life can be given and that gives that life its central meaning … Whereas pursuit of a happy life and career is a secular cosmological way of viewing our circumstance, finding our destiny and giving ourselves over to that is the religious way. (Neville, pp. 215–216)

Cosmic Forces: The Playful Device of Pooh and the Owl

What exactly is *it* that we are discerning? What are the index happenings that become differentially salient in our lives? Each day of our lives can serve as a practice event for our destiny, where we can answer these questions. From the religious view, we answer by discerning God, God's Plan or Will (Hukum), the dance of Shiva, what Allah wishes, the Great Spirit (Wakan Tanka), our karma (Prarabdha), Brahman, the unnamable Tao, the Navajo Fourth World. From the secular view, many possible names emerge. As with religion, why propose only one? Modern philosophers and scientists use such terms as "patterns of connection," "whole systems," "the interconnectedness of all things," "the holographic universe," "the quantum field of consciousness," and the list goes on.

In Quest for Presence, I propose that whatever we call it—both theistic and nontheistic—there is overwhelming evidence that points to cosmic forces that manifest as what happens in our material world. Previous QfP books name and describe these forces in depth: Chaos (randomness, entropy; *things fall apart*), Form (gravity, relative coherence; *things come together*), Time Shaping (intentionality; causality; cause-and-effect; *we make things happen*), and Nurturing Conditions (becoming; co-origination; background conditions that afford emergence; *conditions allow things to happen*).

Every day, "things" (the people, places, and events of our lives) fall apart, come together; they happen because of our efforts and happen because conditions are right. I believe that we can actively discern these forces at work in our lives. However, we often are unaware because our culture overemphasizes the "now" and our current state of satisfaction and well-being: consuming the present of clock-time, one that technology continually carves up into finer and finer segments.

Some research in modern psychology makes the distinction between subjective well-being and ontological well-being.* Subjective

---

* A significant body of research suggests that having a balanced time-perspective (BTP) is associated with greater well-being. BTP refers to the adaptive ability

refers to our own personal and inner experience. For example, "Today, I feel happy in general." Ontology refers to the nature and very existence of our being. For example, "When I look at the ongoing part of my life project, I feel fulfilled." These two types of well-being certainly overlap and influence each other. We have good days, bad days, and everything in between. It is from the whole-time, life project perspective that we may not only glimpse the working of cosmic forces but also, often gradually, gain insight into how they continually shape our past, present, and future. The eternal within the temporal and the temporal within the eternal.

In Book 4, I use the story of Pooh Bear and the Wise Owl to represent how we might discern these forces. Pooh meanders within the day while the Owl observes across the day and longer. It would be a mistake to think that only Owl has discernment. As you read their story, Pooh *truly lives into* the discernment, while Owl creates the conversation, the space. Discernment may come from observation but, in a more intimate way, from living within and sharing life.

We feel that life does not only happen to us but that we are inextricably woven into all the change that surrounds us. We are always changing too. We cannot separate time as something only outside us. So, it is time to quest. Pause. Listen. Contemplate the flow of energy—the Trajectories—across the day and from day to day. As you do, the mystery of time will become increasingly fascinating. You will more fully feel the vibrancy of the exquisite set of changes that are happening, that are your life.

---

to switch between past, present, and future or to see them as one whole blend. These findings parallel Neville's thesis that the three temporal modes are truly together and fragmenting them has implications for a well-lived life. For a review, see Diaconu-Gherasim, L. R., Mardari, C. R., and Măirean, C. (2023). The relation between time perspectives and well-being: A meta-analysis on research. *Current Psychology, 42,* 5951–5963. On ontological well-being, see Şimşek, Ö. F., & Kocayörük, E. (2013). Affective reactions to one's whole life: Preliminary development and validation of the Ontological Well-Being Scale. *Journal of Happiness Studies: An Interdisciplinary Forum on Subjective Well-Being,* 14(1), 309–343.

Trajectories, Time, and Intimacy

The first framework of the eight Trajectories is in *Time and Intimacy: A New Science of Personal Relationships* (2000). I labeled them as emergent *functions* that join the four Forces together and to help explain the dynamics of intimate relationships, how they constitute, grow, change, dissolve, reconfigure, and more. In other words, how couples manage their life together in the face of Chaos and Structure, and how they Shape Time but also learn how to wait and listen for Nurturing Conditions. In that earlier book, my goal was less about the personal journey of rediscovering time and more about helping researchers find a language for understanding and advancing the science of the dynamic nature or intimacy. To be clear, the Trajectories are also functions. Chapter 11 explains more.

So, why trajectory? It is not a simple naming device; much of this book helps unpack its meaning. For now, reflect on the fact that a trajectory is inherently temporal, not everlasting. Even the orbit of a planet changes over time and in its defining path. A trajectory comes and goes, fades, is impermanent. A trajectory has no substance. It is a path *in which* something travels: a planet, an arrow, a lightning bug, a shooting star, a dancer, and you and me.

The prelude to the QfP collection, *The Connoisseur of Time*, emphasizes that the word "quest" is intended to be treated as a verb, a call to action, a setting forth on the path, crossing over the threshold into deep time. As it turns out, we cannot help but do this every day. We are always on some path, traveling in some trajectory. So, in a way, this current book is a call to action. The journey metaphor now has more definition. When you notice Routine, give yourself fully to it and with a beginner's mind of curiosity. When you are thrown off kilter by some Interruption, let your mind sway more slowly than before and notice just how you bounce back. When Timing works—everything comes together—or does not work—you miss an important event—deepen into the bigger picture that is unfolding.

As you quest in these ways, you will do several things, all at the same time. You will develop Presence and discern more of your destiny. You will stumble more into life's Treasures. And you will cultivate an intimate relationship between your temporal self and the eternal.

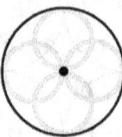

In the frontispiece to this book, Carlo Rovelli, the quantum physicist, explains that time is both ignorance (the quantum view) and suffering (the Buddhist view). From both views, time may not even exist at all.

The problem this book seeks to address can be stated simply: *We don't know what time is but we endure it.*

The solution offered can be stated simply: *There is a language of time that can connect our temporal self with eternal insights. As a result, time is not ignorance. It is knowledge. It is not suffering. It is a treasure.*

Author Note

Quest for Presence, or Q*f*P for short, includes five books. Each can be read independently or as part of the whole; they need not be read in sequence. If you are starting here, welcome! Your journey begins with Q*f*P Book 3: *The Attractions*.

This Q*f*P collection is written and structured to support your sense that the particular book you are reading is just right for you. Indeed, the notion of time in Q*f*P is about being wherever you happen to be.

Readers of Q*f*P like that it has a "choose your own adventure" quality, offering a variety of entry points for engaging with core concepts. If you are new to these topics, I recommend that you read straight through each book. Please pause to review the contemplations at the end of most chapters (or complete the corresponding activities in the Q*f*P companion workbook, or both). It will be helpful to read my personal reflections as well, as they illustrate how these concepts render in real life.

Each book also comes with notes in a research notes section, many of which relate to the science of time or provide references for readers interested in the related concept in the text. Q*f*P is informed by a vast literature in the growing study and philosophy of time. However, these books are not intended to be evidence-based or academic. I am not summoning research to advance a new science of presence. I hope you will explore these notes only when your curiosity outweighs your desire to achieve time competency.

By time competency, I mean the ability to return to living in the present moment of your whole life (staying "on script," as it were).

There are two steps to being time competent. First, you notice when anxiety, worry, longing, or overthinking (your mental future) pull you away from the adventure; or when regret, remorse, self-judgment, or ruminations (your mental past) push you out of the moment. Second, you gently return to the here and now and the feeling that your whole-time is a happening, unfolding, or awesome life journey.

If you are re-entering the collection by way of another starting point, I invite you to reorient and reconnect to your journey. As is the nature of any quest for presence, wherever you are along your path— and whichever book you find yourself reading—there you are.

A final note: The title of Q*f*P changed about ten times as it went into final production. This dynamic is part of the creative process and a contemplation in and of itself. Does the way a book appears—judging a book by its title—make any difference to how you arrived here? I have listed the titles below. I still think they all work. But the world requires us to fix things into a lasting word or image. I hope you find one that resonates with you for now. Perhaps next time, another will resonate with you.

A Quest for Presence, This Happening Life, Time's Precious Weave, Your Journey of Wholeness, Finding Free Time This Whole Time, Recovering Time in a World Addicted to Distraction and *Contemplations for Your Whole Time Here.*

* * *

I encourage you to download a free copy of the preview to Q*f*P on our website www.presencequest.life. *The Connoisseur of Time: An Invitation to Presence* has helped many get a solid grasp of the reason for this journey. You will also find resources and events on our site to support you in your quest.

About the Abbreviation Q*f*P

The *f* symbol between Q and P (a letter f with a descender hook) is the notation used in mathematics to represent functions. Specifically, functions represent how a varying quantity depends on another quantity. For example, the position of a planet is a function of time, or a weekly salary is a function of the hourly pay rate and the number of hours worked, or supply is a function of demand: As price goes up, demand goes down. In our quest for presence, our journey is a function of our presence, and at the same time, our presence is a function of our journey. As you become more present, the experience of life as a happening adventure and unfoldment is more enhanced. As your experience of life enhances, you become more present. The thrill is in the ride, and the ride is in the thrill.

Introduction to All Books

To be present means to be present to the whole-time of your life. Being here now is important. Equally important is your whole life—where you came from and where you are headed. We just don't live in the now. Our whole life is a project of purpose and meaning, a coming into being, a path of sense-making, a place where everything fits together, a journey, a becoming, an arrival, a fulfillment of destiny, a momentous emergence, a cause, a calling, an awakening, and so much more. And all of these occur outside of "clock-time."

Presence happens when we show up and fully engage in this life with all its changes, interruptions, and distractions. Our presence is imperfect. This collection of books encourages you to embrace its imperfections. Our attention faces many challenges: advertisements, attention deficit, abuse, anxiety, aging, and cognitive decline, to name a few. Life is fleeting, a blur. How can you find the time to live it and live it well? Perhaps it's time to embrace the blur of your whole-time here.

This Quest for Presence (QfP) collection is designed to help you reach any number of objectives. This includes the actual letting go of specific deadlines in favor of contemplations that improve your presence. This idea may seem radical in a society oriented toward action, achievement, and accomplishment. As you will discover, this orientation is born out of a narrow-minded, fragmenting, and dysfunctional view that time comprises only "clock-time." A different, contemplative objective would be that you stop long enough to enjoy the rich, full, and precious aspects of this very brief life.

The *QfP* is about making room for uplifts, for positive moments, for glimpses of the amazing wonders and emotions that life has to offer. I call these *Treasures*. My hope is that you will become more inquisitive about these Treasures. Where do they come from? How can you experience them more frequently? Are you prone to experiencing certain kinds more than others? Through the *QfP*, I believe you will get answers to these questions. Your view of time will change. You will have more well-being, wholeness, and intimacy in your life—both with others and with the ever-evolving natural world.

Other objectives stem from these questions. A new perspective may help you be more efficient. To value your time in a new way may give you the motivation and tools to prioritize what matters most. Alternatively, as you discover the big picture of time—as delineated here—you may grow in your sense of spirituality, faith, and transcendence of life's problems. My personal aim for you lies in between these two areas: efficiency and spirituality. This happens by embracing the ordinariness of life by becoming present to it.

Whatever your troubles, a shared presence can also make you resilient and thrive. This quest for presence is meant to be shared. We have arrived here as conscious beings because of cosmic forces that modern physics has only begun to understand. Deterioration of intimacy is the greatest problem of time compression (see my book *Time and Intimacy: A New Science of Personal Relationships* [Erlbaum, 2000]). We cannot appreciate our time without each other. As such, this offering is also a memoir. I hope you get to know me well enough so you feel less alone and more connected. And since we are here, we might as well make the most of it. Together.

Introduction to Book 4: The Trajectories

This book is about the gift of the energies within, and qualities of, your day. The gift of time is one that we can experience in any given day. Yes, this day is a gift given for your presence. You actually unwrap and then peek into a world that lies beyond clock-time. We rarely see this gift because either we fail to recognize or we take for granted the incredibly unique and precious nature of our situation. It is only because of a confluence of several features of time that we are even here and conscious.

Through an extraordinarily unique relationship of the sun to this earth as it turns around its own axis at a particular *pace*, we are given a *rhythm* of light, shadow, and dark, one we have come to calculate as 23 hours, 56 minutes, and 4 seconds. The tilt of that axis also gives us the *transition* of seasons; the *timing* of the seasons and the tides further undergird our ability to discern such timing for purposes of key survival *routines*—agriculture, hunting, and gathering. Further, our appreciation of the moon in its cycle helps shape our prescience, our ability to *schedule*.

All of these—Pacing, Rhythm, Transition, Timing, Routine, Scheduling—have over millennia been steadily written into our nervous system, which has its own set of timings. Yet, despite the rare and beautiful coordination of these features of time, all of us (as individuals, families, and as a species) have to deal with chance, spontaneous *interruptions*, novelty, and the relatively unpredictable weather. There is always, if not often, something new. And such novelty could be our salvation if we were not so stuck in the monotonous security of clock-time. Even the societal chaos brought by power imbalances, human conflict, and trauma can be approached with new solutions. We can awake from the dulling routines, unlearn our old ways, and work with disruption in healing ways. We can be present to the precious nature of our situation.

You may remember waking up as a child with a sense of anticipation or excitement: "I wonder what will happen today?" What followed was a collage of experiences: a flavor folded into a smile, a smile became holding a hand, release of the hand became a fall and a scraped knee, the sun filtered through a laugh, a laugh wafted into a smell, and then there was a longing answered with a cuddle.

Your childhood day happened through the eyes of innocence. Truth be told, every day—then and now—is a gift. At some point, the logic and proportion of clock-time conquered our daily flow and magic. We lost our sense of the flourish and collage. And, thanks to the relentless mechanization and digitization of time, we experience time pressure and time imprisonment, which have increased for all of us, including children.

In fact, in studies on the spiritual life of children, it is common to see they have very little sense of past and future and can be fully immersed in the present with the wink of an eye.* This book is about that wink of an eye. It is a guide to bring you back to the fullness of your happening life that is the textured gift of your day. It is a map of a different type of clock, not one built on the mechanisms of logic and proportion, but instead built on the natural and innate energy of wonder. This is the energy that drives our presence.

So, what is "presence"? You might think being present means alertness, attentiveness, and readiness to perform effectively across

---

* This is the first of several dozen Research Notes that you will find referenced beginning on page 221. Other readers of this book suggested wanting these notes in the back of the book for easy reference but did not want to be interrupted by a citation note. From this point forward, I will not identify each research note and you can certainly go to the Research Notes section anytime.

life tasks and throughout your day. In QfP, we define Presence as being centered in the moment and in life and fully attentive to oneself and one's environment. This happens from both the heart and the mind as a sense of being alive, fully engaged, and attuned to the moment and life as a whole.

When we talk about Presence, we refer to a mosaic: features of time that play and dance during your day—Pacing, Rhythm, Transition, Timing, Routine, and Scheduling. For many, the definition of presence often refers to *the timing* of their day and how they bring attention to time. For example, "I now have some time to pay attention" or "Things got less busy so I can focus on what really matters." But as you shall see, *Timing* is only one of eight different Trajectories that crisscross to create your experience of the day. In QfP, we take as wide a view as possible on Presence and other Soulful Capacities for life. It is not only about bringing Presence to your day, but also to the stream of your entire life, so that the light of your soul can reflect on the ripples of that stream.

The vast majority of current approaches to time focuses on time management, perfect timing, and efficiency. While it is true that we all need to do a better job with using the time we have, in QfP, the focus is less on *using* time and more on *deepening our relationship to* time. We are concerned here with the quality of time, not its quantity.

Yes, a big part of deepening is how we orient to and use the hours we have in a given day. Along the QfP journey, we note that the day is not just about hours, minutes, seconds. In fact, carving up the day as such is a fairly recent convention in human history. Because your soul transcends history, it either needs or deserves to reorient to the many forces that weave your experience of each day, beyond the fleeting hours that call for your awakening.

Most people have very little awareness of the powerful cosmic forces that shape our every experience. Through evolution, society, and culture, we have learned to navigate these forces through the language of time. It is a very specific and intentional language, one that we take for granted because we rarely, if ever, think about the underlying grammar and automatically use the words that our education and culture have given us to navigate with others in our world.

Most dictionaries define "grammar" as the whole system and structure of a language, the rules of how words and sentences are strung together and interpreted. There are almost 100 different uses or connotations as well as idioms for the word "time" in the English language. Every day, swimming in this sea of time, we rarely pause to see how we use this language. *QfP Book 4* invites you to more deeply experience this *grammar of time* as you use the word-label "time" in your everyday life. You are empowered to see time for what it is, to approach it in a less taken-for-granted, automatic, and machine-like manner.

I believe the world would be a more soulful place if, instead of simply using the word "time," we took more care to clarify which context of the term we were using. For example, when someone says "time is an illusion," they are referring to the transcendence of time or, simply, *Transcendence*. When someone says, "I felt pressed for time," they are referring to *Pacing*. "Just in time" often refers to *Timing*. "Let's find a time" often refers to *Scheduling*. "It took some time" typically implies some *Transition*.

These are some examples of the different Trajectories. Our journey in *QfP Book 4* is about first identifying these different qualities of time (understanding and recognizing the Trajectories), and then contemplating how they all dance together and relate to each other. There are many benefits of doing so, including more patience, insight, and sense of well-being, especially when you feel like a slave to time. Paying quiet attention to your ordinary life on this very day, even for a moment, will set you free. You can witness the process of the unfolding of your life.

Day Crafting

Some readers may wish to jump ahead to a five-minute exercise in the Appendix of this book, titled "Day Crafting Tool (Embracing the Trajectories)." Day Crafting will quickly introduce you to the Trajectories and guide you to practice healthy awareness of time, as well as help you develop wisdom about how time works in your life. I highly recommend you practice this exercise across a period of several days. Ultimately, this book seeks to teach you how to pay attention to qualities of time and heighten your perspective so you can appreciate life more. I only use the word "trajectory" to remind us of the deeper forces that give rise to the qualities. At the end of the day (note the double meaning), what matters most is the quality of the time you experience, the quality of your day, and the quality of your life as a whole.

PART ONE
Wise Old Owl and Pooh

After watching the poor bear wander around aimlessly—rushing to and fro—the Wise Old Owl swooped down to Pooh and said:

> "Well, there are many paths in life, and no matter where you go, it helps to every now and then stop and smell the roses... Poor Pooh!"

Pooh, who was growing increasingly concerned, responded:

> "Roses! But roses have thorns and can hurt you. What about honey? Can you find honey on those many paths? There has got to be honey."

Touched by Pooh's never-ending and haphazard quest for honey, the Wise Owl thought for a while on what clever thing he could say to help the poor bear. Finally, he exclaimed:

> "Well, Pooh, you know that it's the other way around: Thorns also have roses. And, if you slow down long enough to look, every path has honey on it."

Pooh, completely ignoring the sage wisdom, quickly became excited:

> "What are we waiting for?! Let's go! Which path do we take first? There are so many!"

CHAPTER 1

Your Day and This Happening Life

The current and subsequent chapters open with a storyline that pays homage to A.A. Milne's original *Winnie the Pooh*, and describes the evolving friendship of Pooh and the Wise Old Owl. The friends' interactions illustrate our relationship with and perceptions of time. This tale is about being fully alive in the blur, rush, or pace of life (Pooh) while also being able to view the terrain of our unfolding (Owl). That unfolding includes the amalgam of *interruptions*, our *pace, routines, schedules, transitions, timing,* and coordinating *rhythms* with others. It also includes stepping aside—smelling the roses—and remembering to *transcend* it all, to not get too caught up in the search for honey, whatever that may mean to each of us individually.

Many Paths

These processes are not incidental to life. They don't just happen. They are an integral part of life that we tend not to see, we avoid, or we take for granted. This book is designed to help you see the entirety of your happening life more clearly.

The many possible paths one can take in this life make this story complex. The processes at work in the background can create more perceived challenges: There will always be *interruptions*. Your *pace* in life may be too slow or too fast at times. Your *routines* may become stifling or outdated. Try as you might to keep control of your time, everything can pile up so that you have difficulty *scheduling* things. And then there are the *transitions* where life requires moving into a new phase.

Your *timing* will not always be perfect. And as much as you may want to get in sync with others and coordinate *rhythms*, that may not work out the way you desire. Because of all of this, you will struggle from time to time to see the big picture, the purpose, where it is all headed, and what it all means. Just like our dear Pooh, you will meander.

REFLECTION

The eight terms used in this book reflect much of what we "get caught up in"—stressed or reactive about—in life. My personal life becomes more navigable when I use one of the eight terms (or a synonym) to name the process at work when it arises. The term reminds me that what is occurring in that moment is a function of the deeper Radiant Forces, and then I can let go and not be so caught up by the event. I see the totality of the situation with fresh eyes.

To be sure, this ability—to label what is happening—takes effort and perspective. But the results are rewarding. In the moment of seeing, a Treasure always arises. Let me give you an example. I will italicize the eight terms that contextualize the processes of time.

When my wife and I were in the process of looking for a new home, I was not as excited as she about moving quickly into the search or making the move. Our financial situation allowed us a window of time before we had to move. I could see the benefits of moving, and I told her I supported the move. However, because I had become accustomed to the *Routines* of my life in the house I called home at that time, I often considered her efforts to be an *Interruption* and quite irritating.

She was acting in full-swing as a time-shaper and continually expressing her intentions. In response to this, because I wanted to entrain with her and fall into a *Rhythm* around this search, I asked her to be mindful of the *Pacing* of her requests to discuss the move. I needed time between each conversation to gather my thoughts and feelings. I expressed that the move represented a major *Transition* in our life. (The new home would likely be where we would spend our retirement years and later stages of life.) On a practical level, finding ways to coordinate with her came down to *Scheduling*: We were both working, and, at that time, I also was trying to write this book. We had to talk about our schedules and find ways to work with our Realtor's schedule.

Ultimately, finding the right home was about *Timing*. In the "sellers" market we found ourselves in, some homes lasted only one day on the market before a buyer placed a bid. Because I saw these processes in play in this home search situation, I was able to remember the trajectory of *Transcendence*. I asked my wife, "Maybe, instead of getting too stressed about having to find a home, we could look at the situation in a different way? What if there is a home out there that is also looking for us—or is being prepared for the right time for us to find it?"

Everything moves along at the right pace and time. I had to keep communicating with my wife (entrain or engage in each moment). Every house we looked at offered new information. Every interaction with the Realtor brought new insights. Regarding the Treasures, I experienced Patience (or do my best to practice it!), cultivated Optimism (again, do my best!), and had moments where my wife and I were aligned in Coherence, during which we found many things in our home search to regard with Adoration. Just being with these Treasures* released me from the stress of the search, and I felt more immersed in life.

---

* Throughout this book, in addition to capitalizing words that refer to the eight Trajectories, I also capitalize words that refer to the Forces (Book 1), Soulful Capacities (Book 2), and Treasures (Book 5).

The Objective (Impersonal) Nature of the Paths

Our usual experience of time occurs along a lesser-seen network of paths, routes, or Trajectories. These are the "processes" that I reference throughout this chapter. I call them Trajectories because they are like energy launched from one cosmic force to another. The eight Trajectories are Routine, Scheduling, Transition, Timing, Rhythm, Transcendence, Interruption, and Pacing. We are always on some Trajectory. When I have problems in any of these areas, I pause to reflect on the nature of the concern. What exactly is Interruption really? What is "bad" Timing? What is Pacing? Transition?

Everything we have been taught about time refers to the pathways on life's surface. But there is a whole lot more going on beneath the surface. As a first step in understanding our deeper self and our cosmic relationship to time, we must accept that our "normal" life—which relies on the clock-time framework of routines, schedules, and calendars—is only one way that time works, with all its thorns and roses. There is more conspiring and weaving below the surface, where the honey is hiding. Once I step back and see that these are objective and impersonal manifestations of deeper forces at work, I am better able to adjust my perception of time. Like Pooh, I can then say, "Well, let's get started looking for that honey!" instead of worrying about the thorns.

This book reveals secrets behind your ordinary life. It shows how everything that happens to you is a function of the deeper dance between the Radiant Forces of Form, Chaos, Time Shaping, and Nurturing Conditions. For example, the Transitions that occur in life arise because the energy of Nurturing Conditions (elements of *becoming* from our past) moves toward the energy of Form (structure) and is *causing* the form of our life to evolve in some way. This is explained in more detail in the last chapter of this book. (See the sections in chapter 11 called "How the Forces Promote Well-Being" and "Inner Paths and Outer Paths.")

Contemplation (Q*f*P 4-1): The Trajectories

As an introduction to this book, please review these questions, some sample affirmations, and a quick study of how sexuality illustrates the Trajectories. As with all Contemplations through the QfP collection, these questions can be used for journaling, group discussion, or a study group.

+ How aware are you that your life has regular or comfortable Routines? What is it that you do most frequently, perhaps every day? What makes these things Routines? How attached are you to your Routines? Which can you let go of?

+ Have you ever experienced that the time was right for you to say or to do something? Or maybe you said or did something and it was immediately clear that the time was not right for it to have occurred? How was your Timing "on" or "off"? In general, do you feel that your Timing for things is good? What about the idea that everything happens at the right time?

+ Have you recently had the feeling that you and those you live or work with were "in sync" with each other? What was the event or occasion where you felt you were all synchronized or "moving to the same Rhythm"? Are there activities that are more likely to bring you that sense of being in Rhythm with life itself?

+ When was the last time you experienced some sort of Transition in your life? It can be any type—one that lasted a day, a week, a month. How are you in Transition right now? What, if anything, are you transitioning toward?

+ When was the last time that clock-time seemed to stop or slow down for you? When did you experience a sense of wonder or mystery, like you were looking down from above your life or Transcending the current moment?

+ When was the last time you set up a Schedule or lived your life with a specific start and end time on an activity so that it did not overlap with another activity (such as at work, home, or leisure)? What was that Schedule? What function did it really fulfill in your life?

+ Have you been aware recently that your day (life and work) had a regular or even pace to it as opposed to a sense that the Pacing was either too slow or too fast? Can you describe days where the pace was "just right" as opposed to otherwise? What made it so?

+ When was the last time you were interrupted, such as on a task, conversation, or project? What was the Interruption? Did you return to where you were before the Interruption? Have there been times in your life when something was interrupted that you never returned to? In which situations do you avoid being interrupted? Why? Does it always work?

Affirmations

Wisdom quotes, or affirmations, provide another way to understand each of the Trajectories. As you review the list below, reflect on which statement resonates with you the most or speaks to you about a current lack or need you have.

+ The Routines of my life support my thriving, my giving, and my receiving the gift of time.

+ Everything in my life reveals right Timing; I am always at the right place and the right time.

+ I easily find my Rhythm at home, at work, and in between; I enjoy swinging with it all.

+ My life is in Transition, always was, always will be; just like everything and everyone else. I fully embrace Transition.

+ Time is an illusion. I give myself permission to Transcend it, to witness the unfolding of life, death, and all in between.

+ I Schedule activities in ways that support my growth, my health, and doing good in the world.

- I step through my days, my work, and my life with an even Pace that serves my awakening.
- I rest secure knowing there are no accidents; when I'm perturbed by an Interruption, I say, "It's just a curve."

A Brief Study of Sexuality as a Reflection of the Trajectories

The sustainment of all life—from the cellular level to the entire organism—rests on sexual reproduction. Human sexuality, and likely most of animal sexuality, can serve as an overview of the eight Trajectories.

All animals have mating rituals, or Routines, whereby they can find time to mate. *Timing* is revealed through the menstrual cycle, estrus, or periods of fertility. The matching of two Rhythms, called entrainment, is required for copulation (the sexual act) to have a greater chance of success. Key phases of Transition are revealed as cells grow and divide in early fetal development as well as throughout the growth cycle.

Orgasm and the actual moment of conception is functionally where individuals Transcend their own particular lives by bringing in a new life to carry genetic information forward in time. From a psychological view, people also experience a Transcendence of time during orgasm. Many couples plan or Schedule their sexual activity as well. Further, how individuals *Pace* their lovemaking is important for sexual satisfaction and orgasm.

Finally, as with anything else, sex has the potential for Interruptions, including disturbances and things just not working right. Interestingly, in many native cultures, marriage rituals include some sort of manufactured barrier, challenge, or disturbance that the partners must navigate and overcome before they can consummate their coupling.

CHAPTER 2

Contemplating the Eight Trajectories

In which Wise Old Owl takes Pooh aside, tells him how attitude is important ("Your attitude is your altitude") and gives him a dedication to remind him why we are all here.*

Do you ever find it difficult to pay attention to the many things that happen in your life? Are you distracted a lot? Are you pulled in different directions? Does your mind wander? Do you have difficulty staying focused on a single task for any length of time? Is your life disorganized? Is it all just a blur?

If you answered yes to any of these questions, this book in the Q*f*P series may offer you some clarity about why you experience your life in these ways. Consider this an invitation to meditate on, to discern, the tapestry (or mandala) of your unfolding life. This contrasts with our tendency, or need, to obey the omnipresent clock that monopolizes our perception of time. Might I suggest that your distraction, confusion, or even your so-called "attention deficit" are good things? Perhaps they are a signal for you to wake up to a different understanding of time.

As you respond to this signal, you will see more clearly how your day is not divisible into hours, minutes, and seconds. Instead, you will appreciate its wholeness: the amazing set of time's ribbons,

---

* I was able to procure this dedication from the Wise Old Owl and it can be found at the end of this very chapter on pg. 30

threads, and filaments weaving your day into the whole experience that makes each day unique, curious, and even wonderful. Instead of feeling the need to worship clock-time, the Q*f*P approach combines the practices of meditation, mindfulness, and presence into a single image, or mandala. This book is designed to help you notice the everyday appearances of time as they show up along eight different pathways, or Trajectories, of your happening life.

The following chapters introduce you to each of the Trajectories and offer tools and exercises to help bring them into focus, label them, and, especially, appreciate them. As you work with the contemplations at the end of each chapter, try to maintain a vitalizing image of the precious weave or tapestry of this unfolding life. A tapestry is created by the overlay of paths of the threads that compose it. The Q*f*P calls these pathways *Trajectories* rather than "lines" or "threads." Let's consider the general definition of the word "trajectory."

> A trajectory is the curved path something takes as it moves through space and as a function of time; a trajectory is defined by the simultaneous position and momentum of something as it moves along the curvature it defines.

Accordingly, the tapestry of life we are imagining is always *in process*; an ever-moving weave of different Trajectories. Fortunately, the Trajectories are not random. Our consciousness and attention actually follow these paths every day. But our attention need not be scattered all over the place. There is a general framework through which the pattern of our day and our life unfolds. The purpose of this book is to give you a big picture and ready access to the framework. Be patient with yourself. Seeing this picture will take practice.

The Underlying Forces

In chapter 1, I mentioned that the Trajectory pathways that create our perceptions of time operate on the surface of life. There also are deeper forces at work. These metaphysical and cosmological forces—the four Radiant Forces—are described in depth in other books in the Q*f*P series. They are briefly defined here to set the stage for your work with the Trajectories. In the following definitions, the capitalized words or phrases in *italics* draw attention to how the eight Trajectories manifest in everyday life, emerging from within and between the underlying forces (Chaos, Form, Nurturing Conditions, Time Shaping).

Chaos (also Entropy, Dissolution): Chaos represents an objective reality that everything is in a state of disintegration. Physicists call this *entropy*. Buddhists call it *impermanence*. We glimpse Chaos in experiences of randomness, challenges, disruption, and the unknown. When Chaos is active in our lives, we are often called to be creative. Chaos leads to our experience of *Interruptions* and disruptions. As a way to help manage or work with Chaos, living organisms develop *Rhythms* and ways of coordinating together. Very often, our ego has an aversion for and tries to avoid Chaos.

Form (also Gravity, Structure, Organization): Form represents an objective reality that everything has a shape, a recognizable pattern, integrity, or coherence. We glimpse Form in experiences of order, regularity, rules, security, organizations, and institutions. Form teaches us that everything in life goes through *Transition*. Also, Form manifests in time as the repetitive *Routines* and habits in our life. Very often, our ego gets attached to Form.

Nurturing Conditions (also Facilitative Conditions, Temporal Context): Nurturing Conditions represent an objective reality that everything is in the process of unfolding, of becoming, of coming into being, or transitioning from one form to the next. We glimpse Nurturing Conditions in organic processes: the experiences of waiting, arriving, growing, or decaying. Nurturing Conditions lead us to discern and understand ideal *Timing* in which to undertake, maintain or stop some activity. Also, it is through Nurturing Conditions that we learn to let go and experience *Transcendence*, that is, the timeless aspects of our existence.

Time Shaping (or Causality, Action): Time Shaping represents an objective reality in which one entity or object has an influence or impact on other entities or events. We understand this force through intentionality, desire, will, and subsequent behaviors. When Time Shaping is active in our lives, we may be called to take action, make a decision to select one behavior over another, or pursue a series of acts. Through Time Shaping, we learn to *Pace* ourselves and develop *Schedules*.

Embracing the Blur

One of the great paradoxes of working with time is that by slowing down, we actually start seeing the blur of life more clearly. We glimpse the Radiant Forces at work. Modern culture—filled with techno-invasion, high-speed everything, fast food, and fast everything—operates at a pace that leads many of us to believe that time is actually speeding up, becoming blurry. Chapter 9, "Contemplating Pacing," goes into more detail on this idea. The truth is that time itself—on the level that we live and work—is neither slowing nor speeding. We have to raise our sights above culture to see things more objectively. And, of course, this takes time. More exactly, it requires exploring (playing with, working with, leaning into) what is more salient, noticeable, or pronounced about eight different qualities of time during your day-to-day life. To aid your explorations, I recommend using the Day Crafting Tool in the Appendix.

In full clarity of our ordinary consciousness, the Trajectories cannot be distinguished from each other. Pace is only one aspect of the whole blur. In full clarity, life is simply a tantalizing blur of teeming events—pulses, electricity, blood, light, fluids, gasses, highways, intersections, emergencies, streams of consciousness, bursts of feeling, reaction after reaction after reaction. Neuroscientists summarize this by saying that we are continuously bombarded by external inputs of various timescales from the environment, and that the brain itself is continuously integrating time at multiple levels. They call this "intrinsic neural timescales," meaning there are multiple timescales in the brain's neural activity. Our upbringing, education, and culture have, at the most fundamental level, evolved to help us organize and make sense of it all.

And the truth is, it does not make any full or total sense. Nor does it have to. The modern quantum physicist Carlo Rovelli concludes the following after his own study of the blur in his book *The Order of Time*:

> The vision of reality and the collective delirium that we have organized has evolved and has turned out to work reasonably well in getting us to this point. The instruments that we have found for dealing with it and attending to it have been many . . . And something of them always escapes from the order of our discourses, since we know that, in the end, every attempt to impose order leaves something outside the frame.

Here, in Book 4 of *Quest for Presence*, and in all the books, you are given your own set of instruments for attending to reality. Instead of seeing that we need a frame (the call to order from the Radiant Force of Form), and to make sense of the disorder (the Radiant Force of Chaos), I ask you to embrace them both as part of the same unified reality. This quest is not only about knowledge and understanding in the literal sense. You are not merely working with a frame. Instead, you are following the threads inside the tapestry—this precious weave of time. This is also a path of intuition, insight, and wisdom; you step back, contemplate, and realize that you are part of the weave and have a role to play in creating it at the same time. You have a map (Book 1), the Soulful Capacities to navigate the blur (Book 2), and a unique Attraction to the journey itself (Book 3).

And now, you jump into the blur, the direct sensory experience, of your daily life. The goal of understanding the Trajectories is not to make sense of daily events. Instead, the Trajectories are reminders of a deeper anxiety every time you feel afraid, anxious, confused, alarmed, or bewildered. These feelings arise because your brain (your intrinsic neural timescales) has only evolved so much to handle what is really going on. Jewish mystics make the distinction between the "watery" world of temporary and material life and the true "crystalline" structure of the temple of eternal life. You can use this idea as a device every time the world disappoints or you feel disillusioned. There is just a deeper (and more beautiful) reality that is tapping against the surface.

The diagram on the facing page provides a visual analog to these ideas about blur. The six different images show a gradual clarification, increasing resolution, or finer focus. In viewing this progression, it helps to remember that we use the word "time" in our daily language for an exquisite array of practical goals (time enough, time to travel, time to stop). It is, according to the *Oxford Dictionary*, the most-used noun in the English language. On the list of the top twenty-five nouns, time is followed by "year" in third place, "day" in fifth and "week" at number 17.

Our continuous reference to time keeps us anchored in this watery, blurry world. Here, in Book 4, you are asked to reflect more carefully on what you exactly mean in the instance where you use the word *time* or related terms (day, week, year) or—more importantly—words like now, happening, happen, sudden, forever—that situate you in your life as a whole. When you make that effort to pay attention, you move to a better understanding or deeper appreciation of the Trajectories.

Again, using the images in the diagram as a metaphor, you may move up a level—from a "6" to a "5" or a "4" to a "3." The six images do not have any specific labels or meaning. They are only provided to depict the idea of gradual clarification: the Trajectories are there, weaving and happening, dancing and twirling, moving in and moving out, creating the tapestry of this amazing happening life that you were brought here to witness. The goal is not for you to move from "1" to "6." Rather, our quest *for* presence is also a quest *in* presence and

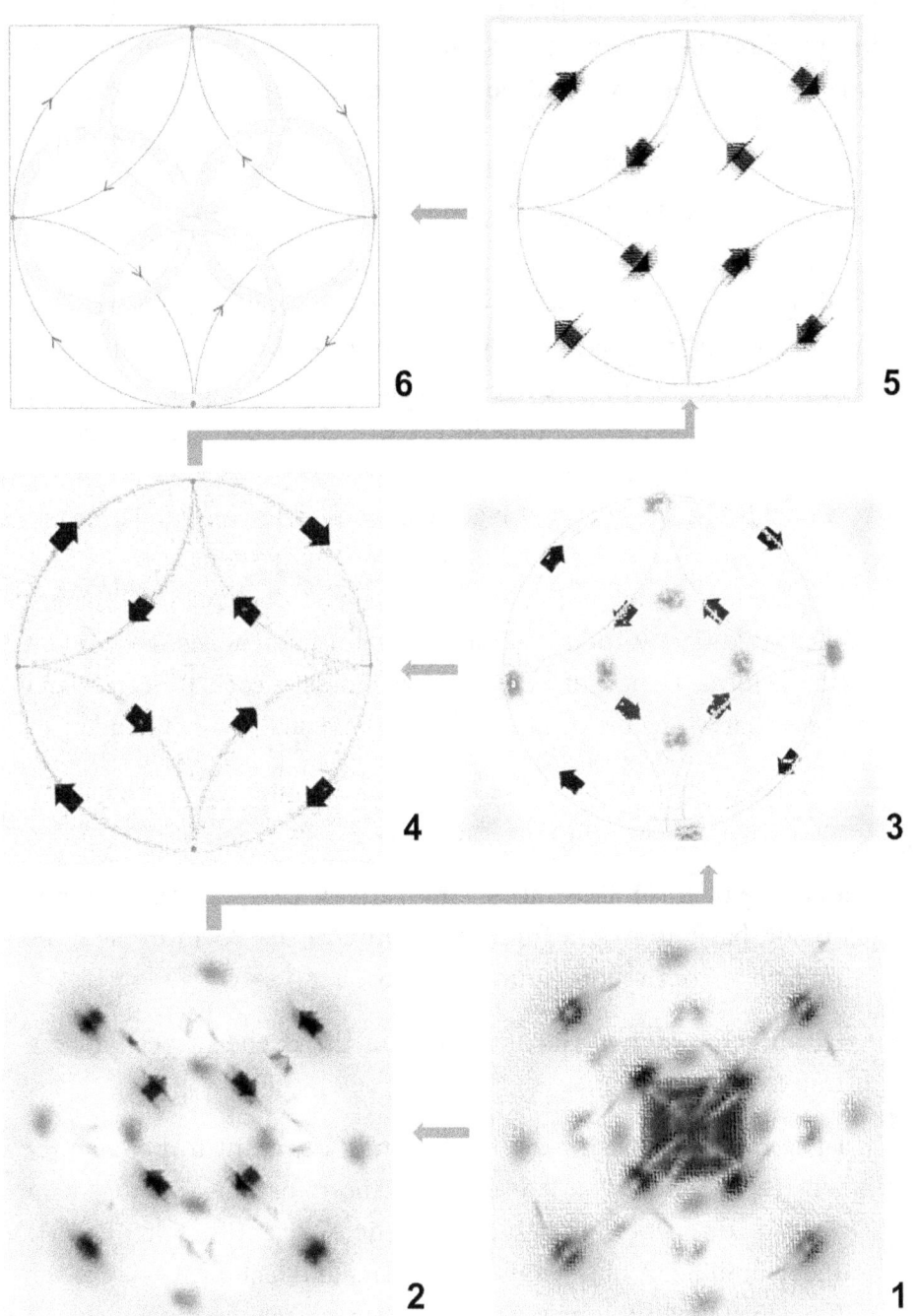

CONTEMPLATING THE EIGHT TRAJECTORIES

of presence. We are not here to achieve some state of Presence in an imagined future. We are here to embrace things for what they are—at whatever level we are—and no matter how confusing, distorted, or blurry they might be.

Navigating the Following Chapters

The Trajectories are routes that operate at many levels in our day. Some are more easily perceived—Routines, Schedules, Interruptions. But all Trajectories have many hidden aspects that our intuitive, somatic, and extrasensory detectors pick up on. We have to remember that every Trajectory is continually at work in our body and in society whether we perceive them or not.

For this reason, the next eight chapters—the contemplations of each Trajectory—are designed to help you study them at metaphorical, symbolic, visual, and more literal levels. I believe in "different strokes for different folks" and use different approaches to help you grasp the ideas. Hence, to raise your awareness of each Trajectory and in a way that works for you, each chapter is structured to include:

✦ a **Pallet** to help you to take a wide and contemplative lens that shows diverse aspects of the Trajectory.

✦ a **Picture** offers an illustration for an artistic perspective. Take time to look back and forth from the Picture to the Poem to view the Trajectory from a more intuitive approach.

✦ a **Poem** that invites you to reflect on the deeper aspects of the Trajectory.

✦ a **Portrait**, which is only a sketch and not meant to be comprehensive or conclusive. It is designed more for those "nerds" who want to dig deeper into a more analytic or scientific ("left brain") understanding. A more multidisciplinary and technical essay of the Trajectory includes a related list of research references, which can be found at the back of the book in a section titled "Bibliographic References for The Essays."

What follows are the descriptions of each chapter segment.

The Pallet begins with a chart labeled "The Dance: Dynamics," which outlines the different relationships between and across the Trajectories. There are many! Consult chapter 11 for more information about these dynamics and their interrelationships. Below is an example chart, which describes what the relationship types are and offers some examples of what you'll find in the next eight chapters:

THE DANCE: DYNAMICS

SAYINGS: Common aphorisms that illustrate how we understand or experience a Trajectory in our life. Examples for Routine include "Humans are creatures of habit," "Get some 'down time' or 'me time,'" and "A walk in the park."

ATTRACTION: Each Trajectory is the surface manifestation of the underlying Radiant Forces at work.* When a Trajectory appears, it is because of the connection between two forces—one active, the other attractive. This is where I'll list examples of these attractions from which a Trajectory emerges.

FUNCTION: Each Trajectory serves the function of connecting the two Radiant Forces between which an Attraction exists. I'll illustrate how the Trajectory fills a specific function on this line.

---

* For readers who have studied Book 3 of QfP (*The Attractions*), it will help to distinguish how the term "attraction" is used in both books. In Book 3, Attraction (capital A) refers to our personal and unique attraction to the fulfillment of our destiny. In Book 4, attraction (small case a) refers to how one Radiant Force is attracted to another. The Attractions (Book 3) unfold and enfold across the whole time of our life journey, the story of our time in this life. The attraction (Book 4) manifests more in our day-to-day experience of time, showing up in our experience of a trajectory—the story of time in our day.

INFLUENCE: There are two paths of influence (inner and outer, described in detail in chapter 11). Each pathway contains a cycle of interaction among four of the Trajectories. This is where I'll name the pathway and interactions a Trajectory navigates.

RESULT: Each Trajectory is a result of the connection between two Radiant Forces. The results relating to a Trajectory will be listed here. For example, when Form and Time Shaping are attracted to one another, Routines emerge from their connection. As a result, we form the ability to Pace ourselves in life. Pacing is the result.

SISTER: Each Trajectory is paired with a sister Trajectory that supports her. For example, Routine helps with Scheduling; Pacing helps with Interruption; Rhythm supports Transcendence; and Timing facilitates Transition.

MIRROR: Each Trajectory has a mirror among its counterparts that facilitates its process. For example, we Transition by virtue of Pacing; our Rhythms synchronize with each other better through Scheduling.

COUNTERPOINT: Each Trajectory also has a counterpoint Trajectory. The counterpoints reflect an ongoing give-and-take between the Trajectories. When one fails to appear, the other loses its meaningfulness, ceases to exist, or reverts to the shadow side of time. For example, without good Rhythm, our Routines become lifeless; too much focus on Scheduling and clock-time prevents us from Transcendence. I'll name these relationships on this line of this box.

In addition, the Pallet segment includes:

1. A functional definition of the Trajectory, along with diverse synonyms and ways the trajectory manifests in the world. By "functional," I want you to have a description whose *function* is to help you contemplate (an important word in our Quest for Presence). Specifically, I want you to have rich and varied features of the specific trajectory in hopes that you will find something that appeals to your own experience and empowers you to see time in a new way. This type of definition varies from the standard form we see in dictionaries, which are always meant to be economical and often less apt to prompt contemplation;

2. Other random samples of how the Trajectory may manifest in daily life. Do not fret if you don't recognize all the references. There are sure to be several that resonate with you; and

3. Brief synopses of topics within the category of the Trajectory.

As with all other chapters in Q*f*P, each one ends with a Contemplation. Some readers may want to skip ahead and complete the contemplation before reading its companion chapter. In this way, you may get a sense of where the Trajectory is headed. Otherwise, just strap yourself in and let the Trajectory take you wherever you might end up.

A Dedication: A Sending Message

To create the right attitude or orientation, I suggest reading the following dedication before reviewing any of the eight Trajectory chapters. The Wise Old Owl gave this to me.

I recognize that all aspects of day-to-day life represent deeper forces at work. By abiding within this recognition, I am able to see the beauty of things unfold in their most clear and natural way.

Each and every day, there is always a bigger picture to my life and the lives of others. I may not know this big picture. Even without this knowledge, the activities and routines of the day unfold according to precise laws.

The unfolding beauty and the precise laws occur on, within, and through specific paths that all of life walks upon.

As I study each path, I see universal qualities that include, but also go beyond, my own life.

As I study each path, I see parallels and comparisons that give me a large sense of freedom. Indeed, we are all—all of humanity and all of life—part of a greater dance.

As I study each path, I become fully present to the moment and the gifts it has in store for me.

As I study each path, I astutely follow all moments and occasions as objective phenomena that arise and pass away.

As I study each path, I am reminded about the original and clear nature of my own conscious awareness that witnesses all events without attachment.

As a result of these insights, I grow and evolve in my wholeness, my life, and my love.

PART TWO

The Trajectories—Pallet, Picture, Poem, Portrait

CHAPTER 3

Contemplating Routine

In which Wise Old Owl observes Pooh as he makes his rounds from hive to honeypot and back again.

THE DANCE: DYNAMICS

SAYINGS: "Humans are creatures of habit," "Get some 'down time' or 'me time,' " "Walk in the park," "Chop wood, carry water."

ATTRACTION: Routine manifests as Form in Form's attraction to Time Shaping.

FUNCTION: The function of Routine is to connect Form to Time Shaping.

INFLUENCE: Routine influences Pacing through Time Shaping.

RESULT: Routine results as Timing, in its own function, connects Nurturing Conditions to Form.

SISTER: Routine is sister to Scheduling. They support and reinforce each other.

MIRROR: The good work born of Routine brings the gifts of Transcendence, or timelessness.

COUNTERPOINT: Without Rhythm, Routine deadens with monotony, our identity fragments, and we grow alienated from nature, biology, and the organic quality of things.

Functional Definition: The choice to treat repetition as either a blind habit (humdrum) or growth through ritual (ecstatic spiral); we can see life's path as either a well-traveled route of sustenance or as a stumbling rut. Our experience of Routine includes feelings of stasis (being stuck, frozen, restricted), as well as comfort, familiarity, trust, dependability, and reliability. Spiritual guides and self-help courses each provide training for tapping into holy, uplifting, or ecstatic ritual or they offer dull techniques. Synonyms or common phrases associated with Routine include: over & over, again & again, karma, déjà vu, samsara, roulette.

Random Samples: Lullabies, "The Itsy-Bitsy Spider," learning math tables, traditions, mellow, tea and biscuits, *The Myth of Sisyphus*, eternal return, comets, comedy shows, dance routines, repetition compulsion, negative feedback loops, addiction, routine maintenance, security systems, weekly meetings, athletic workouts, jogging paths, diets, weekend gatherings, family get togethers.

Here are other common examples of Routine:

Repetition is inherent in Routine and, accordingly, helps to create focus, security, regularity, efficiency, ease, easiness, order, fitness, automation, and project management.

Rituals, in their purest lived and embodied state where we fully show up to their meaning, move us to get in touch with beauty, wonder, goodness, and wisdom. Without the energy of life, ritual becomes a deadening routine.

Work, or time on tasks, wrapped in jobs, wrapped with careers, is a key to understanding Routine as a path toward engaging with life and mastery, toward full participation as a citizen in society. Monotonous and menial work can lead to alienation, withdrawal, isolation, and aloneness.

Addictions of all kinds are defined by a repetitive need for an external substance or process, one we depend on to avoid pain or continually manufacture pleasure.

Because shared social Routines, including leisure, bring coherence and harmony to life, they also produce ease.

Ease: Routines produce an ease in lifestyle because we learn and remember repetitive patterns so we can then reproduce activities easily and readily. Dis-ease emerges when one particular set of Routines dominate others.

Routine provides a foundation for social order, civilization, industrialization, and technology. Routine also provides—through computer language and engineering—advances in the age of information, cyberspace, and artificial intelligence. From our morning bathing and cleaning sequences to the logic of computer chips, our ability to create, communicate, and replicate Routines keeps us and our relationships in an organized state.

Routine speaks to two ironies within the human condition. First, it can lead to either ongoing attachment to the material world or to profound liberation, finding selflessness through the intense concentration or spacious mindset cultivated through regular meditation. Second, with technology, routines can either produce efficiency or dominate our attention so much that we lose connection to the organic rhythms of nature that nurture our health.

ROUTINE

Each opportunity
for waking vanishes
behind our heels . . .

"the same old . . .
the same old"

This day—this chore
your hands—your feet
sleep in their routine

hoping you'll remember

Then the passing moment
Yells "HEY . . . Wait for me!"
craving to be part of
your sweet awakening

You turn to see your
previous self in its rut,

Singing "make your life
like a prayer wheel

or a
rosary

or a mantra"
      ~ J.B.

Portrait: An Essay on Routine

Routine is perhaps the route of all routes. The one that most identifies, defines, and disciplines us to make the best use of clock-time. Consider this quote as a great example of the benefits of Routine:

> *Early to bed, early to rise,*
> *makes a man healthy, wealthy, and wise.*
>
> ~ BENJAMIN FRANKLIN, FOUNDING FATHER, WRITER, SCIENTIST, INVENTOR, STATESMAN, DIPLOMAT, PRINTER, PUBLISHER, AND POLITICAL PHILOSOPHER (1706–1790)

Routine comes from the Old French word (*route*) for "way, path, or course." This is the same path required for the journey—that other French word (*jour*) for "day." Routines clearly simplify our life. But there is more.

On any given day, your Routines may proceed with or without your soul. Is your life alienating or filled with Treasures? Are you taking life's regularities for granted so much that a true appreciation of them would alter your life? These questions are quintessential catalysts in the Quest for Presence. Welcome the Trajectory of Interruption; a life crisis really gets the soul to work.

Routine with soul is ritual, the sacrament, the temple's center. Routine without soul is a habit, a program, the computer's center. Soulful Routine scaffolds artistic creativity, dance, wonder, exploration, and Transcendence. Postmodern Routine is harnessed for engineering, machinery, and infrastructure. In evolution, Routines were born by the pressure to survive, to obtain a habitat (from habit) and predictable nutrition, protection, or warmth. We hunted and gathered. We stored food and retrieved it. We procreated and buried our dead. Today, new routines abound, from industrialization and emergence of the working class and the professions to, more recently, the knowledge worker and the gig worker.

Habits have become a popular topic in the fields of psychology, wellness, and overall work culture. The best-selling book *Atomic*

Habits: Tiny Changes, Remarkable Results explains how, by observing our daily habits, we can choose useful ones, get better 1% each day, and gradually transform our well-being, productivity, and success. The term *life hack* emerged in 2004 to describe any routine work-around or shortcut to increase efficiency. These hacks are often used for time management (see "Essay on Scheduling" in chapter 8). But they also integrate with many life Routines: Keith Bradford's book *Life Hacks* and website (1000lifehacks.com) lists hundreds of strategies in the areas of health, food, travel, fitness, cleaning, school, and other categories.

Routine Seen and Unseen

Routines come from the Radiant Force of Form. Accordingly, you would think they would be fairly obvious, directly perceived, or easy to work with. However, once learned, Routines operate in the background, on autopilot. All education, interestingly enough, is about discovering, creating, and establishing the Routines we need to navigate and succeed in the future of our happening life.

Atomic habits and life hacks speak to our desire to switch out of autopilot and become conscious of how we spend our time. We want to change things up, not go through life with blind Routines we never stop to assess. However, no matter how hard we try, we are creatures of habit. Paradigms shift slowly. Society provides many temporal conventions to keep us in our grooves. Automaticity is inherent within the definition of Routine. Once we learn something (like driving a car), it becomes automatic and less conscious. Society (and the interstate) requires we follow these embedded Routines.

One of the best-known books in the sociology of time is Eviatar Zerubavel's *Hidden Rhythms: Schedules and Calendars in Social Life* (1985). Routines and habits are the core ingredients of the rhythms Zerubavel describes. Indeed, Rhythm is the shadow or counterpoint of Routine for, without Routine, we have no perception or appreciation of Rhythm. That is, we discern Rhythm only when we pay repeated—that is, Routine—attention to the hummings and vibrations of life. Zerubavel outlines four principles of *temporal regularity* in society and culture. These principles describe recurrent, stable practices; eventual performance; the sharing of these practices; and the institutions through which these practices are guided and enacted. In other words: no Routine, no society. And yet they are, as his title suggests, hidden.

The four principles are

1. *rigid sequential structures*: stages we are expected to go through, such as daytime meetups and dinner dates, moving from talking to hugging to kissing to sex;

2. *the expected duration of activities*: implied contracts for how long we should spend doing something (an hour-long class that begins at 1:00 p.m. should end at 2:00 p.m., rather than 2:15 p.m.);

3. *standardized temporal locations:* how behaviors are situated in time, such as eating dessert after dinner or spending time in a waiting room before seeing the doctor rather than after the visit is complete; and

4. *uniform rate of recurrence*: expectations about the frequency and repetition of specific events; meaning a morning ritual includes a series of activities (wake up, get out of bed, drag comb across head, brush teeth, drink tea, and so on). The key words in these principles are "rigid," "expected," "standardized," and "uniform."

The research on Routines tends to suggest that this temporal regularity from society is essential for our well-being. In sort of a beautiful way, Routine coordinates Scheduling (its sister) with Rhythm (its counterpoint). By getting home from work at a regular time and getting to bed at a regular time, we create a regular sleep-wake cycle that entrains with the day. Families function better when its members always know the answer to "When are we meeting up for (fill in the blank)?" These anchors ease the introduction of new routines when changes occur (new school, new job, new route to the store, or moving to a new home). One study shows that putting children to bed regularly with language-based bedtime routines (reading, singing) predicted better health and fewer behavioral problems (anxiety, aggressiveness) two years later.

Infrastructure, Holidays, Celebrations: Our personhood originates from those early childhood routines that establish connection to significant others in our life. Later, society, family, and the workplace provide signposts for locating ourselves in the unfolding schema (see Zerubavel's *temporal locations*). Calendars keep us in touch with others across life's stages (for example, as a feature of culture through cyclic holidays—both religious and secular). Many families and friends meet for birthdays, anniversaries, or reunions and holidays like Mother's Day, Father's Day, or days of mourning. These "days of importance" are named precisely because they connect the calendar, our personal identity (how we see ourselves), and social identity (how we think others see us). The calendar provides a concentric infrastructure from the widest annual events to the weekly rituals to the daily routines like praying, saying affirmations, reading the daily newspaper, or even more frequent routines such as news alerts delivered to our smartphones up to the minute.

Identity: Routines provide the consistency that undergirds personal identity. Reading to a young child at bedtime is one example of a routine for positive child development. Research suggests that a secure sense of self begins early through recurrent and positive parent-infant bonding and many episodes of the separation-attachment cycle. But even if this goes well, problems can occur. Fortunately, society gives us many Routine guideposts to formulate our sense of self, all the way from early childhood to our deathbed. For example, we hang out with the same friends during adolescence; experience the same songs, bars, restaurants, sporting events, and television shows with loved ones and colleagues; establish daily patterns of home activity; travel across the temporal border of work-to-home and back again; and even take side trips along life's way. Security and predictability are good things.

Some argue, however, that Routines can make our lives too rigid, especially if our identities get co-opted by career, work demands, or investment in a path or lifestyle that is not truly resonant for us. A midlife crisis, a sexual affair, sex changes, and lost weekends are examples of self-generated "life interrupted." In these examples, people may take back "their own time" from the normative "time prisons" of society. They step outside the status quo to find themselves.

Subroutines of Self and Shadow: When we follow our own routes separate from others, we differentiate from them. Our journey or life script ensues. This differentiation can be driven *from behind*, by stress and adversity (a.k.a. Chaos). Or it can be pulled *forward* by intention and purpose (a.k.a. Time Shaping). We are a blend of these two scripts. For example, we have subroutines of reactivity ("I will avoid"), adaptation ("I can get through this"), resilience ("I am stronger now"), or mission ("I am ready for more"). These play out in different spheres: gender, career, family, and social identity. The healthy self has fluidity and plasticity across these subroutines, often called "ego states." And sometimes, fissures occur.

I am reminded of the mystery author Agatha Christie. As of 2018, the *Guinness World Records* listed Christie as the best-selling fiction writer of all time. In 1926, when she was thirty-six years old, Christie went missing. She just disappeared. Despite her popular image, she was not found for eleven days. Her autobiography does not mention this event. Biographers offered various explanations: memory loss, traumatic reaction to discovering her husband's affair, a plot to embarrass him, a publicity stunt. To my knowledge, there is still no official answer. After disappearing, she broke from routine by developing a new character in her novels (Miss Marple) with a new writing style, longer books, and her first nonmystery novel.

The affair is the oft-cited culprit. Were Christie's next actions reactive, proactive, or both? Reactively, Christie may have suffered a dissociative fugue state, a behavioral health disorder in which people lose some or all memory of their past, disappear from usual environments, and may leave routines such as family and job. Dissociation suggests a deep need to preserve identity when the journey gets rough. Alternately, there is evidence that Christie staged the disappearance to embarrass her husband. In this scenario, she proactively took back control of her time. The obvious poignancy of this story is its mystery. And there would be no mystery without the routine tropes and styles that combine to make life interesting. Many modern "self-help" books overstate the proactive subroutines. In doing so, they sacrifice the soul—the richer blend that makes this happening life more compelling.

Synthesis

Routines are the forms given from social conventions and days of importance. Like pages in a book, Routines bring coherence to our story, our future, our destiny. Civilization requires the coordination of many routines, a multiplicity of selves, each shaping and shaped by civilization. Many of us have dynamic routines that mutate over time as we learn from stress and our own initiative. When we see the full context of our journey, we appreciate the unseen harbor of routines provided by the love of our parents and the many signposts of society. However, as an unseen thing in itself, Routine can turn into alienation and nihilism, divorced from the context of all Trajectories.

Like other Stoic philosophers, Epictetus (first and early second century) taught that reason, our own autonomy, and our ability to choose Routines are what build character. He wrote that "capability is confirmed and grows in its corresponding actions, walking by walking, and running by running . . . therefore, if you want to do something, *make a habit of it*" (italics added). Also, "One person likes tending to his farm, another to his horse; I like to *daily* monitor my self-improvement" (italics added).

Stoic philosophy grew at a time when people questioned the power of Zeus and the other gods as the government. The self as its own source of action came into greater relief. Epictetus was himself a slave. His philosophy helped him rise above "the state" of his life with great discipline of habit and Routine.

There has been a resurgence of interest in Stoicism (read Ryan Holiday, Sharon Lebell, Lawrence Becker, Massimo Pigliucci). This popularity may be due to modern culture's focus on the aspirational self (such as selfies and Facebook). Indeed, some studies show increases in perfectionism and narcissism in recent decades. Either way, the modern "self" is very different than the one described by the original Stoics.

Modern Stoics are sometimes atheistic and take Stoicism out of its deeper spiritual context, such that some critics argue against what they call "life-hack stoicism." Consider these quotes from the Greeks: "You are a fragment of God himself" (Epictetus); "A sacred spirit dwells within us, and is the observer and guardian of all our goods and ills" (Seneca); and "He is living with the gods who constantly displays to them a soul that is satisfied with the lot assigned to it" (Marcus Aurelius, *Meditations*, Book 5).

As discussed elsewhere in this Quest for Presence, whether you are an atheist or not, the Radiant Forces will continue to weave within and around you across your journey. To know the Radiant Forces (*QfP Book 1*), we develop the Soulful Capacities (*QfP Book 2*) and study the Attractions (*QfP Book 3*). The QfP contemplations help us to see what is hidden, to become *observers* and *guardians* of the interweaving Trajectories and help us deeply know *the lot assigned to us*. Routine helps us regularly join with others to cultivate Acceptance, Presence, and Flow. Together, we discover meaning, those Synchronicities hidden in the Routines and from the Treasures we share together.

Contemplation (QfP 4-2): Routine

The contemplation of Routine uses the "Time Adjustment Protocol" from *QfP Book 1*. First, reflect on each of the following steps of the protocol as applied to Routine:

1. You already have habits and routines. How can you make the most of the Routines you have to help you enjoy life more and give you a sense of coherence in your life?

2. What regular or dedicated practice do you include in your Routine that enhances your spirit, sense of meaning or purpose, or joy?

3. How can you stay awake and alert within your Routines so you can neither fall asleep, nor get distracted and instead stay present, enjoy life, and witness the Treasures?

4. How do your habits support your purpose, your values, your calling, cause, destiny?

Second, think about any Treasure you experience, either as part of your daily routine (meals, waking, working, retiring) or as part of a ritual or day of importance, whether a birthday, anniversary, holiday, seasonal event, memorial, or other day that has personal meaning. Imagine that any Treasure you experience from a day of importance can be part of your Routine or vice versa. Write the Treasure in the starred spaces below, and think of ways to remind yourself of it at points in your Routine. For example, what positive feeling or uplift do you experience—which may even be unique or characterizes—a birthday, an anniversary, a civic holiday (such as Labor Day), or others? The sixteen Treasures discussed in the Q*f*P series are Spontaneity, Momentousness, Fulfillment, Clutch, Optimism, Effortlessness, Ordinariness, Coherence, Adoration, Resonance, Patience, Preciousness, Savoring, Poignance, Release, and Awe.

Instructions: In each of the seven ANNIVERSARY boxes below, first reflect on an experience you had or will have in the category. For example, recall a recent birthday or anniversary event or imagine an upcoming event. Note the positive, uplifting, or stirring feeling you have in association with that event. You can write that feeling in the box. Also, review the list of 16 Treasures. Which Treasure comes to mind? Next, do the same for the four DAILY ROUTINE boxes.

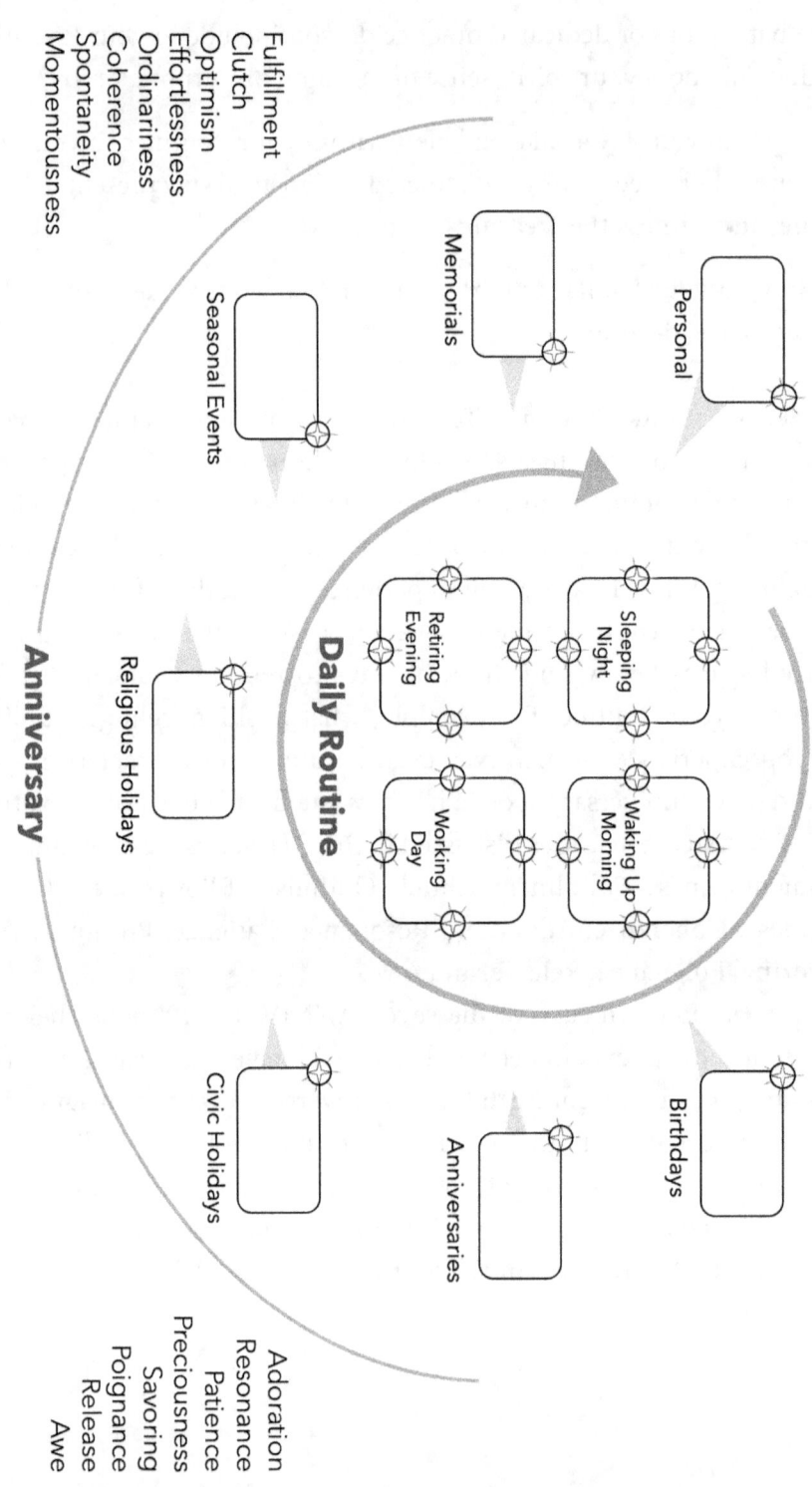

CHAPTER 4

Contemplating Timing

In which Wise Old Owl and Pooh, sitting down to share a cup of tea, reflect on the age-old wisdom of the statement, "It is always time for tea." And, in which, Pooh asks "But isn't the best time for tea honey season?"

THE DANCE: DYNAMICS

SAYINGS: "There is no time like now," "The time has come," and "Make good time."

ATTRACTION: Timing manifests from Nurturing Conditions in Nurturing Conditions' attraction to Form.

FUNCTION: The function of Timing is to connect Nurturing Conditions to Form.

INFLUENCE: Timing influences Routine through Form.

RESULT: Timing results as Rhythm, in its own function, connects Chaos to Nurturing Conditions.

SISTER: Timing is sister to Transition. They each facilitate the expression of the other.

MIRROR: The good guidance born of Timing helps us embrace the gifts of Interruption.

COUNTERPOINT: Without Pacing, the gift of Timing loses meaning, and we become shackled to clock-time.

Functional Definition: Timing occurs whenever we have a positive sense of *when*; that is, when we experience the duration of an event or time window (a day, a season, an orbit) in a way that brings a sense of rightness, matching, efficiency, effectiveness, or co-order (coordination) to the relationship between self and others or self and the situation. This includes beginning and ending as expected, meeting at the right point in a process, or arriving and leaving at the "right" time. Timing is a moment in which otherwise separate entities (self and other) come together to cocreate a Form and experience Flow as a singular unit.

Random samples: Musical chairs; punctuality; windows of opportunity; syntony; cooking times; being in the right (wrong) place at the right (wrong) moment; trapeze; catching all green lights; catch the train; visiting a place (museum, restaurant) at the opportune period for best viewing, seating, service; satellites; space travel (calculate best time for docking, launch, landing, and other key procedures). Examples of inopportune timing include oafishness; blurting; missing a beat; missing a connection; accidents; botching; over- or undercooked.

Other examples include the following:

Mindful or right action involves sensitivity to the optimal time to say or do something in a way that brings about a sense of fit, flow, or collaboration, whereas mindless action will lead to awkwardness or feeling off-kilter. At the same time, successful robberies and pickpockets occur because of the perpetrators' mindfulness of the right time to strike.

Meetings and *conversations* all depend on Timing. Attunement to Timing includes finding the opportunity or making the decision to meet or not, coming together or going apart, of leaning in and potential for helping, knowing when to collaborate and when to hold back and let others act, sensing when to speak and when to listen.

Diplomacy depends on Timing. Dr. Bo Bennett, social psychologist, entrepreneur, and author notes, "Diplomacy is more than saying or doing the right things at the right time, it is avoiding saying or doing the wrong things at any time."

Relationship problems occur when Timing is thwarted through impatience and impulsivity.

Timing of life transitions (see more in chapter 6, "Contemplating Transition") has been the focus of some research which suggests that cultural norms and age shape the when or "best" time for life-course rituals (such as first sexual intercourse, voting age, first job, end of formal schooling, marriage, first child, last child, retirement).

Time of day and time of life (see section on "Binding" in the "Essay on Timing") has been shown to play an important role in a vast array of human activities for human performance, cognitive tasks, creative work, and teamwork.

Of all the Trajectories, Timing is where our attention to surrounding conditions is the most relevant. Being in "syntony" means the state of being normally responsive to and in harmony with the environment. Syntony is the epitome of Timing.

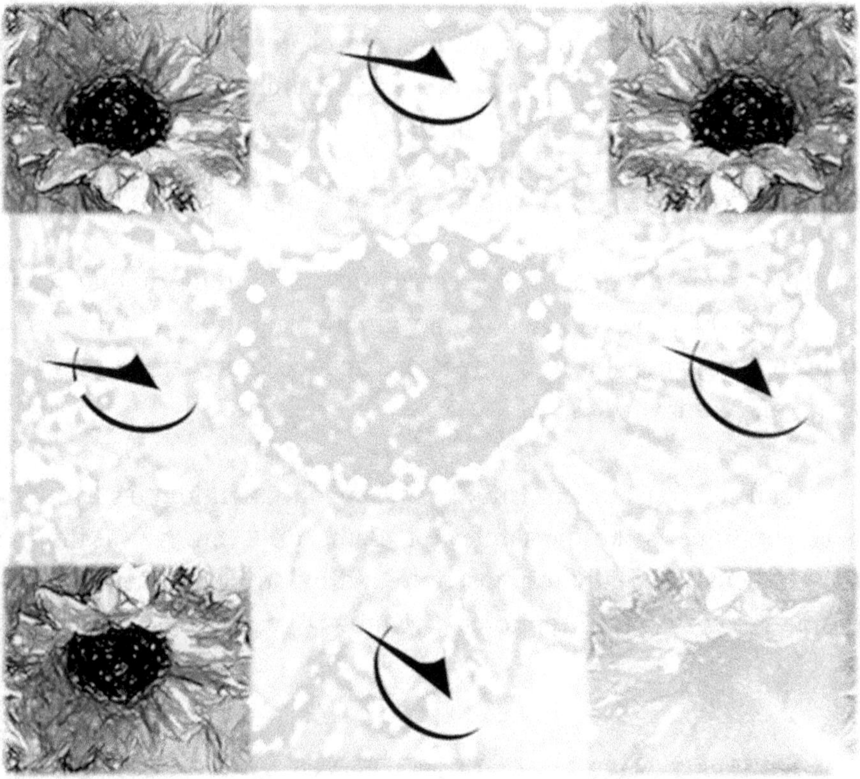

TIMING

I

remember sunlight as an
occasion on each leaf
that summer in Tuscany.

I remember light that way.

Like glancing up from my desk in the back of
the room in third grade and meeting your eyes,
like showing up just as the sun made a jewel of
a dew drop on a blade of grass.

I remember these moments when
things come together.

When the student is ready, the teacher comes.
When lovers find each other.

When insight comes from the silence, we, give,
ourselves.

All is right timing.

It has never been any other way

Light and the way things

come together:

birds on a wire,

spiritual friendship,

and joy.

~ J.B.

Portrait: Essay on Timing

The time is now! But time for what? Let's start with tea. Tea requires heating water to a certain temperature. Many teas require the right brewing time to maximize flavor and benefit. *Very specific and previous conditions* have to prevail so the tea can be savored. And make sure it's not too hot before taking that first sip!

This simple example shows how our experience comes from our actions and the *Timing* of *two* occasions. First, there is the previous context (cultivation of tea plant and drying, teapot, fire, teacup), which includes our actions (gathering the tea, lighting the fire). Second, there is the act of drinking and, most important, the savoring of the tea. Our experience gains meaning from preceding conditions. The art of tea can mimic the art of living. Life is a happening affair. Meaning comes from Timing. This is not the meaning that comes from words on a page. Rather, it is the understanding and deeper insights that come from the moment. All Synchronicity comes from Timing.

Timing is really about the Form our lives take as conditions allow our life to take Form. We are part of those conditions. Being deeply Present to life means getting out of our own way so we can participate in the story as it unfolds. Otherwise, we really don't take the time to appreciate the tea. It is sort of an amnesia. Consider this poem, which shows that tea has different effects depending on *the point in the sequence* of drinking.

> *The first cup moistens my lips and throat. The second shatters my loneliness. The third causes the wrongs of life to fade gently from my recollection. The fourth purifies my soul. The fifth lifts me to the realms of the unwinking gods.*
> ~ CHINESE MYSTIC, TANG DYNASTY (FROM "THE BOOK OF TEA")

I wonder, what tea was around in the Tang Dynasty that lifts one to the gods!? Perhaps I was born at the wrong time?

Timing and the Journey

Imagine you are going on a journey. A native wisdom guide has mysteriously shown up to take you up a rugged, uncharted mountain. The two of you are connected by a cord. You need that cord and the threads that bind it together in case you lose your footing or your way. The mountain is big, so you start with small steps. By journey's end, you will have a big view of how Timing works. For now, let's focus on the cord that tethers you to the guide. Imagine the cord is made up of the many different Timings of your life.

Let's start with simple daily threads in that connecting cord. When do you take a shower? When do you start preparing a meal? When do you leave your house to make sure you pick up the kids, make it to an appointment, or catch a bus, train, or plane? When is the right time to exercise, take a nap, wake up, and go to sleep?

What about those medium-size strings? When do you ask for a date, kiss, propose marriage; request a raise or send out a resume; buy or sell a stock; get the right medical treatment or vaccination; start a new diet; take a vacation; initiate a project?

Go bigger. When do you make contact with an estranged family member or friend; seek confession; return what is long due to another person; ask for or grant forgiveness; prepare for your own death? And look back. When did your stars align; when did you meet the right person, find the right job—just at the right time? Did you know it at the time?

These "whens" suggest Timing is about *right timing*. We connect with nature and the rhythm of society as we wind through life's days, phases, and turning points. But as that cord connects us to our guide, Timing will eventually bring us to a summit where we discover an appreciation of all life's Timings—whether right or wrong, good or bad. The thread of our soul, weaving unseen in that cord, is really leading the way.

Our ascent requires navigating clocks provided by nature, society, our culture, and perhaps esoteric and spiritual signposts we find along the way. We are on a journey, with a guide, a cord that connects us, and the winding, circuitous, and dangerous path up the mountain. Of course, the journey here is the journey of your soul; the guide is your higher self, that part of you that has deep insight and wisdom about your life; and the cord is all those Timings that make up the moments of the journey.

As we age, we eventually will need to let go of that cord. We will see the Timing of this entire life lies beyond the detailed threads, the different situations of our life, from the mundane to the profound and sacred. We will have to surrender to that moment when the guide says, "This is the right time for us to take a break. Join me for some tea."

Defining Timing

Before we take that tea break, it will help to define Timing. For starters, here are five different ways that Timing works in our lives.

1. The Timing of *nature*. Everything has its own time, in and of itself, whether we are present to witness it or not. For example, green leaves reappear in the spring.

2. The Timing of *our day*. We have routine touchpoints: waking up, eating breakfast, leaving for work, using the restroom, and so on. Here, we often talk about how our day is well-timed or whether we are on time—or *not*!

3. The Timing that *requires us to* act (Routine). Daily tasks require Timing, or we will lose the opportunity. Drive through the green light and stop on the red, take the bread out of the oven after 45 minutes, or—for the sake of others we are about to meet—brush our teeth and use mouthwash! Even with our best intentions, bad Timing occurs.

4. The Timing of *opportunity*: Life presents auspicious moments to take decisive action, to "seize the day." For example, you ask your future spouse on a date just before a rival suitor has the chance.

Consider this quote from an anonymous survivor of the Holocaust: "Timing is all about guts and luck."

5. The Timing of *existence, of our life (purpose and meaning)*. This is the deepest, most soulful definition. We ponder the question, "Why was I born at this time?" and contemplate our calling, destiny, or legacy—that is, the Quest for Presence!

Clearly, the definition of Timing depends on context. At any moment, all of these definitions blur, blend, and intertwine together. Discernment is required to give our attention to any of them. Our ability to be present requires that we see the context, select a thread from among this twining cord of our proceeding life. Most of us require a guide—a teacher, therapist, or coach—to help us discern. More about this later.

Similarly, nature has its Timing with seasons, tides, and biological and hormonal cycles. Some times are more optimal for planting, finding food, harvesting, and many acts that support well-being. In an achievement-oriented culture, the right decision must be timely. But where did that moment come from? It would not be there without previous conditions, some accumulation of other moments. Contrast seizing the day with the well-known verse in Ecclesiastes 3:1, from the Geneva Bible of 1599 translation: "To all things there is an appointed time, and a time to every purpose under the heaven."

Contemporary Definitions: This contrast, between Timing *with* and Timing *without* us, is at the heart of understanding Timing. Let's compare three definitions drawn from contemporary dictionaries. Timing is:

1. A selection for maximum effect of the precise moment for beginning or doing something.

2. A selection or the ability to select for maximum effect of the precise moment for beginning or doing something.

3. The ability to choose the right moment to do or say something, or the time when something happens.

The first and second definitions are from *Webster's Collegiate Dictionary*, the ninth (1983) and tenth (1996) editions, respectively. The third is from the current online version of the *Merriam-Webster Collegiate Dictionary* (2022). Note an obvious change from the earliest (1983) definition, which only included "selection" of the moment. The next (1996) added "the ability to" select. The most recent used "the ability to choose" and completely dropped the generic select. As an important counterpoint, here is the current (2021) *Oxford Advanced Learner's (The British) Dictionary* definition of Timing: "The act of choosing when something happens; a particular point or period of time when something happens or is planned."

This comparison is itself a mirror of the very thing we are describing: the importance of context, of *when* you happen to look up the definition. Imagine if only one of these definitions was available to you because of *the time* you consulted the dictionary or even read this book. When you were born and even recent changes can make a difference in how timing is defined. For our purposes, in our Quest for Presence, both of these definitions are important: 1) the *ability to choose* (which requires you, an individual agent with choice), and 2) the more abstract *point in time when something happens* (which does not require you, an actor or decider, at all).

Happenings have their own opportunity to express themselves, whether we notice them or not. It is *Webster's Contemporary American English Dictionary* that moves progressively toward ability and agency for *maximum effect* and moves away from this more abstract sense of Timing as inherent opportunity. In the United States and many Western cultures, Timing is more about effect, an outcome, and even a perfect one at that. In fact, research shows that from 1989 to 2016, students in the US, Canada, and the UK expected more and more perfectionism from themselves and others.

Timing Is Neutral: Sure, there is *right timing*. However, in itself, Timing is neither right nor wrong. It is the objective or neutral moment pregnant with potential. It is how we orient to that moment that gives it meaning. Do we take decisive action, or do we follow our intuition? In astrology and for all sorts of divination (such as tarot cards, palm reading) the future is teeming with many right and wrong Timings. The stars will or will not align. Intuitive, wisdom-oriented, and esoteric perspectives can relax compulsive views of time. With Timing, we are called first toward intuiting the emerging form. Action then serves that intuition.

Different from Scheduling and Rhythm: Remember that Timing emerges from Nurturing Conditions. The conditions of our lives bow down, *in their own time,* to the next sense of order in our lives. When we align and synchronize our lives, chances improve for happiness, health, and success. As described below, research shows how time-management tools increase alignment. But we cannot fully control it, nor should we. Scheduling and good habits are certainly helpful. But it would be a mistake to think that all that is good, beautiful, and right, comes only from our own efforts at Time Shaping.

There are also differences between the Timing of showers, buying stocks, and preparing for death. Each reflects a different bandwidth of Rhythm. While Timing is of the moment, Rhythm is of nature, birthed from many interactions of life on this planet. Timing can come from attuning to Rhythm and even foreseeing the emergent form of the next vista in our life journey. Timing arises in our awareness as a readiness to peek around the bend. We might know *when* we are ready. More often, it is the *when of time* that finds us ready. We can prepare for the right time by following a Schedule and a Rhythm. However, when we least expect, our mountain guide may pull us off the path.

Timing: Binding, Finding, Guiding

Let's return to our journey and that connecting cord. Eventually, as we "learn the ropes" in life and from teachers, we may not need that cord. We obtain a certain level of mastery and can travel the paths, go up and down at will. We still may want to have the guide near us. And there will be *times* when we explore on our own—whether through guts, luck, or chance.

In ancient Greece, two words defined time: *chronos* (χρόνος) and *kairos* (καιρός). Zeus, the chief god, was the youngest son of Chronos, who represented time's quantitative, sequential, and forward movement that existed in the void before anything. We seek to measure chronos with moon phases, hourglasses, clocks, and now digital timers. Kairos, the youngest son of Zeus, represented qualitative, deep-time; the time of opportunity, the auspicious and fleeting moment, grace, or stumbling into adventure.

It is worth nothing that Zeus, the father of most heroes in Greek mythology, is the center-point between Chronos and Kairos. The hero's challenge requires navigating the situation or surface plot of our lives, failure and success, as well as the deeper counterpoints and opportunities of fortune. Kairos is related to the Greek word *kara* (head). A *kairos* is a time when things "come to a head," requiring decisive action. In our metaphor of journeying up the mountain, chronos is like the cord, the guide, and the well-worn paths. In contrast, kairoi are those moments when we go off on our own and experience what is actually happening.

Binding: Having studied time for a while, I can select any number of articles or books to support ideas I might write about. Here are four books, all of which I recommend for their wealth of insights, tips, and tools about timing.

1. *How to Stop Worrying and Start Living* (by Dale Carnegie, first published in 1944 and since selling over 16 million copies);

2. *Timeshifting: Creating More Time to Enjoy Your Life* (by Stephan Rechtschaffen, published in 1996);

3. *Time Management from the Inside Out* (by Julie Morgenstern, published in 2000); and

4. *On Time: Finding Your Pace in a World Addicted to Fast* (by Catherine Blyth, published in 2017).

These books inspire you to make the best decisions about time. They emphasize how to approach time to reduce stress (Carnegie), to be more present to life (Rechtschaffen), to take better control of one's schedule (Morgenstern), and to just savor time and one's life more (Blyth).

As "timing" would have it, another book was published just while I was crafting this section: *When: The Scientific Secrets of Perfect Timing* (by Daniel H. Pink, published in 2018, is a *New York Times* and *Wall Street Journal* bestseller). Pink's book offers much of the same advice as the others. It also provides a nifty framework based in science, drawing from more than 700 studies from such fields as economics, anthropology, endocrinology, and social psychology. See the table below, A Timing Framework: Adapted from *When: The Scientific Secrets of Perfect Timing* (2018). It provides a condensed version of some key features he shares about Timing. Pink describes the best times for performance, for beginning and ending tasks, and for avoiding the midpoint slump.

A Timing Framework: Adapted from *When: The Scientific Secrets of Perfect Timing* (2018)

CATEGORY OF TIMING	KEY FEATURES AND SCIENCE-BASED ADVICE
Our Daily When and Performance	
The Best Time to Perform a Task Depends on: • Daily Energy Cycles • Alignment of Three Factors: Chronotype, Time, and Task. (Scientists call this alignment the "synchrony effect.") A chronotype is a natural preference for when we wake and sleep. Most alert in early part of day (Lark), late in day (Owl), or no preference (Third-Bird)	Varies across the day for most people. Know that your energy, mood, and sociability generally increase from waking until noon, take a dip after noon until between 5:00 p.m. and 7:00 p.m., and then rise again.
	Know that your type influences best performance times whether you are a morning-oriented person (lark), evening-oriented (owl), or "third-bird" (in between).
	Know your pattern chronotypes have different peak times for performance: (A) Peak → Trough → Recover: If you are a lark or third-bird, it is best to work in the morning; or (B) Recovery → Trough → Peak: If you are an owl, it is best to work later in the day.
	Know your task peak times are best for high vigilance and problem-solving tasks. Tough times are best for mundane tasks. Recovery times may be best for creative and insight-oriented tasks.
The Importance of Preparing, Pausing, and Breaking	In addition, your ability to perform depends on having breakfast, recognizing the danger of trough (low energy) periods, and preparing for them; making sure to take any type of break (micro-breaks and breaks for moving; nature and social breaks and mental gear-shifting); and taking perfect naps.
Beginnings, Endings, and In Between	
The Best Time to Begin (a task, a life milestone or turning point)	Some days and times are better for new endeavors.
	We can craft our own turning points in life.
	It helps to meet certain milestones before marriage.

CATEGORY OF TIMING	KEY FEATURES AND SCIENCE-BASED ADVICE
Midpoints and Motivation (when energy or inspiration flags or declines)	Set and keep the right goals.
	Effective teamwork requires synchronization: aligning with leadership, building bonds, enhancing cohesion, shared mission.
	Find a mentor. Be grateful. Have self-compassion.
The Best Time to End	We tend to kick it into high gear when nearing the goal.
	Structure things of importance toward the end.
	In communication, best to end on a positive note.

Note: These categories are condensed from the first five (of seven) chapters in Daniel Pink's book. Pink, D. (2018). *When: The Scientific Secrets of Perfect Timing.* New York: Riverhead Books

From the science Pink synthesizes, a pattern emerges that casts Timing as inseparable from its catalyst of Rhythm, or the entrainment of two clocks. Right timing depends on entrainment, on synchronizing our habits with the rhythms of the day, our life, and each other. Interestingly, in his final chapter, Pink references or alludes to a number of soulful qualities and Treasures, such as Awe and Poignance. The last two sentences of the book are: "I used to believe that timing was everything. Now I believe that everything is timing." It is as though Pink had to walk with Chronos in order to find Kairos.

Finding: Many studies fall outside the massive amount of research that Pink and his researchers were able to assemble. "Context is everything" completely outdoes "Timing is everything." This, for the very fact that "the right time" depends on a host of preceding and overlapping factors. John Smith, in a 1969 essay in *The Monist*, writes, "Kairos . . . means *the time when a constellation* of events presents a crisis to which a response must be made." We often fail to respond because we don't take *the time* to see the constellation. Timing requires seeing both the tree and the forest.

The wide variety of research includes work in organizations, social discourse, creative writing, rhetoric, and psychoanalysis. There are studies on the timing of mergers and acquisitions, the right time to announce layoffs, the use of timing in conversations to indicate power, or bad timing, the timing of internet use, the timing of moving to a new home, the timing (or age) of important life transitions (driver's license, first marriage, first child) and even—going back to the beginning of this essay—the time of showering. The latter study, by Gram-Hanssen et al., researchers at Aalborg University in Copenhagen, found that the "practice and timing of showering" was influenced by its *meaning and purpose*: for cleaning, as a mental break, as a chance to be naked together, to conserve energy of hot water use, after exercise or work that was dirty, before going to the office, and others.

This showering example proves the point of all the studies alluded to thus far. There appears to be no such thing as a universal "perfect time" for many things that matter in life. Each life, in the context of its very unfolding, is unique. Sure, there are social and biological norms. The point of our personal journey is its *personal* nature. We have to find the time that works for whatever *purpose under heaven* we walk into, are called for, or are thrown up against. And most of us need help.

Guiding: Our many-threaded cord includes a time for everything. We can walk with Chronos and with Kairos. Timing may emerge on its own accord (it's not about us) *and* result from our previous efforts (it is about us). We can keep an eye out for right timings (see the table *A Timing Framework* on pages 60–61), and we can listen for auspicious spontaneity. We can listen not just for this day or phase in life but for the symphony that is our entire life. But the ability to hold these different perspectives is difficult to develop. We need a guide. Moreover, life happens, our timing gets thrown off, the cord breaks loose, and we seek help.

Harold Kelman, the founder of the Institute of Psychoanalysis, wrote the essay "Kairos: The Auspicious Moment" (published in 1969) when he was sixty-three and reflecting back on his work with dozens of clients, most of whom he had seen in therapy for many years. He reports that many patients will say, "I see what you mean, why didn't you tell me that before?" In fact, he had told them many times, but either they were not ready or Kelman himself had not been sensitive to the right time to provide the insight and decisively firm in his delivery. He also describes the need to "hit bottom" for many alcoholics who don't start recovery until the auspicious moment of awakening.

Fast forward to today, and we find a vast amount of research on psychological readiness to change. Coaches, therapists, and counselors learn how to structure their sessions for the right time to say things to enhance client readiness. Every day across the globe, millions of people receive such professional help. And, to no small extent, the needed shift depends on Timing. People also go to church, on retreats, or workshops. Many people gain deep insights, even epiphanies, in kairos time. But when they return to the world of chronos, they struggle with the pressure of life and cannot apply their discovery . . . until the right time or with the right help.

Synthesis

There is a greater message through all the binding, finding, and guiding—all the help we receive in the Timings of this life. At the deepest level, each of us is tethered to a guide or many guides. For many, it is the one guide of a higher self (God) that the religious historian and philosopher Mircea Eliade describes in a section titled "The 'God Who Binds' and the Symbolism of Knots" in his book *Images and Symbols*. These bindings often manifest in the form of all the friends, family, lovers, teachers, mentors, and therapists who have taught us and are teaching us now. All is coming at the right time, whether we knew it or not. Timing has always tethered us to the Form of the moment while the next thing happened and only because conditions of our life made it so.

So at a deeper level, Timing really is about perfection: Holy Perfection. Most spiritual paths call us to pause along the way and reflect on the Timing of this life. It is not only about reaching the summit. Timing brings our attention back again and again to the path, no matter where we happen to be (or which dictionary defines Timing). Every mountain has a summit and the perfect path toward it.

In finishing this essay, it may be fitting or "timely" to consider one last set of questions: Why were you born on this planet at *this time*? What is your purpose for being in the world *during this generation*? Our human species may be around for quite some time. What's so special about now? We are confronted with claims every day that climate change, pollution, overpopulation, and disease will lead to global disaster, if nuclear war does not break out first.

Because of these *prevailing* conditions, Stewart Brand, founder of the Long Now Foundation, suggests that we really need to carry with us "the clock of the long now." It is a symbol of the organization's purpose, which is to slow down our accelerating culture and encourage longer-term thinking about social responsibility going 10,000 years into the future. From this perspective, every decision we make—all our cords bound together—will have a lasting impact for generations to come. From this "Long Now" perspective, both Timing and the choices we make will have a big impact—catalyzing and evolving all meaning—for the very distant future.

So where is your cord leading you? What can you do in this moment (now and in the long moment that is your lifetime) to advance your purpose for being here in this time? This is not a challenge, but rather a reminder to look closely at the threads that make up your cord. Where have you been? Where are you heading? Make no mistake; your actions may be nurturing the future conditions for someone else to save the world.

I invite you to join me for some tea, and maybe we will figure this thing out together.

Contemplation (Q*f*P 4-3): Timing

The preceding essay uses the image of being led up a mountain by a guide who is your higher self. In that image, you are connected by a cord. Using this image as a metaphor for your life, consider journaling or discussing answers to these questions.

1. Where is your higher self taking you at *this time* in your life? What threads in the cord must you keep? What can you let go of? Can you let go of the cord entirely?

2. What is happening now in your life that feels as though it is the right time to be engaged with an activity, relationship, career, or project? Would you describe that engagement as binding you, guiding you, or finding you?

3. Imagine that you get to the top of the mountain and look back at all the different *times* in your life (for example, starting times, best times, midpoints, ending times). What do you notice? How many of these timings were "perfect"? Explain what made them more or less right, wrong, perfect, or imperfect.

Reflection

I had not planned to write a personal reflection in the midst of these chapters and essays on each of the Trajectories. But as Timing would have it, those Radiant Forces and Synchronicity compelled me to share this following story. I should mention that of all sections I have written in the five volumes of the *QfP* series, the essay on Timing was the most challenging. I was overwhelmed by the complexity of the concept. It took a long time to contemplate all the meanings of Timing and discern what needed to be said. As it turned out, the day after I put what I thought were my finishing touches on the above essay was Valentine's Day, and something unexpected happened.

My initial reflection in this book describes my pending move to a new home along with my resistance to the transition. To be completely honest, it was very hard for me. I missed the routines of my daily walks, access to a river trail, and the close proximity of a coffee shop and other conveniences. After a year, I still resist some aspects of fully moving in. Nonetheless, I had been in our new home for more than a year and was continuing to write this book. I completed the essay on Timing, so the next day I turned my attention to more "moving chores"—shifting parts of my office and books onto a new bookcase. It was then that I noticed sheets of paper stuck in between the pages of one of the books.

The papers were those I had received from the cemetery where my Jewish paternal grandparents are buried. They list the dates of Yahrzeit, the anniversary of the day of death according to the Hebrew calendar. Looking at the list of dates, I discovered that the next day to honor my paternal grandmother (Augusta Eichenhorn Bennett-Gussie) was, in fact, the very day I discovered the papers: Sunday, February 14, 2021—Valentine's Day.

My immediate feelings were a combination of awe, guilt, and excitement. Awe from witnessing the very Timing of Synchronicity that I had just written about, and excitement because I again had stepped into the unfolding of this happening life that remains a primary motivation for writing this book. But the feelings of guilt—a very awkward sense of flagging conscientiousness—were far more complex and had to do with the meaning and customs of Yahrzeit, the fact that I had just finished the essay on Timing, and the felt presence of Grandma Gussie. As soon as I saw the date "February 14, 2021," I felt she had caught me red-handed! Let me explain.

The main custom of Yahrzeit requires lighting a candle designed to burn for twenty-four hours as a way of honoring and celebrating the memory of the departed person. The candlelight represents the soul, and the prayer associated with the lighting is about sending love and goodwill to the soul of the departed. It always has been a beautiful and deeply moving moment for me, and I try to remember to light Yahrzeit every year for family members who have passed.

Everything hinges on the "try" in that last sentence. First, I light Yarhzeit more often on the day of the departed's birth and not their death because it is easier for me to remember. As noted, the list of dates was buried in a book on my bookshelf. Second, I don't always do it on the exact day, but rather, I am often prompted to do so by thinking, "Sometime around now, I should do this." Third, and this has something to do with being raised Jewish, I say to myself, "Well, at least I am doing it, and I love doing it, so it doesn't really matter that I get the custom perfect. Besides, who's watching?"

Well, as it turned out, Grandma Gussie was watching!

And she sent a twofold message to me in that moment. First: "Who do you think you are writing about Timing, Mr.

Know-It-All, Big Shot! You have no clue!" It was almost as though she, or some higher power who kept me working on the essay until that very day, was waiting for the right Timing to send me the message that, indeed, we—all of us—can only barely glimpse the wonder and complexity of Timing. Kairos is truly ephemeral. Good luck trying to nail that one down!

The second message was even more powerful or poignant. In 2021, my grandmother would have been gone more than twenty years. And yet, when I saw it was Valentine's Day, a shiver ran up and down my spine, and I had goosebumps. According to the Hebrew calendar, this was the only time in my lifetime that her Yahrzeit would fall on Valentine's Day. The only time. This co-alignment of the Hebrew timeline and the secular "day of importance" had never occurred before and would never occur again for me.

And while there are many meanings associated with Valentine's Day, I am most drawn to its connection to chocolate. My grandmother and I had a special bond when it came to chocolate. I remember sharing our love for chocolate very early on. When I was five or six, she would tell me, "If I had to choose one way of dying, it would be by drowning in a vat of chocolate." Toward the end of her life, I would sneak in small pieces of chocolate every time I visited her in the nursing home when she was in her confused state of dementia. In short, when it came to the bond of us, there was never enough chocolate around. So the Timing of her Yahrzeit on a day I associate with chocolate had a particularly powerful impact. The fact that it also aligned with the work I was doing on this very subject enhanced its meaningfulness and inspired me to share.

Thanks, Grandma, for finding me that day and for your unbinding guidance. Perfect Timing!

CHAPTER 5

Contemplating Rhythm

In which Poor Pooh sleeps for days after downing a whole pot of honey and, after waking, meanders around the forest with a terrible pain in his tummy. This horrid sight prompts Wise Old Owl to, once again, console Pooh and explain the importance of paying careful attention to the rhythms of nature, which include Pooh's tummy.

THE DANCE: DYNAMICS

SAYINGS: "The beat goes on" and "keep time" (maintain the beat in music).

ATTRACTION: Rhythm manifests from Chaos in Chaos's attraction to Nurturing Conditions.

FUNCTION: The function of Rhythm is to connect Chaos to Nurturing Conditions.

INFLUENCE: Rhythm influences Timing through Nurturing Conditions.

RESULT: Rhythm results as Pacing, in its own function, connects Time Shaping to Chaos.

SISTER: Rhythm is sister to Transcendence. Each expands and deepens our experience of the other, and our access to each is facilitated by the other.

> **MIRROR:** The good wisdom born of Rhythm helps us use Scheduling to foster well-being.
>
> **COUNTERPOINT:** Without Routine, Rhythm mutates into mania, a frenzied disconnection from self, others, and nature.

Functional Definition: Alternating emphasis of durations and periods—coming/going, hard/soft, shadow/light, or ebb/flow. This also includes the entrainment or synchronization of two separate Rhythms that overlap and diverge (again and again, as in a cycle). Refers to personal Rhythms (hormonal, sleep-wake, activity-rest, social-private cycles), and natural Rhythms (seasonal, monthly, weekly, daily). Rhythm gives us an aesthetic sense that things move together in time and includes symmetry, coherence, collaboration, and well-being.

Random Samples: Nursery rhymes like "Patty Cake"; symbiotic give-and-take; pendulums; circadian rhythms (24-hour biological cycles); breathing; waves; lunar tides; play; jazz; improvisation; syntony; rhythm method of birth control; dance; syncopation; spherical symmetry in seed and flower patterns; synchronization of Routines with others, society, the "collective"; seasonal migration; poetry. Here are other examples of Rhythm.

Cycles in Nature are core in many native wisdom traditions. There is an understanding not only that it is the right "time" for something to happen (see chapter 4 on Timing) but that this time will come again (and again), so there is a sense of Acceptance (not "pushing the river") and a willingness to live one's life in *accord with* (in "Rhythm" with) these cycles (as with Timing, see Ecclesiastes 3:1 in the Bible).

Cadence is defined by Dictionary.com as rhythmic flow of a sequence of sounds or words: *the pattern in which something is experienced*. For example, the frenetic cadence of modern life contrasts with the soft cadence of a hypnotist's voice or a guided meditation (a slight rising or falling in pitch of the voice). Even now, you can adjust the cadence of your reading.

Geological and Cosmological Timeframes reveal long Rhythms. The "supercontinent cycle" is the periodic coming together and going apart of Earth's continental crust, believed to complete a cycle every 300 million to 500 million years. Recently, the physicist Roger Penrose proposed the Conformal Cyclic Cosmology (CCC). CCC claims that the entire universe goes through a cycle of expansion (dispersal of energy and galaxies) following a Big Bang and will contract again. The Big Bang that created our current universe is not the first to occur. There may have been many more before and since. The time between one and another is an *eon*, estimated as much longer than our current universe (estimated at 13.8 billion years) has been in existence.

Equanimity, or a state of mental balance or evenness, recognizes the inevitability of cycles. There will be periods of trouble, failure, and loss, and these will be followed by phases of less difficulty. Equanimity recognizes that our actions (efforts at Time Shaping) may or may not result in desired outcomes and, likewise, that conditions may or may not be right for things to occur.

Engagement: When we (in body and mind) are fully in Rhythm—in synch, in syntony—with others, we are fully engaged. Technology, social media, time pressure, excessive Routine, or anything that thwarts this "in Rhythm" is a major cause of disengagement, alienation, and apathy.

Of all Trajectories, Rhythm is most *experiential;* we directly know the Rhythm of heart, of breath, of digestion. Rhythm offers an experience of connecting to Life (capital L) in a most sensory, somatic way. It connects our Rhythms with others and with all life. In society, the function of Rhythm provides opportunities for coordination. Rhythm arises within the field of Coherence: the heart and mind cohere.

RHYTHM ENTRAINMENT

it was amazing the time you came up to me
   hands flailing jumping up and
your eyes scattered with all kinds of light and
there you were and there i was
turning into your just being there and laughing
   belly out loud all raucous and wildness and
   heart pounding away like two rocks dumped
   from high up into a clear mountain lake and
   so we watched the
two sets of ripples of stream light move out
from their centers and perfectly
interlace again and again
hearts beating
in
rhythm

                                            ~ J.B.

Portrait: Essay on Rhythm

Every living thing is a latticework of timekeepers. There are so many wonderful Rhythms in nature and many wonderful Rhythms within us. For human beings, the three biggest biological clocks gift us with waking and sleeping, breathing in and breathing out, and the beating of the heart. All are synchronized in intricate ways, held together by the daily Rhythms of our planet. There would be no Rhythm without day and night.

Long before mechanical clocks, we were held by vibrations, deep Rhythms in nature—organic, pulsing, and born from light and air. Despite the Chaos and challenges they faced, our ancestors kept breathing through the cycles: night and day; the traverse of sun, stars, and moon; and the seasons. No need for ticking seconds, minutes, and hours. Before the artifice of timekeepers, society teemed with an array of pulses: in our bodies, with the clan, near the animals, from the tides. Light, with its alternating patterns, made our species dance with the world. Rituals honored cycles of birth, death, and animal migrations. We marked Rhythm through offerings made to deities.

Rhythm has always been a tribal leader, a mentor. Our consciousness of it anchors our senses to the ancient whispers of the soul. A modern life of Routine that has no Rhythm is soulless. Conversely, Rhythm without Routine is untethered frenzy. Rhythm brings a familiar, organic security that protects us from inevitable disturbance and nourishes our bodies. A healthy society rests on institutions that protect that Rhythm. Of all daily Trajectories, Rhythm is the most rooted in our biology, our cells, and our evolution—from the very beginning.

But fast forward to a world with a more fragile ecology. Many problems arise when things get wobbly. Like many living systems, we now require an even finer tuning to maintain a health-giving Rhythm. This tuning, technically called entrainment, is how a coordinated array of biological "oscillators" in our mind-body system synchs up with cyclic changes in our natural environment. These ancient cycles of day and night correspond to light and dark or "circadian" rhythms. As well, the seasonal cycles of hot/cold and wet/dry link to a wide set of oscillators in our brain and nervous system.

You can sense this when you stop and listen to nature. You also can find entrainments when you reflect on your own story. The contours of your own presence journey are defined by alternating lines of success and failure, happiness and sadness, gain and loss. We also entrain with each other, especially those we love, live with, and parent. Married partners and couples coregulate in many ways: turn-taking, conversational Rhythms, daily hormonal cycles, and synchronized heartbeats when sleeping. We coordinate better with the exchange of affection. Many of us learn a positive attachment style from parents who synchronized with our emotions while we were very young. This social entrainment of Rhythm is important to our well-being and success in life. Technology may disrupt some Rhythms, but we find health by dancing, literally and figuratively, together and in recalling times when we entrained with others.

But it is hard to stop, listen, dance, and reflect. We have less access to natural Rhythms. The culprits are industry, technology, the emission of artificial light, and the "24/7" background beep of the internet. I said "beep," not "beat" (more on that later). Extensive night-shift work and exposure to unnatural electric light disrupts otherwise healthy biological Rhythms. The term for this is *circadian misalignment*. Things get out of synch: sleep and wake times, lack of alignment between sleep/wake cycles and eating Rhythms, hormonal cycles, glucose metabolism, and mood. Misalignment causes a variety of both physical and psychiatric problems. For example, social media use at night has been linked to problems with sleep hygiene and mental well-being. Fast food leads to overeating and obesity.

The Wisdom of Rhythm

*One can ascend to a higher development only
by bringing rhythm and repetition into one's
life. Rhythm holds sway in all nature.*

~ Rudolf Steiner, Austrian spiritualist and educator
(Waldorf Schools)

To fully understand the role of Rhythm as our mentor, several terms need definition. First, Rhythm is too often defined in the abstract as a regular, repeated pattern of movement, sound, or light. The pattern is characterized by alternations between strong and weak elements. When we think of Rhythm, we think of music, like the drumbeat or bass of a jazz band's rhythm section. But it is also integral to poetry, dance, architecture, and, perhaps most important, to language and communication. In all languages, the cadence of speech, emotional terms, and facial expressions convey meaning beyond words.

But Rhythm is not abstract. It never occurs in a vacuum. It is always connected to something else. In the Quest for Presence, we also rely on connection. Presence connects to life, with its own set of rhythms. Rhythm is always a synchronization with other oscillators that show up in our journey. Therefore, two more terms need definition. These are *oscillate* and *entrainment*.

The term *oscillate* comes from the Latin word for swing, as in vibrate or pitch back and forth. A biological oscillator is any cellular system that leads to a periodic rhythm. Most living organisms have an intricate web of oscillators. There are millions upon millions of oscillators in our genes, neurons, sensory and visceral organs, and muscles.

Entrainment, as explained by one group of scientists, is

"the process through which two oscillators are attracted to each other by virtue of their interactions. The term entrainment is often used to refer not only to the case of perfect period and phase synchronization, but also to the tendency toward that state, perfect synchronization being just one specific case of entrainment" (Damm et al., 2020).

The second sentence of the definition speaks directly to the relationship between Nurturing Conditions and Chaos. Nurturing Conditions always receives the force of Chaos through Rhythm entrainment. Perfect synchronization is rare and not always ideal. Things wobble.

We are conceived because of entrainment. Newborn feeding patterns often start out erratic but eventually become entrained. Our growth is itself a signature of adapting to life's Rhythms. Wisdom is knowing that we rarely hit the same or perfect tempo—from day to day, with others—in any given day. It also is knowing, as the previous definition explained, that people are attracted to the state of synchronization, symmetry, of being in tune with life. Each of us, to varying degrees, yearns to dance with vitality, excitement, and spontaneity. This attraction is the very same discussed in *QfP Book 3* on the Attractions. We ever tend toward synchrony. Wisdom comes from knowing when synchrony occurs, our distance to it in time, how people differ in their knowledge of it, and how to help them find it. Rhythm entrainment may sound technical, but is a central player in our empowered language of time.

The Master Oscillator: Scientists have demonstrated that a certain cluster of brain cells entrains with the cycles of day and night. This cluster—called the *suprachiasmatic nucleus* (SCN)—exhibits cyclic activity based on light-dark cycles. We now know that every cell, not just the SCN, oscillates. Moreover, molecules oscillate in the most basic element of all life: the genetic structure and genome. All mammals have both a central and built-in oscillator (the SCN) and a vast array of peripheral or distributed oscillators. The health of our entire brain-mind-body system results from the central and peripheral coordination of all these rhythms, our circadian system. Finely tuned cellular rhythms underlie the microbiome, metabolism, sleep, cardiovascular function, aging, and cancer. Ordinarily, this coordination has its own autonomous rhythm. Poor health habits, such as drug and alcohol use, can disharmonize the system. However, even with changes in the environment, that master oscillator always finds its way back to harmony.

Feedback Loops and Consciousness: We wake to light. For thousands of years, philosophers and spiritual teachers have equated consciousness with light. Poets use rhythmic verse to highlight this connection. Our consciousness depends on built-in rhythms in the SCN. And it is all due to light. Our brains exhibit distinctive states of rhythmic frequencies through the day and when we sleep, all influenced by the SCN. These brain waves are well-established correlates of wakefulness, consciousness, dream sleep, and deep sleep. Circadian rhythms are disrupted in disorders of consciousness. This includes dementia and Alzheimer's disease as well as unresponsive wakefulness syndrome and minimally conscious states.

The SCN has a core region that receives input from the retina. This retinorecipient core transforms light signals from photoreceptors. Phototransduction moves that information to the surrounding *highly rhythmic shell region* of the SCN. This shell is continually sending signals and receiving feedback from oscillators in tissue all over the body. We wake to light and are sensitive to thousands of gradations of light. This sensitivity is coregulated in our breathing, brain, temperature, heart, muscles, and endocrine system. These homeostatic feedback loops get expressed as electrical rhythms in our brains. In short, we could not be conscious and present to our bodies without Rhythm born of light. Light even affects the SCN of totally blind persons.

Personal Biorhythms: There are individual differences in rhythmic tendencies. I am talking about chronotypes, as reviewed above in the essay on Timing (chapter 4). This is not the pseudoscience that claims differences between emotional, intellectual, and physical daily rhythms. A chronotype refers to individual differences in preference for morning or evening sleep onset. Theoretically, extreme morning-oriented people ("early birds" or "larks") wake up when extreme evening-oriented individuals ("night owls") fall asleep. Research indicates that most of us (65%) fall in between these extremes. Studies suggest that an "evening-ness" orientation is associated with worse performance and mood disorders. "Morning-ness" orientation is associated with having a more conscientious personality and greater life satisfaction.

But this is not always the case. The science again suggests context (Nurturing Conditions) matters. There is wide variability due to the type of performance (for example, requiring alertness versus creativity) and type of environment—our "temporal niche" and "zeitgebers." A temporal niche refers to those times during the day, week, month, or season when we are most active. Bats and owls have a strong temporal niche in the evening. A zeitgeber is an environmental time cue such as sunlight, alarm clocks, or social interaction that trigger entrainment to a 24-hour cycle. So, again, Rhythm goes hand-in-hand with entrainment. On one hand, those with a strong chronotype (an extreme early bird or night owl) might seek out, construct, and maintain temporal niches and zeitgebers that reinforce or help manage morningness or eveningness. For example, night owls can shut out stimulation before sleep. On the other hand, zeitgebers may modify our chronotype tendencies. Most of us, in the middle, entrain to these cues and manage quite well.

Synthesis

The force of Chaos brings randomness to oscillations. The force of Nurturing Conditions brings a receptivity, a tuning in to these changes. When these two forces meet, we reset and either find a new Rhythm or reestablish an old one. This is our happening life. We cannot only tune into the disruptors; we also must respond to them. The philosopher Rudolf Steiner wrote, "Only man is permitted to live without rhythm in order that he can become free. However, he must of his own accord bring rhythm again into the chaos."

Entrainment falls within the realm of "our own accord." It emerges from feedback loops between the master oscillator, other peripheral oscillators in the body, social features, and changing cues of light and dark. We keep on dancing with these changes. We are inherently beings of Rhythm, and our health depends on how well we keep dancing.

Technology, social media, a fast pace, and travel keep those beeps coming. We have to learn to get back in touch with our beat—our own internal, ancient, and soulful Rhythms. In fact, this is the purpose of Nurturing Conditions, of contemplation, and of taking a step back when too many Rhythms accumulate.

Remembering our Quest for Presence within the beating Trajectories, we get out in nature; relish the sun; exercise; practice yoga, meditation, or Qigong; have a friendly cup of tea; or get active with art, cooking, or gardening. Pay attention to that master oscillator. Remember that harmony is the norm. Take more breaks. Construct your temporal niche. Stay conscious. Find the wisdom of the beat. Recently, due to frustration with the COVID-19 pandemic, a friend asked for my advice about falling into a rhythm. I responded:

The only thing you need to listen to is the hum of nature, outside, away from the voices, into the heart, where you rediscover the true meaning of Rhythm, from which all those voices come. Stay there as long as possible. Visit as often as possible. Be Rhythm as often as your heart can possibly take.

Contemplation (QfP 4-4): Rhythm (Entrainment, Being Synchronized)

Rhythm is essential because it connects us to nature and each other. Using the diagram on page 82, determine your own temporal niche, and find a way to get back to the beat of your life. First, take the Quick Rhythm Inventory, located in the center of the diagram. If you find yourself lacking in Rhythm, look to the top of the diagram for some suggested activities. If these don't help, look to the left (Pace) and right (Timing) sides of the diagram. If you need even more help, look at the bottom of the diagram and consider letting go of any Routines that may be hurting your Rhythm.

Next, move your eyes to each of the dots in the black circle (center, up, left, right, down). Develop a rhythm to your eye movements. Put on some music to help. Start using your hands. Move your hands in a similar pattern: from in front of you, move them up, then left, then right, then down. Repeat in rhythm with the music. Get up and dance, swing, boogie. If you can take a few minutes to do this—finding the beat and staying active with it—you may realize that you just constructed your own temporal niche. Dancing is its own temporal niche. Consider sharing this niche by dancing with others.

Find the Beat
Construct Your Own Temporal Niche

What activities give you more rhythm (music, dance, exercise, hobbies, cooking, gardening, reading, writing)?

A Quick Rhythm Inventory

- ❏ I am sensitive to the rhythms of my life.
- ❏ I feel in touch with my own body.
- ❏ I feel good about the natural rhythm of waking, getting active, lowering my energy, and sleeping.

- ❏ I am sensitive to the rhythms of significant others in my life.
- ❏ I digest my food well.
- ❏ I rest well and awake refreshed.
- ❏ I feel a flow and regularity to the rhythm of my day.

Pace Feeds Rhythm

How can you pace your life to be more "in rhythm" with nature?

Rhythm Feeds Timing

How can being "in rhythm" help you find time to just be (relax, unwind)?

Are you so stuck in your routines that you have lost a sense of beat, tempo, rhythm, and vitality in your life?

Routines Can Shadow Rhythm

CHAPTER 6

Contemplating Transition

In which Wise Old Owl finally manages to bring Pooh to sit with him on the highest branch of the Old Oak Tree where they can watch the sunset, the fading light, and the emerging stars together. And Pooh, inspired by the transition of color and light, exclaims: "This is almost as sweet as honey!"

THE DANCE: DYNAMICS

SAYINGS: "Here today, gone tomorrow," "The sands of time," and "The time is passing."

ATTRACTION: Transition manifests from Form in Form's attraction to Nurturing Conditions.

FUNCTION: The function of Transition is to connect Form to Nurturing Conditions.

INFLUENCE: Transition influences Transcendence through Nurturing Conditions.

RESULT: Transition results as Scheduling, in its own function, connects Time Shaping to Form.

SISTER: Transition is sister to Timing. Each facilitates the expression of the other.

MIRROR: The transformation born of Transition helps to Pace ourselves to best use the time we have left.

COUNTERPOINT: Without Interruption, life's Transitions become endless and overwhelming.

Functional Definition: The process of moving through probabilities and phases of that which is and that which will be. Transition is seen in systems (metamorphosis, evolution), perspectives (from near to far), life (birth, growth, death), consciousness (sleep-to-wake to higher levels of awareness), history (premodern, urbanization, industrial, post-industrial), or narrative (scene setting, tension, climax, getting closure, resolution). Transition includes emergence, phasing, conversion, passage, and arrival. All transformation is Transition but not vice versa. We move from potential to actual and fuse the temporary with the possible. All things, events, and situations have a transitory nature.

Random Samples: Metamorphosis; learning; molting; waystation; eclipse; menopause; equinox; working through the barriers to self-compassion; growing pains; changing of the guard; decay; quantum phase transitions; half-time; intermission; "Transition words" (therefore, subsequently, indeed); breakthrough; dreaming; amphibians; Bardo states (from Tibetan Buddhism refers to a state of existence between death and birth); purgatory.

Initiations: Increases in consciousness, maturity, or responsibility are significant Transitions marked by initiations in cultural rites. It helps to distinguish outward initiation of ceremony from its raw, organic, and naked form, without cultural garment and with potential for epiphany. Here, Transition is a vivid slice in time, taking a slice from the pie that is the continuity of life.

Surface and Deep Transitions: Religious confirmations, Bar Mitzvah, Bat Mitzvah, engagements, graduations, weddings, funerals, memorials, christenings—rituals can all be on the surface of life. In contrast, consider a suddenness of awakening that marks the Transition from one phase of consciousness to another (such as a religious conversion). This is symbolically captured by the icon of *vajra* (thunderbolt) in Buddhism, symbolizing a diamond-like destruction of ignorance.

Liminality (from the Latin word līmen, *meaning "a threshold"):* Liminality is that state of consciousness or the state of the soul when we experience confusion, bewilderment, or disorientation. This is seen in the middle stage of a rite of passage or the experience of being "betwixt and between" in our journey of growth.

Phases: Sudden change contrasts with graduated change, as seen in stages and phases. When heated, water shifts from solid (ice) to liquid to gas (steam). Psychologists describe change in health behavior (denial-to-contemplation-to-taking action) and grief (denial, anger, bargaining, depression, and acceptance). In mythology, the hero's journey: departure (the call to adventure), the threshold (for example, finding a mentor), the challenge or trial, transformation, and return.

Evolution and Development in Life: All life is constantly in transition. Within individuals, a myriad of developmental windows and Trajectories unfold from conception to birth to life to death. Species evolve from simple to more complex organisms with increasing size of the brain.

Response to Adversity and Recovery: We can learn to move across stages of dealing with adversity: succumbing (depression, stress disorder), addiction (releasing tension as a way to cope), getting by or tolerating pain, finding coping tools, becoming resilient, and thriving. Those recovering from addiction also may go through phases (moratorium, awareness, preparation, rebuilding, and growth).

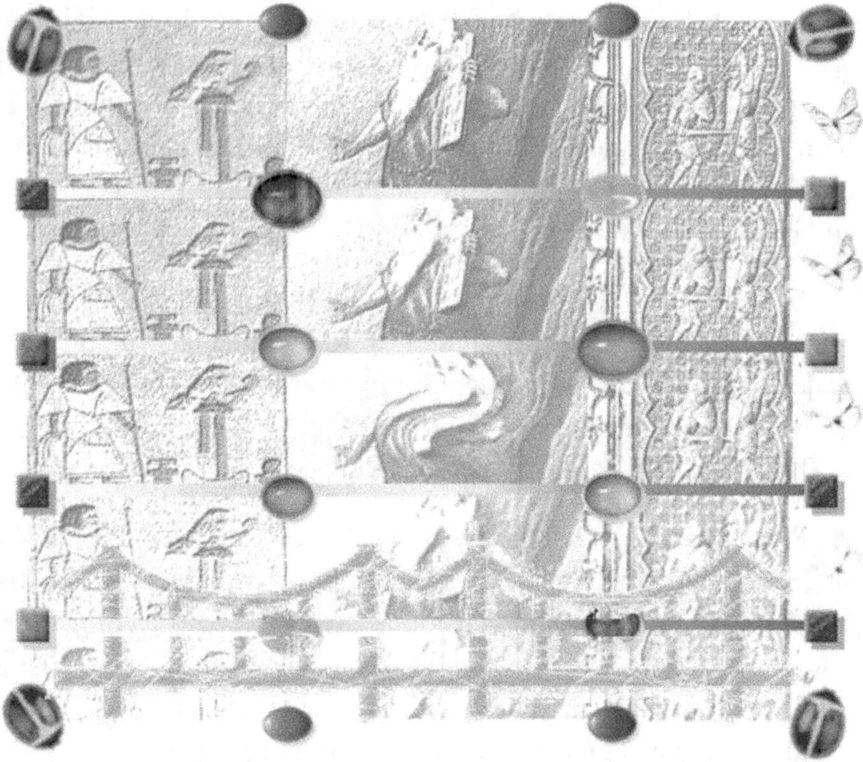

TRANSITION

The players grieve the curtain's last
The dusk enfolds the sun
Footprints fade on the beach
Even character and glory wither on history's vine

And the stars recede

You were once called to surrender in this lapse
This. Yet another transition from Eon to Eon
Now
Devote your Attention to what is happening
This next day here
    A planet swirling out somewhere else
We all fade
We all merge
We are struck through like jewels with stars
Now
Devote your Attention to what just happened
This past day here
    History gradually resided
    Somewhere else

Now, can you let your higher Self
Throw your smaller self into the
knowledge of all
    This, void and metamorphosis?
    The coming and going of the moment, the day,
      this very life?

~ J.B.

Portrait: Essay on Transition

Everything is either moving into, going through, or emerging out of some Form at every moment and for eternity. All things become something other than what they are now. We acknowledge Transition every time we say, "Life is a blur" or "That went by so fast" or "I can't believe that happened already; how did I miss it?" Transition is the attraction of Form into the welcoming arms of Nurturing Conditions—welcoming this instant. As you read this, realize you have arrived on life's welcome mat. It is *essential* to know that the day you were born, you were invited to a grand reception, a majestic occasion, of this incessant Transition we call "life and death"—but it is one of many layers of Transition.

Every transition implies an inflexion or turning point. This point initiates a phase and a movement of some element, organism, or system into and through that phase. The transition can happen *within* that element, as when water turns from liquid to ice or to steam. We witness a movement from one state to another. The Transition also can happen *to* something without actually changing its state, just as the earth's shadow creates the moon's phases. And the system can completely alter in its entirety, as a caterpillar becomes a butterfly or as a living organism passes into death and disintegrates.

The turning point is often natural and routine: the seasons marked by equinoxes or solstices; the infant rising up on its own feet and later taking first steps; the water heating to 212 degrees Fahrenheit. These inflexions arise from previous conditions and result from prior accumulations and developments, each with some degree of predictability. This level of predictability seen in Transition stands in contrast to its counterpoint, the Trajectory of Interruption (or disruption). With Interruption, the turning point is more sudden and unpredictable.

Either way, every Transition has an inflexion and a phase. In daily activity, we typically focus on the happening instant—the chore, conversation, or routine. This instant is part of a situation. And the situation is always part of some phase. With practice, it is possible to bring our attention from the instant to the situation and the phase. We would not be able to plan for the future, strategize, and invent without an understanding of Transition.

A Taxonomy of Transitions

There is a taxonomy of Transitions just as there is a name and a place for organisms within the hierarchy of biology—from the broadest level of kingdom to division (phylum), class, order, family, genus, and species. The grand divisions of Transition discussed here include impermanence, metamorphosis, evolution, development, alchemy, chemistry, relationships, narrative or story, and the journey of the soul. Of course, it is the last on this list that concerns us most here. The fullness of our soul's journey partly depends on recognizing and embracing the previous eight in the list.

Many modern-day writers in psychology and self-help talk about "life transitions"—phases and stages of growth, critical periods, turning points, and even "disruptors" that signal an unpredictable change from one life chapter to another. Each of these reflects a greater intelligence at work—the weave of the nine divisions of Transition. We are ever subject to the unfolding reality of our lives, regardless of how much we believe we can control that unfoldment. That reality is great, supreme, and awe-inspiring. Reality is the kingdom of kingdoms that awaits our presence.

Impermanence: Impermanence is the great Transition. Our first sense of impermanence often births anxiety about as well as our fear—and denial—of death. From the "transitional object" of a child's teddy bear or blanket to the fetishes and addictions of adults, human beings are innately aware that Transition is inevitable. A transitional object is a material possession that an infant gives special value to and helps the infant move out of the early-attachment phase with the mother.

As we age, our sense of impermanence and the awareness of death grows and often becomes more acute. We may begin to understand that everything dissolves. At the grandest scale, impermanence is named *Mahapralaya* (Grand Dissolution) in Hindu cosmology. In Sanskrit, *Pralaya* means dissolution, reabsorption, destruction, annihilation. And the cosmos includes many regions (for example, the classes in our taxonomy), each one eventually dissolving. *Mahapralaya* occurs when all regions return to an unmanifest state. Time ceases to exist. Everything returns to its origin. There is no more kingdom.

A central tenet of Buddhism is *anicca,* impermanence of the entire phenomenal universe. The Buddha urged human beings to pay attention to the four most visible signs or classes of *anicca*: old age, sickness, decay, and death. Through the practice of mindfulness of breath and sensation, and with compassion, we witness change wrought by impermanence. Centering ourselves in Nurturing Conditions, we watch the unfolding of this happening life.

So, on one hand, we have the unimaginable great extinction. On the other hand, we have meditation practice. What about everything in between? How can we understand all these different classes or levels of impermanence? Let's return to the example of water. Without water on planet Earth, there would be no life. Indeed, some believe that the preservation of water on earth is due to life. Water is a great example because it Transitions both in terms of its own state and as part of a cycle. As a state, water transitions from ice, to liquid, to steam. As a cycle, water transitions from condensation in a cloud, then to rain, on to evaporation, and to rain again.

Water shows us the most obvious and ubiquitous of all Transitions on this planet. And yet, it will not always be so. Eventually, over millions of years, and most likely due to increases in solar luminosity, all the water on Earth will evaporate. Most scientists believe that this is what happened to water on the planet Mars. Just pause for a moment and reflect on the idea, with Mars as a comparison point. Water will eventually leave planet Earth. And yet, it is because water breeds life that we are even able to have the next group of Transitions to be discussed.

Evolution: The Transition of evolution refers to a special change from a simple to a more complex or advanced state. The caterpillar-to-butterfly transition is an interesting example because there is a lot of research on the evolution of butterflies, especially their coloration, mating, and other qualities. Research on butterfly evolution points definitively to the role of hybridization and coevolution as integral to the transition from simple to advanced. Hybridization is the process of combining different varieties of organisms to create a hybrid. Coevolution refers to the ongoing relationship between butterflies and the plants they feed from; both support each other in their evolution. All species, including our own, have evolved because of these types of connections. We never evolve on our own. According to Etymonline.com, the online etymology dictionary, the word *evolution* comes from the Latin *evolvere*, "to unroll, roll out, roll forth, unfold," especially of books.

Development: Development implies a Transition toward some purposeful future state. Phases become distinctive levels or stages, with each new level having greater freedom, consciousness, meaning, or purpose. The philosopher Aristotle used the term *telos*, meaning the potential or inherent purpose or objective of a person or thing. From the context of development, Transitions are not merely random or born of Chaos. Of all our divisions, development provides the clearest example where we see the nurturing aspect of Nurturing Conditions. Some degree of support, facilitation, nourishment, or cultivation is required for an organism, thing, or project to develop toward its fullest form. The modern philosopher Ken Wilber (2000) integrated a vast array of ideas about development. This includes stages of cognitive growth (for example, from preconceptual to advanced logic); self-development (from instinctive or reactive to integrated and objective); and moral development (from amoral and narcissistic to altruistic), as well as in terms of spirituality, eroticism, art, ethics, religion, and others. The hierarchy of needs developed by Abraham Maslow ascend from physiological to safety to belongingness to self-esteem to self-actualization to self-transcendence. Inevitably, Transition results in transcendence (timelessness) through the activity of Nurturing Conditions in its attraction toward Chaos. Maslow also talked about "peak experiences" as potential turning points where we glimpse higher levels of being.

Metamorphosis: Metamorphosis is often defined as a change of the form or nature of a thing or person into a completely different one by natural or supernatural means. While impermanence is the completion of all form, metamorphosis is a complete change of form—but only if we can see the transformation as a witness standing outside. The great futurist and inventor R. Buckminster Fuller wrote, "There is nothing in a caterpillar that tells you it's going to be a butterfly." From the perspective of the caterpillar, once it goes into that cocoon, it is impermanent. Again, depending on our temporal context (Nurturing Conditions), what appears as impermanence reveals itself to be a transformation into something else.

Alchemy and Transmutation: Readers may be critical of reference to Gnosticism and alchemy. However, alchemy provides insight into our topic of Transition, specifically as related to the soul and our intention to navigate phases of our soul's awakening. Gnosticism, derived from the Greek word *gnosis* (meaning "secret knowledge"), refers to knowledge of transcendence or mystical experiences arrived at through internal, intuitive means to overcome material existence. Historically speaking, alchemy was an offshoot from Gnosticism and refers to medieval chemistry and the science of transmutation of base metals into silver or gold. Alchemists believed in the quest for a universal panacea, a life-transcending elixir, and the quintessence of universal wisdom. *Transmutation* refers to changing lead (a base element) into gold (a higher vibrational element), or the "philosopher's stone." This was an outer alchemy.

Psychologist Carl Jung described an inner alchemy. For Jung, alchemy was an articulate metaphor for the process of *individuation*, the phases of personality development from fragmentation into wholeness. Individuation can be activated through intuition, creativity, imagination, dreams, and reflections on art, poetry, fiction, and metaphor. In contrast to the classes of Transition described above (evolution, development, and the rest), the transmutation of alchemy involves a deliberate intention to "work with one's self" and the matter of one's life—especially difficulties, adversity, unresolved issues, and areas that one has resisted assessing ("one's own shit"). Alchemy describes different phases through which we transform our neurosis into a powerful source of internal inspiration, wholeness, and well-being; otherwise known as the philosopher's stone of one's psyche.

Three specific phases and seven subphases of transmutation of the inner alchemy provide a roadmap in our Quest for Presence. They include the *nigredo* (a "dark" or black time, composed of calcination, dissolution, and separation). This is often a period of great despair, a dark night, hitting a wall or hitting bottom. *Nigredo* requires one to pause or slow down and assess the shadow side of one's personality. In the separation subphase, we distinguish conscious thoughts and feelings from unconscious motivations. We awaken to see our false ego is not our true essence. The *albedo* or "white" phase refers to cleansing or purification. We empower our true essence to express itself. Albedo contains conjunction, fermentation, and distillation. Fermentation is also known as putrefaction or decomposition. It is where we witness the rotting of the dead self. We look squarely at our character defects, vices, selfishness, and begin to let go of (distill) them from our essential self. The last phase, *rubedo* (the "redness" for vigor and vitality), involves coagulation. This is where the whiteness of the purified self is fully invigorated with life. One attains self-mastery, self-realization, and a sense of abiding wholeness.

Chemistry: The alchemists, working between the thirteenth and eighteenth centuries, are seen as the precursors of modern chemistry. There is a fundamental process in modern chemical science called the *transition state*. Technically, a transition state is a very short-lived configuration of atoms at a local energy maximum during a chemical reaction as described in a reaction-energy diagram. It is a "point of no return" that lasts for only a few femtoseconds (quadrillionths of a second) and where a molecule is transformed into a new product. In a brief essay on transition states, contemporary organic chemist James Ashenhurst (2025) explains that maximum energy is akin to the point of maximum pain. He uses the analogy of the character Remus Lupin in the Harry Potter series. When Remus changed to his werewolf form at the full moon, "fangs and hair had to grow, the spine curled, the hands became more pawlike and the fingernails lengthened into claws . . . You can imagine that the extent to which Remus disliked transforming into a werewolf was proportional to the pain involved. That point of maximum pain—where Lupin is half-man, half-werewolf—is a lot like a transition state."

Personal Relationships: In my book *Time and Intimacy* (2000), I describe eight theoretical models of relationship development from social psychology and marriage and family studies. These models suggest relationships transition with a specific order of phases. Importantly, these theories indicate that couples rarely adhere to a sequence. They can skip a phase completely (for example, first kiss goes directly to marriage without any real courtship). Sometimes they continually cycle through break up and repair over a long period before either ending the relationship or making a commitment. And, in the case of families, especially step-families, the whole family system continually reorganizes with important turning points (such as childbirth, new job, children entering school, or death of a grandparent). Fast forward twenty-one years, and new research on relationships formed through social media now suggests specific transitional phases. In early stages, people move from instant messaging to cell phones as a relationship progresses. Study participants cautioned that it was important to wait for a period, engaging by text messages before moving forward with a more intimate phone call. Timing (the sister of Transition) is important when navigating transitions even in social media courtship.

Narrative and Story: Consider the above descriptions. Are they stories? A story requires 1) both a plot and characters who, through their actions, advance the plot; and 2) sufficient details about setting so as to transport an audience to a different time and place. A story contains elements that allow us to empathically enter into the time of the developing narrative. All stories contain characters and transition points, often where we can engage emotionally. For example, characters grow up, fall in love, achieve their goals; or they lose their way, fail, experience tragic loss; or they forgive or are forgiven, redeem or experience redemption, end up in jail or are released into freedom.

Synthesis and the Quest for Presence

Across all the above examples of Transition, a pattern emerges that stands above and outside our own agency. Conditions are ever bringing us on and on to the next stage. The quote from Shakespeare that "All the world is a stage" in *As You Like It* begins like this:

> *All the world's a stage,*
> *And all the men and women merely players;*
> *They have their exits and their entrances;*
> *And one man in his time plays many parts,*
> *His acts being seven ages.*

The remainder of this famous soliloquy describes those seven ages: infant, schoolboy, lover, soldier, adult, middle-aged, and feeble senior. But the overarching context for this metaphor is the stage, the conditions that allow the plot to unfold. Without the stage to begin with, there would be no forms entering and exiting.

Consider another opening line in a Shakespeare soliloquy: "To be, or not to be, that is the question" in Act 3, Scene 1 of *Hamlet*. This, perhaps the most-quoted line in all of English, also occurs in a broad context, which those who quote it often do not know. As explained toward the start of this essay, every instant of our life nests within a situation which nests within a phase. Hamlet does not question existence earlier in Act 1, Scene 1, nor later in the final scene of Act 5. Hamlet's soliloquy is an inflexion point. It begins to consider, but never really answers, the question posed in previous acts of the play: "Is Hamlet mad?" Instead, the soliloquy helps us understand Hamlet's motives for later actions.

Specifically, the last lines of the "to be or not to be" speech presage Hamlet's last lines of the entire play. As he lies dying, Hamlet asks his trusted and intelligent friend Horatio to stay alive long enough to "tell my story" to others. In the "to be" speech, Hamlet points out that most human beings are cowards because they fear death and so fail to take required action. The entire play becomes a contemplation on the purpose of life, the actions we take, and the need to leave a story behind us before we Transition to death.

The Quest for Presence is then one of meaning. Life Transitions may be viewed as either metamorphosis, evolution, or development. As a central character in those Transitions, you can bring courage, intentionality, and deliberate action, steering your future through alchemical changes that result in more wholeness. Through all these lenses, it is unlikely that you will change in an instant like a molecule in a transition state. It is more likely that a story unfolds that seasons you and deepens your wisdom.

In every religion, contemplation of impermanence is the basis of awakening and salvation. Faced with the knowledge of this transitory life, many teachers exhort us to pray, meditate, repeat a mantra, make devotions with earnestness—daily if not many times during the day. Of all the Trajectories, contemplation of Transition inevitably brings us to an awareness that time is fleeting. There is work to do on this stage, in this story, forever and ever. Stop ruminating about "to be or not to be." Your story is now. Live it.

Contemplation (QfP 4-5): Transition

The following exercise is based on the work of Metzner (1980), who describes different metaphors of self-transformation. This contemplation is both a meditation and a prompt for you to journal or spend time with a coach or spiritual teacher reviewing your responses. Start by taking a moment to get quiet. Reflect on the readings in the essay above and the differences between impermanence, evolution, development, and metamorphosis. Next, in a slow and meditative voice, repeat the four phrases in parentheses in the diagram below "All is transitory. All is evolving. All is developing. All is transforming." Repeat this sequence several times—at least ten times.

Next, reflect on your own story. Where are you in the Transitions of your life? As you do so, repeat the metaphor statements listed below. You may use the stem "I am moving . . ." to begin each statement. For example, "I am moving from Dream Sleep to Awakening." Repeat this sequence several times. You will know when you feel complete with this exercise.

Next, sense for yourself which statement or statements resonate most with you, if that feels right. Finally, within that statement, sense for yourself what transition state, point of inflexion, or turning point presents itself for you right now. What Transition is happening in your life right now?

Impermanence (All is transitory)

Evolution (All is evolving)

Development (All is developing)

Metamorphosis (All is transforming)

FROM **Dream Sleep** to **Awakening**
FROM **Imprisonment** to **Liberation**
FROM **Fragmentation** to **Wholeness**
FROM **Separation** to **Oneness**
FROM **Being on a Journey** to **Arriving** at a **Destination**
FROM **Being in Exile** to **Arriving Home**
FROM **Seed** to **Flowering Tree**
FROM **Death** to **Rebirth**
FROM **Darkness** to **Light**
FROM **Impurity** to **Purity**

Transition State
Inflexion Point

My Story

CHAPTER 7

Contemplating Transcendence (Timelessness, Time Transcendence)

In which Wise Old Owl, seeing Pooh starting to guzzle down yet another pot of honey, swoops down and grabs Pooh with his talons and then climbs higher and higher into the sky. And, in which Pooh experiences an awe and wonder he never knew and a deep appreciation for his friend.

THE DANCE: DYNAMICS

SAYINGS: "It's time to let go and let God," "Time works wonders," and "Time heals all wounds."

ATTRACTION: Transcendence manifests from Nurturing Conditions in Nurturing Conditions' attraction to Chaos.

FUNCTION: The function of Transcendence is to connect Nurturing Conditions to Chaos.

INFLUENCE: Transcendence influences Interruption through Chaos.

RESULT: Transcendence results as Transition, in its own function, connects Form to Nurturing Conditions.

SISTER: Transcendence is sister to Rhythm. Each expands and deepens our experience of the other, and our access to each is facilitated by the other.

MIRROR: The insight of Transcendence helps us to learn and detach from Routine, habit, ritual.

COUNTERPOINT: Without Scheduling, Transcendence can lead to social withdrawal, being out of touch with reality, a deterioration in mental status, delusion, or schizoid thought.

Functional Definition: The process of lifting above, letting go, and having faith. With Transcendence, there is simultaneous insight into life as both nurturing and chaotic. Also includes self-observation with inner stillness; to witness events pass in a detached way; touching or joining the mystery and interrelatedness of being, the unity or wholeness of all things. Every moment is transcendent, a portal to timelessness. From Transcendence of now to transcendence of self. Rising above just working for survival. Standing above the ups and downs of life.

Random Samples: The lives of the Saints; love; unity; wholeness; balloons; vacation; inspiration; everlasting; reconciliation; destiny; get high; rainbows; clairvoyance; near-death experiences; prophecy; past life; metacognition; unfathomable; ineffable; hard act to follow; conceptually, in biology, life transcends all other levels: life includes domain, which includes kingdom, which includes phylum, which includes class, followed by order, family, genus, and finally species; movies *It's a Wonderful Life*; *Groundhog Day*; *Interstellar*; *The Arrival*; *The Time Machine*; *Castaway*.

While Transition is a linear movement across phases, Transcendence moves beyond time. While Rhythm arises in the field of coherence, Transcendence is apart from but abides with great care over the field of coherence. The Transcendence of clock-time lies *within* the Trajectories and is not unique. It is as essential as Routine or other paths, and more about our experience of *no* time, being lifted out of our daily concerns, of time actually stopping. Most children experience sheer delight, giving themselves fully to the moment. And most adults have a memory of this experience.

Maslow's 1969 essay on *Various Meanings of Transcendence* (Journal of Transpersonal Psychology) describes thirty-five types of Transcendence, three specific to time transcendence. First, instead of seeing oneself as one is now, seeing oneself as a meaningful and symbolic part of a succession of those who came long before us and who will come long after us. Second, we can feel a sense of closeness with inspirational leaders, saints, and philosophers who died long ago but whose "spirit" still lives on in ways we connect to. Third, see ourselves as working hard now for the benefit of future generations to make a contribution to our successors, to leave a legacy. We are each part of a lineage that can carry the spirit and leave a legacy.

Connection and Unity. Transcendence often means connection and unity, not necessarily a belief in a divine force, God, or higher power. We sense a connection to something greater, a belonging with everything, an enjoyment of selfless giving to others, a purpose that outlives us, and simple joy in being alive. People experience these qualities as part of life. Transcendence can be more "mundane" and does not necessarily mean a vivid mystical experience or religious conversion. In a general 2006 survey, 45% of respondents indicated that "joy lifts me out of my daily concerns" at least on "most days" if not more often; and 85% have felt this way sometime in their lives.

Letting go. We can detach ourselves from any one perspective, approach, viewpoint or paradigm; from persuading or having to get a point across; or from our current level of ego development. There is a realization that one's identity is not what one previously thought it was.

Cognition of the deep past and the deep future. We can remember experiences or information learned in the distant past as well as imagine events or experiences that might occur in the distant future. This ability provides the sense that one's current "I" is not all that is, was, or will be. While Time Transcendence may rest on our thinking, it is often accompanied by an emotional experience of immersion, awe, inspiration, or ecstasy. For many, holding on to an enduring set of values, principles, or moral code, or having deep faith allows them to think past any current circumstance and follow a cause or calling.

 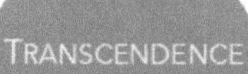 

Transcendence

Your capacity to separate & see things from two sides: Truth is better than that	Spirit's capacity to join all things in the tumult, fire of time: Truth is burning in that
Your desire for light, to move beyond this world Joy is better than that	Spirit's desire for you to move beyond this world Joy is burning in that
What could you know of forces at work for millennia to bring you to us meeting now?	An entire galaxy swirled, sang & died. Stop now & listen. Can you hear it?

~ J.B.

Portrait: Essay on Transcendence (Timelessness)

The most important idea to remember about timelessness, and probably about this entire book, is that timelessness is itself situated within and is entirely woven into the whole fabric of your daily mandala. It is right there, smack dab in the middle, alongside your Routines, Schedules, Interruptions, and every other happening. Think about those moments when time just disappears, when you enjoy losing track of time, or when you are just fully present without worry or regret. Every day we hover around and sometimes dip into that experience of connection, of letting go, of touching into the deep past or iridescent future that transcends this moment, the eternal now or the Holy Instant.

Timelessness is where you enter into the treasure world of life. You recognize the paradox of Transcendence. At any moment, you do not "rise above" the world, but instead become so fully immersed in it that the sense of connection becomes a deep realization of unity. Unity has always existed and will always exist. You simply are one with your surroundings, with others, with the world, and with the universe. There is no separation at all. Your feelings of connection are no longer about you being connected to another. Instead, the veil lifts. You see the pervading and underlying dance of the whole mandala. Transcendence becomes Routine. Routine becomes Transcendence.

As you reflect on this idea—that timelessness is always part of your day—you may wonder why we human beings don't take more time to cultivate this awareness, teach it to our children, or create methods and institutions that formalize our access to this deeper awareness. You may also wonder about those who suffer from poverty, mental illness, addiction, oppressive labor, or slavery. How can timelessness be important to them?

First, human beings have made extraordinary efforts to cultivate awareness of timelessness through the province of sacred ritual, spiritual ceremony, and religion. The Jewish Sabbath is a "time" set apart from all other times to contemplate timelessness. Second, in actuality, much of our understanding about timelessness comes from those who have suffered, not only from spiritual teachers or religious devotees. Biographies from survivors of concentration camps, and from those recovering from depression and mental illness reveal instances of unity, transcendence, or timelessness.

It is also necessary to see that Transcendence has less to do with happiness or satisfaction *with* life and more to do with meaning and fulfillment *in and beyond* life, beyond time. Studies show that while those living in poverty are less happy than others, they do report having more fulfilling and meaningful lives, usually as a result of their religious orientation. Countries that provide economic wealth tend to beat the drum of Routine and productivity at the expense of Transcendence. People feel alienated and disconnected even though they have secure wealth. This has been called "affluenza."

In other words, our failure to give attention to Transcendence and timelessness as part of our day-to-day life represents a tear in the weave of our mandala of Trajectories. This is often understood from the quotation in the Bible (Matthew 16:26, NIV): "What good will it be for someone to gain the whole world, yet forfeit their soul? Or what can anyone give in exchange for their soul?" This can be translated to say: "If you remember that timelessness is always there, you will never forfeit your soul while you go about your day."

It is important to know that similar messages exist in other wisdom or religious writings. In Buddhism, the Heart Sutra is probably considered the most profound, widely known, and commented on. It ends with this mantra; in Sanskrit:

> "gate gate pāragate pārasaṃgate bodhi svāhā,"

(pronounced ga-tay, ga-tay pa-ra-ga-tay, pa-ra-sam-ga-tay bo-dhi sva-ha). While the mantra is never translated in repetition in English, it loosely translates as "Gone, gone, gone beyond, gone completely beyond, enlightenment, svaha." Another translation by Zen teacher Judith Ragir reads:

Gate, gate—beyond thought
Pāragate—beyond personal identity
Pārasaṃgate—beyond constructions of Time
Bodhi—awakened awareness gone beyond individual consciousness
Svāhā—ohh, ah, wow!

Connecting with the Previous and the Forthcoming

All the books in the Quest for Presence series discuss the transcendence of time, or timelessness. The remainder of this essay will help you make connections to key ideas I have discussed in other books. You need not have read these books or read them in order to benefit from this section.

Time's Precious Tapestry and the Forces that Weave: When we look at the very big picture of this happening life, we see the Radiant Forces, our Soulful Capacities, and our Attractions all weaving together to create the experience of the wonderful unfolding that is our own very precious life. *QfP Book 1* introduced the Time Adjustment Protocol as a method or tool to help us glimpse this very big picture. Here are the four steps of the protocol.

1. You are already here; you might as well make the most of it (while it lasts).

2. Don't take any of it too seriously, except for a regular and dedicated practice that enhances your spirit, sense of meaning or purpose, or joy.

3. Every moment, you have the opportunity to see things as they really are.

4. Stay focused on taking positive steps toward your objective, and then sit back and enjoy the journey of your life.

Timelessness is an essential aspect of this protocol. In the Time Adjustment Protocol, we recognize four features or processes given to us as human beings: birth, death, time, and timelessness. All four are essential. Time, as an illusion, is more than a steady march from birth to death. We miss out on life if we focus only within this frame of sequential clock-time. Timelessness helps us break out of the frame—much like breaking out of prison or having the "Get Out of Jail" free card in the game of Monopoly. Time no longer monopolizes our life. The four practices of the protocol help us make the break.

The Soulful Capacities: A Soulful Capacity refers to our innate and ever-present ability to experience the precious weave of life and the Radiant Forces, especially as those forces manifest in our experience of life's Treasures. *QfP Book 2* describes and provides practices for the four capacities of Acceptance, Presence, Flow, and Synchronicity. Through these practices, the experience of timelessness brings us either upward into the realm of the spirit or downward into the province of the soul. Moving up, timelessness has the quality of evanescence, effervescence, and dissipation; time just evaporates as we practice the Soulful Capacities. Moving down, timelessness brings us into contact with ancestral, archetypal, and deeper patterns that have great soul weight and helps us see the current civilization as just a small speck in the grand scheme of the cosmos.

Each of the Soulful Capacities takes us out of the linear time of mind, ego, narrative, and attachment to our stories and identities. The time of the soul waits for our ego to transcend itself and the mind's attachment to the past and future. Through Acceptance, we experience forgiveness (transcending the past), patience (letting go of the present), and fulfillment (being fully with life). Through Presence, we immerse ourselves into life with so much purpose, intention, and body-centeredness that clock-time ceases to be a burden and instead becomes a tool or a source to help us further our goals. Along with the joy and aliveness of Flow, time just fades into the background. Moments of Synchronicity give us glimpses into the grand scheme of the cosmos. With great clarity, we understand that there is so much more going on than clock-time can ever come close to measuring.

Each of the Soulful Capacities ultimately brings us to an

experience of the timelessness of the soul. As explained in *QfP Book 2*, those who work in hospice and with death and dying often have a sense of timelessness that comes with self-transcendence. In a 2010 article, Dr. Christine Jonas-Simpson explains: "As a nurse prepares to be present with someone who is dying or deeply grieving there is a penetrating shift in focus to the now moment." She describes the *timeless transcendent presence* that emerges in this focus and refers to the writings of Eckhart Tolle. Tolle explains that the mind will always try to control the time of past and future and so it perceives the timeless Now as threatening.

Attractions to the Path: Most of the time, you may not experience *timeless transcendent presence* because you get caught up in mind, ego, and personality. But your personality may help you transcend. *QfP Book 3* introduced the idea that your personality has its own unique Attraction to the spiritual path. Most of us has have a curiosity, an interest, or a yearning to get in touch with the soul, experience Transcendence, or understand "our brief time while here." Alternatively, life throws us into unexpected situations (see chapter 10 on Interruption), and we are compelled to explore more.

Either way, we are attracted to a higher state of aliveness and Transcendence. This Attraction happens in unique ways and our entire life—our evolving mind-body-spirit system—adapts and organizes over time in accord with this unique Attraction. *QfP Book 3* describes nine different Attractions and provides self-assessments and contemplations to enhance your insight and use of them. These Attractions are like a system of personality, except that our Attraction to the spiritual path is not about a single set of character traits that endure over time. Instead, we are drawn to something that moves us beyond time and, in following that Attraction, our life trajectory takes on a deeper quest of its own.

The purpose of identifying your own unique Attraction (related to the nine described in *QfP Book 3*) is to cultivate an ability to observe, to witness, and to stand apart from the drama and changes of life. In other words, we each have an observing self or inner witness that can detach from the mind, ego, and personality and see these for what they are instead of simply reacting to them. We might enjoy and even need to be or do a certain way, whether to create, organize, take action, connect with others, or challenge. Instead of overidentifying with these or stubbornly doing life our way, we can transcend our identity. In so doing, we have greater access to timelessness and may even see how the various archetypes of personality are themselves timeless and beyond our own ego.

Archetypes are gateways to timelessness. As defined by Carl Jung, an archetype is an unconscious image or pattern of particular characters that potentiate and reflect universal principles. Authors described any number of archetypes, such as Child, Warrior, Lover, King, Magician, Martyr, or Mother. Caroline Myss describes more than seventy different archetypes in her work on sacred contracts. For example, the Alchemist embodies the principles of alchemy as described in chapter 6. We tap into the timeless pattern of the Alchemist whenever we engage in the alchemical work of turning our stress, neurosis, addiction, or any psychological problem into a positive resource. Similarly, we may access the deep wisdom of any archetype during our day.

The Treasures: *QfP Book 5* provides stories and descriptions of different life Treasures. A Treasure is an experience—a state of consciousness—wherein one witnesses the value or preciousness of life *as it is happening* and in a way that brings a sense of uplift, wholeness, or Transcendence. In the Quest for Presence, the Treasures alter our sense of time; we become more present. The Treasures are not "out there" in the future. Treasures are uplifts that occur at the intersection of the Soulful Capacities and the Radiant Forces. Even in the midst of depression, we can experience Treasures every day.

In essence, the Treasures are those moments on the path where we—through spirit—experience the evanescence and dissipation of time or—through soul—glimpse the deeper patterns that define life and the cosmos. It would be a mistake to think that the Quest for Presence is a linear quest in time to obtain a Treasure. Instead, it is the gift of timelessness in every Treasure that sparks or propels our

Attraction to begin with (see *QfP Book 3*), reminds us of the need to practice a Soulful Capacity (see *QfP Book 2*), or helps us to see the great unfolding of this precious happening life (see *QfP Book 1*). The Treasures of life help us Transcend Time in many ways.

Synthesis

Philosophers make the distinction between Transcendence and immanence. Immanence refers to the idea that the world of the spirit always permeates the ordinary world of the mundane. Everything that happens (that unfolds over time or that is remembered and enfolded in your personality) is infused with spirit, soul, and essence. In contrast, theories of Transcendence often hold that timeless and divine qualities exist outside the normal reality of our everyday life.

In the Quest for Presence, this distinction between Transcendence and immanence falls apart. As stated in the beginning of this essay, timelessness or the experience of transcending time lives and breathes along with the rest of the neighborhood of the Trajectories. It dances within the precious weave of life in all of its features and threads.

Contemplation (Q*f*P 4-6): Time Transcendence (Timelessness)

Time Transcendence and the experience of timelessness can happen in many ways during our daily life. As you review the above, reflect on how timelessness is accessible through the random samples provided (love, inspiration, near-death experiences); from connection, letting go, and cognition of the deep past or future; or from contemplation of time's precious tapestry, the Soulful Capacities, our Attraction to the path, archetypes, and life's Treasures.

Exercise: By yourself or with friends, select anyone of the topics listed below. Journal or talk about how the topic is a gateway to timelessness, and share an experience that relates to the topic. For a discussion group, ask each person to discuss a topic not previously selected.

A daily uplift	Immersed in a movie	Nostalgia
Playing	Making love	Grieving a loss
Time of leisure, idleness	Connecting with nature	Reliving a trauma
A spontaneous activity	Listening to, making music	Talking to elders
Humor/time spent laughing	Studying a saint	Reading spiritual literature
Immersed in a book	A daily chore (such as cleaning)	Being with a pet
Being with a child	Finding solitude	Watching a sunset or sunrise
A synchronistic meeting	Flowing at work or in a task	Off the beaten path
Forgetting about time	Losing oneself in anything	Reconnecting with the past
An enduring principle	Caring for the elderly	A calling, cause, or legacy

CHAPTER 8

Contemplating Scheduling

In which Pooh remembers his recent flight with Wise Old Owl and wonders why Owl is always so on time and organized while Pooh just shows up when he feels it's time to show up. And, in which the Wise Old Owl tries to explain the difference between living for today versus tomorrow and all the steps in between.

THE DANCE: DYNAMICS

SAYINGS: "At the appointed time," "Ahead of schedule," "On schedule," and "Behind schedule."

ATTRACTION: Scheduling manifests from Time Shaping in Time Shaping's attraction to Form.

FUNCTION: The function of Scheduling is to connect Time Shaping to Form.

INFLUENCE: Scheduling influences Transition through Form.

RESULT: Scheduling results as Interruption, in its own function, connects Chaos to Time Shaping.

SISTER: Scheduling is sister to Routine. They support and reinforce each other.

MIRROR: When Scheduling our time in such a way as to bring more well-being into our lives, this well-being comes from how

> our schedule brings rhythm into our lives, with each other, and with nature.
>
> **COUNTERPOINT:** Without Transcendence, Scheduling can lead to a fixation on goals and outcomes, as well as exhaustion, burnout, and disrupted Rhythms.

Definition: Budgeting or appointing clock-time time to tasks, activities, and recreation or aligning activities with organic, inner, or cosmic time, or both. Honoring the resulting matrix (calendar). Such actions shape relationships that occur during and after a schedule is made. To witness the matrix of events that comprise the occasions of our lives. To respond to this matrix with mindfulness so that a series of events has a proportion, order, and sequence to them (not cluttered, random, or dense). Living alone, with others, or in a family is a significant factor in how and what we Schedule.

Random samples: Aesop's fable "The Ant and the Grasshopper," time management, cooking timers, calendars, holidays, harvest, bookmarks, timelines, priorities, day planners, to-do lists, quarterly goals, time pressure, overtime, 24/7, nine-to-five, clock in/clock out, work shift, roster schedules, time budget, full-time, part-time, stretch breaks, work-life balance, date night.

We schedule and consider future probabilities to give order, to accomplish, produce, work, and prioritize work, leisure, self-care, and social connection. Of all the Trajectories, Scheduling—and behaving with Schedules—is where most humans "spend" time.

Density. We can overschedule, under-schedule, or live in a border between Schedules. Overscheduling leads to overwork, which can lead to death. In Japan, *karōshi* is the sudden death of those working more than eighty hours of overtime a month. Often, *karōshi* comes from meaningless, spiritually empty work. Under-scheduling often relates to quality or leisure time. Leisure time has three types:

a) solitary (reading, exercising, listening to music, hobbies)

b) time with family or friends (date night, visiting, dining); and

c) interaction in institutionalized settings (volunteering, neighborhood activities, sports events).

Schedules are influenced by culture, values, and trade-offs between investing outward clock-time in different areas or in attunement to Schedules that occur in more inward "organic" time.

Work-Life Borders. Many studies focus on work-to-life conflict, life-to-work conflict, or spillover from one area of our life to another. In contrast, work-life borders is where we all have our own private psychological and internal "space" that we can return to many times during the day. We can schedule time for being inside the border.

Values/Priorities. Henry David Thoreau wrote, "It's not enough to be busy, so are the ants. The question is, what are we busy about?" We enrich our lives when we prioritize, Schedule from our values (family, spirituality, service, and others), and focus on our purpose.

Work-Family Alignment. Scheduling is the most ordinary of all Trajectories. Because it comes from behavior, it is the most under our control. Yet given our borders and priorities, we have to intentionally align our activities with what matters most to us. Alignment is the effortful use of time to support well-being in ourselves at work, at home, and in society.

Inward, Organic, Cosmic Time. Depending on culture and belief, people follow alternative schedules to attune to inward time. For example, in Chinese medicine, energy (Qi) cycles through meridians in our bodies at different times of the day. In astrology, people seek best outcomes and plan pursuits based on solar, lunar, or planetary events.

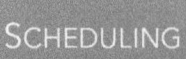
SCHEDULING

Advancing toward the pause

the tides weave the womb

for our first schedule

the tides weave the womb

receding from the Pause

~ J.B.

Portrait: Essay on Scheduling
(Schedules, Time Management)

We think that the appointments we make bring about the occasions of this happening life. But, just as often, it is the occasions that afford the appointments we make.

Scheduling is the relatively conscious process of creating a temporal structure and through the use of specific tools: a calendar, to-do list, reminders; a schedule itself. Compared with other Trajectories, Scheduling has three unique characteristics. First, it most obviously demonstrates the relationship between two of the Radiant Forces, in this case, Form and Time Shaping. Specifically, Scheduling occurs whenever Time Shaping creates Form: a sense of order to the day, month, year, and so on. Second, Scheduling is defined by the future or what researchers call "future time perspective"—our beliefs about the future. Finally, Scheduling is the most accessible to our consciousness as it requires clock perception and manipulation of the aforementioned tools. Intention and forecasting give us more control over time.

And because of the apparent control schedules give us, Scheduling benefits us in many ways, especially our self-efficacy. Our attention swims in a society with all kinds of time gadgets. Time-management systems control our attention so we can be more efficient. Scheduling always involves intention, a desired goal, and the belief that we can control time. But Scheduling is *one* way, not the *only* way to reach a goal. In contrast to the other Trajectories, time is something to manage instead of *let go of* (Transcendence), *tune into* (Rhythm), or *wait with* (Transition). If Schedule is our primary way to time, we can start to think that we can control the time of others. This is a slippery slope for narcissists, jealous partners, and toxic bosses who make efforts to control everyone else's time.

The research on time management falls into two categories: personal well-being (self-help and success) or work-related performance. It is important to emphasize a few things before describing these studies. They often ignore the impact of society, culture, and economic class. For the vast majority of people, time is often thought of in terms of the distinctions we just made: how much of one's clock-time is spent for personal well-being or for work. Of course, this distinction is blurry for those who work at home. Either way, our attention is drawn to the Trajectory of Scheduling in our action-oriented, future-oriented, consumer-oriented and fairly structured culture. While the other Trajectories are as important as these two, our culture dampens awareness of them.

An overemphasis on Scheduling, without honoring the other Trajectories, is the basis for a great deal of illness and, ironically, productivity problems. *QfP Book 1* listed some of these: burnout, anxiety, depression, stress disorder, workaholism, and suicidal thinking. At the same time, given any culture, it is very difficult to function and contribute to the world without some ability to schedule unless you are a robot. Indeed, the study of alienation in modern society is tied to how individuals feel they have no control over their time.

With regard to culture, the degree to which one has influence over one's time (discretionary time) is referred to as *temporal capital*. Such capital tends to increase for those in higher professional classes or with higher socioeconomic status. But even managers in highly demanding jobs have as much limited time as first-line employees or workers requiring two jobs to make financial obligations. Thus, while Scheduling, in and of itself, gives rise to Form, the forms and structures of society strongly influence whether and how much we can actually manage our own time.

The rise of industry, the digital age, and now the knowledge economy shows ever-increasing pressures on efficiency. Several books describe these cultural factors in great depth. For example, Melissa Gregg, in her book *Counterproductive,* decries the prevailing focus on productivity and how it isolates workers and dims any collective efforts as a measure of success. Time management covers up modern problems of precarity in the knowledge economy—unpredictability, job insecurity, and the lack of material or psychological welfare. To understand the origins of this focus on efficiency, read Robert Kanigel's biography of Frederick Winslow Taylor, who is considered the father of industrial engineering. To see its impact on stress and economic burden, read Jeffrey Pfeffer's *Dying for a Paycheck*.

Scheduling: A Multifaceted Jewel

To think of time in terms of efficiency is akin to seeing time as money. Doing so causes stress. But it is important to remember that all the Trajectories, in and of themselves, are objective or neutral. Problems arise only when we forget the intricate feedback loops between the Trajectories. Scheduling does not always have to be about work-time optimization. In fact, research on future time perspective (FTP) shows that those with stronger FTP have greater well-being, hopefulness, and a positive outlook on the future.

Scheduling (time management and FTP) is the most explicit, socially negotiated, and mentally accessible of all the Trajectories. Accordingly, it is the most studied Trajectory in psychology, business, and education. The key hypothesis is that if we manage our time better, we will be healthier, more productive, and achieve more. To test this, scientists have developed psychological measures of time orientation that show strong relationships with how we schedule. We now know that scheduling is multifaceted, with many components, and also has distinctive relationships with outcomes of success.

Scheduling and Well-Being: A recent review of many scientific studies served as the basis for this section (Aeon, Faber, & Panaccio, 2021). The authors first explained that time management is generally done to meet one or more of three goals: *structuring* (scheduling and planning their activities), *protecting* (setting boundaries or limiting time in activities), and *adapting* (being responsive and flexible to one's time structure).

From the review: Thirty research studies found a significant positive relationship between the degree to which people manage their time or receive time-management training and well-being. This relationship was found for life satisfaction, positive physical health, mental health, optimism, well-being, and job satisfaction. This same review also examined the relationship between time management and distress in fifty-eight studies. While relationships were less strong, the more one manages time, the less boredom, negative emotion, anxiety, work-life conflict, and stress one has. These studies do not prove that time management causes these outcomes. Some experimental studies suggest our well-being can be improved through a time-management course or practice.

Scheduling and Performance: The same review identified twenty-one studies that examined time management in relationship to work performance and a whopping seventy-six studies that looked at academic performance. For work performance, the relationship was stronger for behavior-based performance (such as being more motivated, proactive, and involved in your job) than for results-based performance (such as being seen as performing better and showing outcomes). Still, both of these relationships were significant. Importantly, there is a significant body of research on procrastination, and the review also found that greater time management was associated with less procrastination in both workplace and academic settings. The academic studies also showed significant relationships between time management and GPA, test scores, and student motivation, but not with standardized tests.

Orientation to Time Management: The above review reinforced earlier studies showing that time management increases with one's self-efficacy, self-esteem, or conscientiousness and that these personality factors apply to time management regardless of age, gender, or other demographics. This finding is consistent with the idea that Time Shaping aligns with the sense that one has the ability to cause things to happen in the future by how they shape the time they have. This sense of control seems to be increasingly important for the online or internet environment. Students' performance in online learning is based on how regularly or steadily they log in to their courses rather than on the amount of time they study online. Also, internet addiction is defined, in part, by whether people spend more time online than they want, hide this fact from others, and keep telling themselves "just a few more minutes," which results in their work suffering. Because these studies strongly point to individual differences in time management and time orientation, the next section explores these differences in more depth.

Individual Differences in Future Orientation and Management of Time: There are dozens of research studies that further highlight distinct facets of our orientation toward Scheduling. See the following table, *Examples of Measures of Time Management and Future Time Perspective*, which provides a summary of the different measures. In addition, a large review of 212 studies by Kooij and colleagues (2018), helps to further clarify different dimensions of FTP. This means that individuals vary in how much they have each of the following in their outlook to the future: *Time orientation,* or our focus on the past, present, or future; *extension,* or how far into the future people project; *continuity* (or planning), or how much we anticipate both the immediate effects and long-term consequences of a potential action; *density* (or clarity), or the number of goals we plan to obtain in the future and associated level of detail; and *directionality*, or how much we see ourselves as moving forward from the present moment into the future.

These distinctions, along with others highlighted in the table, clearly show the many faceted ways in which we orient to, feel about, and manage our time now and in the future. The studies show that some of us are more hopeful and optimistic than others as we go about our Scheduling and time management. In addition, some of us are more impulsive as we act on our plans, whereas others delay gratification.

EXAMPLES OF MEASURES OF TIME MANAGEMENT AND FUTURE TIME PERSPECTIVE

MEASURE	SUBSCALE	REPRESENTATIVE ITEM (ADAPTED)
Time Management		
Time Management Behavior Scale (Macan, 1994)	Planning (Goal Setting and Prioritizing)	I set deadlines for myself when I set out to accomplish a task.
	Mechanics	I keep a daily log of my activities.
	Preference for Organization	At the end of the work day, I leave a clear, well-organized work space.
Time Structure Questionnaire (Bond and Feather, 1988)	Sense of Purpose	My time has great use and value.
	Routine and Planning	The activities of my day fit together in a structured way.
	Present Orientation	I don't spend much time thinking about the future or opportunities I have missed.
	Effective Organization	I have trouble organizing the things I have to do. (Reverse scored)
	Persistence	Once I start an activity, I persist until I have completed it.
Time Management Questionnaire	Short-Range Planning	I spend time each day planning.
	Time Attitudes	I feel I am in charge of my own time by and large.
	Long-Range Planning	I have a set of goals for the entire quarter.
Future Time Perspective		
Consideration of Future Consequence Scale	Future Concern	I consider how things might be in the future and try to influence those things with my day-to-day behavior.
	Immediate Concern	I only act to satisfy immediate concerns, figuring the future will take care of itself.

MEASURE	SUBSCALE	REPRESENTATIVE ITEM (ADAPTED)
Future Time Perspective Scale (Carstensen and Lang, 1996)	Research does not clarify if this scale has more than one dimension.	Most of my time lies ahead of me.
Zimbardo Time Perspective Inventory (ZTPI)	Future Orientation	I complete projects on time by making steady progress.
	Present Hedonism	I make decisions in the spur of the moment.
	Present Fatalism	Life today is too complicated; I prefer the simpler life of the past.
	Past Negative	Painful past experiences keep being replayed in my mind.
	Past Positive	Happy memories of good times spring readily to mind.
	Transcendental Future	My body is just a temporary home for the real me.

Synthesis

In their book *The Time Paradox* (2008), authors Zimbardo and Boyd explain that while people increasingly use time-saving devices, they paradoxically experience feelings of having less time. Their proposed remedy is to adopt a balance (see Zimbardo's Time Perspective Inventory at bottom of the table). A healthy orientation toward time involves a high past-positive and transcendental future orientation, moderately high in future and present-hedonistic, and low in both past-negative and present-fatalistic orientation.

Since the publication of *The Time Paradox*, we have seen an explosive use of time-robbing technology through social media, smartphones, and the emergence of the anytime/anywhere "mobile self." There have been some efforts at time-perspective training and therapy. But it is not clear how effective these are against the onslaught of the new time thieves. Problematic smartphone use has been identified as a concern for 25% of children and young people. In their review of over sixty studies, Sohn and colleagues (2019) found a consistent relationship between problematic use and deleterious mental health symptoms including depression, anxiety, and poor sleep.

Fortunately, the reviewed research gives us guideposts and warning signs as we move from Time Shaping into the future structures of our lives. We all have limited temporal capital. The Trajectory of Scheduling helps us spend it wisely. We just need to be wary of the forms we create and mindlessly use: those smartphone apps, social media, and 24/7 planning devices. These forms result from or aid schedules, and they are not ends in themselves. There may be other appointments waiting for us. We can adopt a transcendental future perspective. American Pastor Mark Batterson says, "You are someone else's miracle! God is setting up divine appointments, and it is our job to keep them."

It helps to remember our quest and the precious weave. From this perspective, all the above findings are best viewed in the multifaceted and objective context of Scheduling as a Trajectory. We often get caught up in schedules rather than let schedules work toward a higher purpose. The author Annie Dillard wrote, "A schedule defends from chaos and whim. A net for catching days." Again, the research is clear. We can strengthen our positive sense of self by using schedules to reach goals. Time Shaping helps us rise to life's challenges and leads to fulfillment. We can get so good at using time that life becomes effortless. Fulfillment and Effortlessness then become the Treasures in the days we catch.

Contemplation (QfP 4-7): Scheduling

This next contemplation invites you to reflect on these questions. How much do you use daily logs, calendars, planners, or schedulers? How often do you take your time with them during your day? Where does your daily Scheduling behavior come from?

The preceding essay reviewed some of the time-management and time-perspective research (see the table *Examples of Measures of Time Management and Future Time Perspective*). Some of this is organized into the boxes shown in the diagram on the facing page. As you review the bulleted statements in the boxes, reflect on what factors drive you to be more or less focused on Scheduling.

+ How does your philosophy and value of time influence your Scheduling?

+ Does your orientation to future, present, or past influence your Scheduling?

+ Are you more oriented to short- or long-term planning?

+ Does your Scheduling support your well-being?

+ How can you use the diagram on the facing page to take a step back, reenvision your use of scheduling, and establish a healthier orientation toward Time Shaping?

+ Do the arrows in the diagram make sense? Would you draw them differently?

Philosophy

- ☐ My time has great use and value.
- ☐ I feel I am in charge of my own time.
- ☐ My body is just a temporary home for the real me.
- ☐ Time is just an illusion.

Time Horizon Orientation

- ☐ Most of my time lies ahead of me.
- ☐ I influence my future with my day-to-day behavior.
- ☐ The future is very important to me.
- ☐ I make decisions on the spur of the moment.
- ☐ I never put off till tomorrow what I can do today.
- ☐ All that really matters is this day.
- ☐ Painful past experiences keep going through my mind.
- ☐ Happy memories of good times spring readily to mind.
- ☐ I think about the past a lot since it helped me get here.

past — present — future

Planning Range

- ☐ I focus on planning my day or week.
- ☐ I focus on planning the quarter ahead.
- ☐ I focus on planning the whole year.
- ☐ My plans are organized for several years ahead.

short ↔ long

Scheduling Behavior

- ☐ I set deadlines for myself.
- ☐ I keep a daily log.
- ☐ I fit the activities of my day together in a structured way.
- ☐ Once I start an activity I persist until it's done.
- ☐ At the end of the work day, I leave a clear, organized work space.
- ☐ I use a calendar or scheduling device often throughout the day.
- ☐ I make adjustments to my calendar or scheduler during the day.

My Well-Being

- ☐ I am happy with my life.
- ☐ I am present to the happenings of my life.
- ☐ My day flows easily.
- ☐ I feel a sense of well-being throughout my day.

CONTEMPLATING SCHEDULING

CHAPTER 9

Contemplating Pacing

In which both Pooh and Wise Old Owl visit another part of the woods where they watch the rabbits, the gophers, and the bees. Owl tries to explain the different paces happening in front of them: "Bees are the busiest animals in the whole world. Rabbits get bored easily, so they eat to stay busy. And gophers stay busy all year long and don't sleep in the winter like you do, Pooh!" Of course, Pooh misses the big picture and exclaims, "I guess bees have to stay busy so there is enough honey around, right?"

THE DANCE: DYNAMICS

SAYINGS: "Take one's time," "A stitch in time," and "All in good time."

ATTRACTION: Pacing manifests from Time Shaping in Time Shaping's attraction to Chaos.

FUNCTION: The function of Pacing is to connect Time Shaping to Chaos.

INFLUENCE: Pacing influences Rhythm through Chaos.

RESULT: Pacing results as Routine, in its own function, connects Form to Time Shaping.

SISTER: Pacing is sister to Interruption. They calibrate and set limits on each other.

MIRROR: The stability, homeostasis, and culture born of Pacing allows us to Transition well.

> **COUNTERPOINT:** Without Timing, we would not know when to slow down or speed up, and our Pacing would be ever subject to disruptions and the whims of Chaos.

Functional Definition: The degree to which we both consider and regulate how much time or length of time—along with pauses—to devote to an activity, task, or recreation. Our intention to pace ourselves influences the form of our relationship with others—neither too slow nor too fast, but following a rate that accords with well-being, sensibility, security, safety, and sustainability. To give witness to the natural pace of energy circulation, the buildup and release of energy (thoughts, words, acts), and to respond with sensitivity to that natural circulation (non-intrusive, patient, careful). Simply, the speed of movement.

Random samples: Aesop's fable "The Tortoise and the Hare"; pace of life; back-and-forth in basketball game; courtship pace → time to first kiss → initial sex, etc.; impatience—pacing anxiously; rate of eating ("fast food"); move with ease/dis-ease connotes that pace is off; compare pacing in jitterbug versus waltz, play in golf versus stock car auto race; foraging and hunting in animals (varies by animal, hunger, season); unwinding; procrastination; heart.

Finding the "right" pace may be the root of well-being, the secret of fulfillment. Mindfulness of Pacing is the antidote to rushing, busyness, workaholism, and general slavery to the fabricated press or density of time. The better we pace, the more effective our Scheduling will be. The more effective we schedule, the more we can time our activities (our entries and exits) to be in harmony with those around us. The better our Timing, the more we can enjoy the Rhythms of life.

Mistaking speed for success is a paradox of modern amenities. Actually, we have more joy and fulfillment when crafting space (s p a c e) between events. Our presence to life is associated with moving at the right pace. Significant differences in pace occur across cultures and countries on Earth. Pace of life is faster in colder, more individualistic, and more affluent countries. Procrastination in one context may be viewed as a pause, siesta, or delay in another context.

Acceleration or Deceleration. Sociologists claim society has sped up in three ways: technology (for example, disruptive innovations), social rules (such as the proliferation of new gender roles and innovations in dating), and pace of life. In the workplace, we more quickly exchange information (emails, texts), are expected to get things done more quickly, and have fewer break times. Time urgency is a risk factor for cardiovascular disease. However, one social geographer also claims that the pace of many aspects of culture and society is gradually decelerating. In his book *Slowdown,* Danny Dorling reviews research that shows "slowing growth" in a wide swath of areas: population growth, fertility rates, data and knowledge production, technological innovation, gross domestic product, and capitalism. The only things that appear to be speeding up are climate change and increasing temperatures, which appears to be a function of our lack of presence to nature and to our environment and how we treat it.

The Slow Movement. Growing efforts to slow down have emerged in response to accelerated pace in many cultures throughout the world. These efforts are generically referred to as *The Slow Movement*, and all advocate for a cultural shift toward slowing down life's pace and reconnecting with nature and each other. For example, there is a Slow Food movement, a guide for the Slow Professor, and Slow Tourism. As one example, the increased use of social media and smartphones is countered when individuals post guidelines for turning off one's phone during the day, limiting the use of certain notification applications, or otherwise limiting use of communication technology.

Anxiety. Anxiety has been defined as a future-oriented emotion involving distress about what may happen; when anxious, we overestimate how long things will take. Anticipation of negative events causes the imagined rate of those events to speed up (faster pace) in our minds.

Of all Trajectories, Pacing seems to be one we believe is most under societal control. In this light, modern technology distances us from nature. Consider this quote from Emerson: "Adopt the pace of nature: her secret is patience." Time to think "biocentric"—we are ourselves nature.

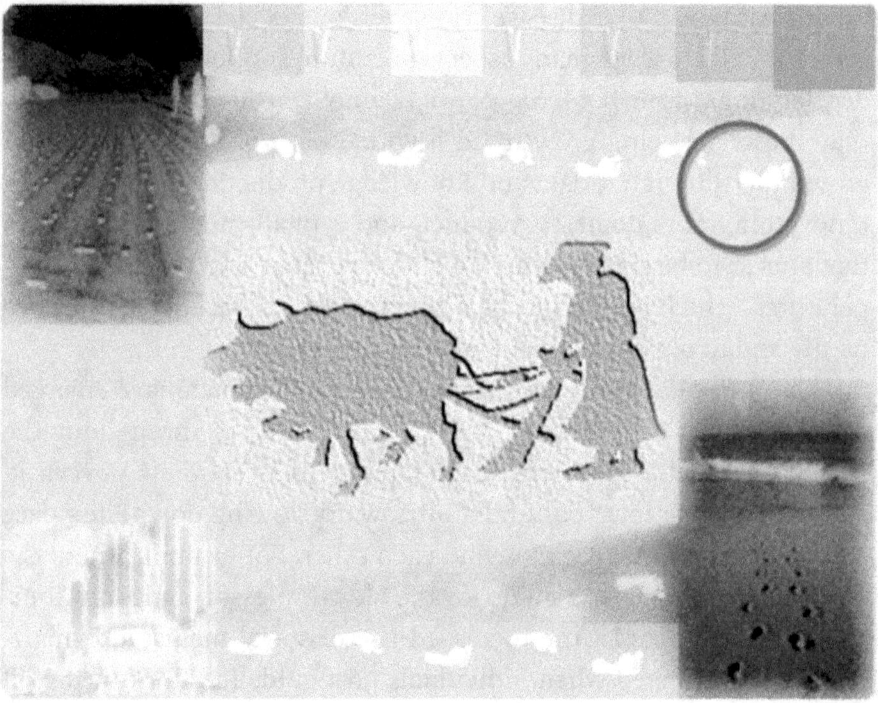

PACING

A glacial

patience

inscribes the orbits and
patterns of all meeting:

gaze back at the rows:
    friends
    events
    turnings

    how well they marked that one long
    stride
    that brought
    you here.

~ J.B.

Portrait: Essay on Pacing

What if I told you that the entire cosmos, and everything in it, is expanding and contracting, breathing in and out, circulating energy at its own pace ... and that you are part of it? Moreover, this pace is not always even. There are bumps and hiccups. In other words (and the science of cosmology supports this), there is no such thing as equilibrium. Never was. Never will be. Energy flows in everything. While there may not be any sustained stability, one thing is for sure: The entire universe, especially every living thing, is filled with "pace-makers." Pace is happening.

I understand that a hiccupping cosmos may not be a pressing concern for you. However, in the Quest for Presence, we are each called to find the right Pace for us at this time in our life on this earth. To that end, and for the benefit of those who are impatient (hello!), we profit from a responsive awareness of the influences of life's many "pace-makers." This includes both internal (within the body or somatic) and external (societal and technological) timers, clocks, or driving factors. With contemplation, we can stay mindful when external factors interrupt our Pace. Human beings are genuinely complex, psychospiritual, and dynamic systems. This means we can learn to dance with and even control many diverse pacers, each pulsing at varying rates or tempos as they come in and out of our daily life.

You might hear claims about the benefits of slowing down versus speeding up, how acceleration is oppressive and outside our control. We are enslaved by the gods of Frantic, Punctuality, Schedule, and Calendar. But look closer. In the Quest for Presence, it helps to resonate with the regularity, coherence, and life-giving quality of Pacing. This will be more useful than regarding fast-paced activity as some looming monstrosity. It's time to stop worrying about its intensity, speed, or tempo. Actually, one study showed that people in countries with a faster pace of life are no less happy than their slower-moving neighbors. Wherever you live, the Pace of your soul can inspire your slowing, steady your rate, and reveal the natural Pacing of your personality.

Faces of Pacing

Pace is typically defined as a regular, steady, and continuous speed for walking, running, or moving. Tempo is typically defined as the rate of speed or pacing out and is often used to refer to music (adagio, largo, presto, or allegro). Both of these set limits or create a boundary around the press of Chaos. We are hard-wired for tempo, we can modulate it, and our revolving planet, the sun, technology, and society shape it. In the modern technological era, our biological clocks sometimes (often?) become more attuned to clock-time than to natural Rhythms of the sun and the seasons.

Limits: Our well-being depends on the regularity, coherence, speed, and control of Pace. The human heart beats, on average, between 60 and 100 beats per minute. This average range slows as we age. Depending on the health of the individual, problems occur if the heart rate gets too slow or too fast. While individuals vary, there is an upper and a lower limit to the pace of the heart. Human beings generally require between six and eight hours of sleep per day. This average range lessens as we age. Depending on a variety of factors, chronic increases and decreases in this range may signal problems (examples include depression, sleep disorders, and workaholism). While individuals vary, there is an upper and a lower limit to sleep requirements.

Homeostasis: These are just two examples of biological systems—heart rate and sleep cycles—that require operating within a range of speeds and have built-in neurological mechanisms to maintain that range. Those mechanisms actually reflect the two points of our breathing-in and exhaling-out cosmos. For example, the heart has two groups of cells—the sinoatrial (SA) node and the atrioventricular (AV) node—which alternately serve to contract and expand the muscles of the heart. These nodes are influenced by the two branches of the autonomic nervous system (ANS) which continually send signals to either speed up or slow down the heart rate so that blood can be circulated and flow through our entire body.

I provide the above detail to remind you of the amazing complexity of our bodies. The systems that regulate our sleep and waking cycles are equally complex. *Homeostasis* is the term used to describe a steady state of conditions that maintain the optimal function of a living system, so when changes occur, regulators kick in to maintain a balance within a "homeostatic" range, always between two set points. Otherwise, these systems can exceed a threshold of Chaos and breakdown. By Pacing ourselves, we stay connected to these natural homeostatic regulators. Pace is a source of connection.

As individual human beings, we have some ability to control these regulators through practice, biofeedback, and a variety of lifestyle choices (exercise, diet, and meditation among others). Much of this occurs through the ANS, processes that afford us the ability to speed up or slow down our fight-or-flight reaction. We can even speed up or slow down our mental sense of tempo through daily techniques (like listening to slow music). While we can succumb to external "temporal regulators" in our environment, we are also a resilient species. Studies show that, despite technological acceleration, our Pace is fairly reliable when it comes to maintaining a relatively invariable heart rate and always finding some way to get regular sleep.

Fast or Slow: There is a constant debate about the relative benefits of living life at a slow or fast pace. For example, while pace of life may have increased in some societies in recent decades, other research suggests that there may be a slowing or plateau. Other data suggest that, for cities to maintain health, there needs to be an ongoing acceleration of Pace or economic and social structures would collapse.

Researchers define pace of life in various ways, including 1) work-leisure patterns in society or the degree to which we take time to intersperse leisure activity with work; 2) walking speed, postal speed, clock accuracy; and 3) a combination of speed required to do work, avoiding the piling up of work, having enough time, and falling behind. Studies have shown that as cultural pace increases, so does the rate of insecure romantic attachments. Increased work pace is associated with stress, symptoms of poor health, use of medication (such as painkillers), and increased risk for cardiovascular disease.

From a public health perspective, the increase of life pace in the last century was generally a good thing. Between 1875 and 2000, data from many countries showed a general increase in life expectancy with relatively even increases in the year-to-year pace of this change. Even with the global influenza pandemic of 1918–1919 and other "interruptions" (such as malaria outbreaks and HIV), there was an overall increase in the pace of life expectancy that is attributed to medical and public health innovation.

Culture: Each culture has its own normative "pace-maker." For example, scholars have described the achievement-oriented "American" character as "Keeping up with the Joneses." Americans are willing to tolerate risk and uncertainty to maintain a "status" of living, if not a quality of life. In contrast, the "European" character focuses more on compassion, community, and getting along for the sake of security and orthodoxy. This is partly influenced by governmental regulations on vacation time. The European Union requires more vacation time, while in contrast, the US is the only industrialized country where employers are not required to provide paid vacation.

The emergence of the Slow Movement (Slow Food, Travel, Tourism) appears to be a homeostatic reaction to acceleration and restrictions on leisure time. The Slow Movement is represented as any social effort in a group of individuals who advocate for the slowing down of cultural pace. Historians suggest that it began in 1986 as the Slow Food movement. The political activist and culinary expert Carlo Petrini protested against the opening of a McDonald's restaurant near the Spanish Steps in Rome. Since then, there have been efforts made at slow marketing, slow fashion, and even the slow office. The advent of the COVID-19 pandemic has, ironically, accelerated these slowing efforts.

Burnout and Work: Burnout, as defined by researchers, is a syndrome that includes feelings of emotional exhaustion (drained, frustrated, fatigued), depersonalization (lack of caring, callousness, and hardened by work), and low self-efficacy or competence (ineffective, lacking positivity and energy for job). Research indicates that exhaustion is predicted by high levels of work pace over which employees have no control. When it comes to the overall syndrome of burnout, work pace may still be important but less of an influence than being treated fairly, supported, and given a manageable workload.

Even with a demanding work pace, other factors can reduce a negative impact on burnout. This includes *time adequacy*, where workers feel they have enough time for home, family, and community; and *schedule control,* having the autonomy to make decisions regarding the duration and timing of work, including where work is done. Finally, workplace interventions can promote more flexible work arrangements and increase adequacy and control, reduce burnout, and improve well-being. In other words, we have greater well-being when we have the flexibility to attend to the diverse pacers of work and home and not just get locked into endless monotony.

Pace-of-Life Syndrome: You might be interested to know that human beings are not the only species that can experience burnout. Evolutionary biologists have hypothesized a pace-of-life syndrome (POLS), which predicts a continuum of Pace across and within species. According to a 2018 article in *Nature* magazine, "Individuals on the 'fast' end of POLS continuum grow faster, exhibit higher metabolism, and are more risk-prone, but die earlier than ones on the 'slow' end." Again, this stuff is really complex, partly because proof for the hypothesis varies across—and I did not count or review them all—hundreds of studies. One key idea from the POLS literature is that human personality—how we differ from each other—is partly due to how we allocate, parcel out, and space our energy across the lifespan. Some of us live hard, run on empty, and die young. Some mosey along. Most of us are in between.

Heart Rate Variability: In the final analysis, it helps to remember your relationship to your own body. An overwhelming body of research indicates that, with little practice, people can regulate their heart rate variability (HRV). HRV is the variation in time between consecutive heartbeats. It is universally accepted as a marker of ANS activity. Across each successive heartbeat, our heart rate constantly changes due to changing needs and demands, for example, movement, breathing, stress, emotions, exertion, and cognitive or intellectual tasks. Hence, we return to homeostasis.

HRV is sort of a marker of our calibration for homeostasis. When the beat-to-beat changes are widely varied, it means that our heart is getting feedback and adjusting: we are healthier. The healthier the ANS, the faster you are able to switch gears, showing more resilience and flexibility. Research has shown a relationship between low HRV and worsening depression or anxiety. A low HRV is even associated with an increased risk of death and cardiovascular disease. Training in HRV biofeedback exercises the balance between the two aspects of our ANS: sympathetic and parasympathetic. We become less anxious, less stressed, more present, and more adaptable with life.

Synthesis

In summary, a wide array of factors influences personal Pacing in our Quest for Presence—from culture and work to our nervous system and our heart. The arising of Pace depends on two counteracting nodes, switches, or pulses. One signals us to start, move, speed up, expand, or open. The other says stop, be still, slow down, contract, or close down. Pace is defined by the duration between the first and second signal. At times and for any number of reasons, life may feel like it is speeding up. We can move too fast, get ahead of ourselves, and burn out. Other times, we feel things are taking too long or even that life is moving so slow that we lose a sense of purpose and meaning. The lesson of Pace is that the extremes of these two situations are often unsustainable. Something has to give. We are called to innovate, reset the Pace, or perhaps some Synchronicity pops in and does it for us.

The pace of life varies in complexity from one time to the next in history, across cultures, and both across and within individuals. At the same time, it is through the regulation of Pace—our agility and responsiveness to change—that we bring some order to the Chaos. We have many choices and can find agile Pacing, even with highly demanding work conditions that restrict our Pace or with inherited character traits that make us impatient (hello again!). The relationship between Time Shaping and complexity is defined by how our intentions and actions bring a Pace to our lives. Ultimately, we can at least understand that complexity is a given. We can learn to Pace ourselves. Then, even in the midst of great turbulence and challenge, we can rise to the occasion and experience Effortlessness and Fulfillment. And maybe even some Patience.

Contemplation (Q*f*P 4-8): Pacing

The following questions are for journaling and group discussion. For each question, ask others to do the same and compare notes. Ideally, do this exercise with people from different age groups (grandparents, Gen Z), races, and background. Next, review the suggested websites.

1. First, reflect on your surrounding culture and your regular day-to-day activities during the *work week*. Rate how much you feel the Pace of the world around you is, from "1" (slow and easy) to "10" (accelerated and hectic).

2. Next, see yourself as standing apart from culture. Focus on your own Pace. Imagine that you paced your day during the *work week* in a way that was natural for you, one that you prefer. Again, on the same scale of 1 to 10, rate your own natural Pace.

3. Do the same ratings for Question 1 and 2 above but this time substitute "weekend" for "work week." After doing so, you will have four numbers: your rated Pace of culture and your preferred Pace for the work week and weekend.

	← Slow and easy					Accelerated and hectic →				
	1	2	3	4	5	6	7	8	9	10
Pace of work week										
Pace of the world around me	1	2	3	4	5	6	7	8	9	10
My pace for the work week	1	2	3	4	5	6	7	8	9	10
Pace of weekend										
Pace of the world around me	1	2	3	4	5	6	7	8	9	10
My pace for the weekend	1	2	3	4	5	6	7	8	9	10

4. Compare the four numbers. Reflect and journal on these questions:

- ✦ What do you notice about the pattern of responses?
- ✦ Where do you have any choice, agility, or responsiveness?
- ✦ How do the ratings relate to your current level of energy, well-being, and life satisfaction?
- ✦ Would you or could you change anything? Explain why or why not.

5. Consider these sites:

https://www.slowmovement.com/

https://www.slowfood.com/

https://slowfoodusa.org/

https://www.sloww.co/about/

CHAPTER 10

Contemplating Interruption

In which, following a terrible storm, Pooh looks sadly upon the fallen trees, the many blocked trails and paths, and the damage to many of his friends' homes. So moved by their plight, Pooh tells Wise Old Owl where he has hidden his secret stashes of honey so he can share it with them. All the animals come together and share tea and honey as they plan their recovery. "Thank you! We love you, Pooh!" they cheer together.

THE DANCE: DYNAMICS

SAYINGS: "There are no accidents," "Crunch time," and "Sticking point."

ATTRACTION: Interruption manifests from Chaos in Chaos's attraction to Time Shaping.

FUNCTION: The function of Interruption is to connect Chaos to Time Shaping.

INFLUENCE: Interruption influences Scheduling through Time Shaping.

RESULT: Interruption results as Transcendence, in its own function, connects Nurturing Conditions to Chaos.

SISTER: Interruption is sister to Pacing. They calibrate and set limits on each other.

> **MIRROR:** The attention, rightness, or perfection born of Timing helps us welcome Interruption.
>
> **COUNTERPOINT:** Without Transition, life would be a series of Interruptions. We would never get our bearings.

Functional Definition: Alterity, disruption, perturbation. Any break, delay, postponement, or cancellation in a sequence or system that you agree is the reality (sole or shared). Interruption reveals the force of Chaos to those attached to action and outcome of action. Each of these—discontinuity, accident, jumping, stalling—serve up the moment to the perceiver and appear longer than usual. An Interruption to the ego is opportunity for revelation to higher self. In time's great expanse, an Interruption arises as a wakeful moment, a new chance.

Random samples: Humpty Dumpty; trauma; a jangle of lightening; a tangle of wreckage; a scattering of glass shards; disequilibrium; divorce; breakup; unwanted phone calls; uncontrollable; suddenness; loss; asymmetry; missing data; surprise; adversity; intrusion; explosion; being invited "out of nowhere" to an event; flight delays; earthquake; spark plug; postponement; drop-in visitors; unpredictable; cattywampus; willy-nilly; discontinuous; dissipative systems; fractals.

One word cannot convey this Trajectory. Chaos is tricky: to alter state, position, or direction; to perturb anything that is otherwise homogenous or steady, has direction (like a stream), or a back-and-forth component (like conversation). *Alterity* and *perturbation* are distinct aspects of Chaos. Grief over loss is where we most intimately work this Trajectory. Resilience comes from Interruption.

> *Storms make trees take deeper roots.*
> ~ Dolly Parton (American Singer-Songwriter)

Alterity. Something comes into our lives that is "other," strange, opposite from our Routine, breaking the Rhythm, causing a

Transition. But by meeting the other—the stranger—we become present to what is odd, off-kilter, or weird. The encounter of the other can bring novelty, spontaneity, a calling, an obligation, empathy, and gratitude. Hence, Interruption is inherently positive; it catalyzes growth, a new journey, or seeing things in a new way. It gets us outside ourselves and can awaken compassion.

Perturbation. Three theories about the universe and the way things work give perturbation a starring role: cosmological perturbation theory, complexity theory, and chaos theory. In common language, *perturb* means to bother, vex, trouble, unsettle, throw into confusion or disorder. In physics, it means to slightly modify the motion of an object. In astronomy, it means to modify the motion of a body by exerting a gravitational force. In mathematics, it means to modify slightly, such as an equation or value. Comparing the common with scientific definitions shows both "objective" and emotional realities. Epictetus wrote: "People are not disturbed by things, but by the view they take of them."

Conversation. Both alterity and perturbation affect our talk with others. An overlap, talking at the same time as the other in conversation, can be seen as an Interruption causing irritation, or it can be interpreted as "being in synch with" the other speaker. It depends on the tone used. This is called *prosody* or a sense of rhythmic turn-taking. The frequency of back-and-forth interruption is even a sign of intimacy and can create a rhythm to the conversation (see chapter 5 on Rhythm).

Grief. Grief unmakes and remakes the self. Research suggests that we do not go lock-stepped through specific phases after loss. We each have uniquely complex Trajectories and oscillate between making sense, sadness, restoring a bond, reminiscing, loneliness, and so on.

Resilience. The process of bouncing back or restoration following a disturbance and learning and potentially growing from that disturbance.

INTERRUPTION

Today you learn there
are no accidents;

Every rip & tear & drop
    of grief is a sign that
        lifelines do stretch out

far past boundaries of comfort

When interrupted in thought, speech or deed
stop inside the pause

live an
entire
life
there.

                                            ~ J.B.

Portrait: Essay on Interruption
(Disruption, Perturbation, Alteration)

What if I told you there is a very good chance that something will happen today that will, at the very least, interrupt your ordinary routine, perhaps even completely and totally throw things off course? It could be anything from an intrusive nuisance in your otherwise perfect day (an unwanted text message) to an accident or brush with death. Insurance policies sometimes label the latter "Acts of God" (from *force majeure* clauses); an event due to natural causes without human intervention and that could not have been prevented by reasonable foresight or care. Ironically, what one can say with certainty about the Trajectory of Interruption is that uncertainty is a certainty. Everywhere. At any time. Think global pandemic!

If this causes you to feel anxious, it helps to know that Interruption (born from the force of Chaos) is the mirror image of Pacing (born from the force of Time Shaping). What Pacing controls, Interruption unfolds. Learned helplessness occurs when we are persistently interrupted in our efforts to reach a desired goal. We try to Time Shape. We get Interrupted. This keeps happening; we eventually give up. Anxiety and depression set in, *unless* we *perceive some control* over the event and *find some level of predictability*. Fortunately, there is fairly good evidence that our ever-increasing abilities at control and predictability led to the evolution of our human species. So, as with everything else about time, let's consider Interruption our friend. Or, at least, an enemy that can become our friend.

By coincidence, I am writing this section during the COVID-19 pandemic. Many people feel anxious or depressed because their life has been interrupted. They have difficulty finding a new Routine. They can neither plan nor Schedule for the future, predict how long quarantine might last, or gauge its impact on their livelihood. In other words, their Time Shaping has been thrown for a loop. But not everyone feels this way. Research suggests that during lockdown, people maintain well-being and a positive mood through regular and paced habits: daily exercise, religious coping, connecting with nature, and getting outside.

There is some comfort in knowing we can pace ourselves through Chaos. When you are going through hell, keep going. Nonetheless, Interruptions can last for such a long time that, if we don't adjust, something has to give. The press to adjust is the basis for mutation. If we cannot coordinate our inner resources with the new environment, disruption emerges from within, often the genetic pressures of adaptation. Let me explain that at a more personal level. One frustration after another can result in explosive anger. One loss after another can result in depression. Repeated addictive binges can result in death. So, sometimes, we are ourselves the cause of our own interrupted life.

Sensations of Perturbations

Interruption is typically used to refer to a stop, break, or disjuncture in a line, a continuity, or an expected sequence. Disruption is a bit more dramatic, conjuring images of riots, disturbances, problems, and even destruction. I prefer to use the term *perturbation*. It seems more neutral to me and can apply to both Interruption and disruption. Plus, theoretical physicists and astronomers like to use that term too! In physics, perturbation is defined as "a deviation of a system, moving object, or process from its regular or normal state or path, caused by an outside influence." In astronomy: "a minor deviation in the course of a celestial body, caused by the gravitational attraction of a neighboring body."

Death may be the greatest of all Interruptions or, perhaps, just another perturbation in the Trajectory of our soul. I discuss more about death in the section on Transcendence. However, one phenomenon is worth noting here. In her article "Why Do We See Dead People?" Patricia Pearson describes the experience that many people have following the death of a loved one. These are experienced as unexpected, yet very real, visitations or gentle intrusions rather than grief hallucinations. Increasingly, grief therapists are treating these as real and valid experiences rather than dismissing them.

In the precious weave of this happening life—and death—we make an effort to view everything as a dynamic system, as gifts that spark our presence. Especially when the shit hits the fan! So, let's just assume that every Interruption or disruption refers to, at some level seen or unseen, a perturbation in the system. Same for when we are disturbed, rattled, or when we feel messed up, out of sorts, off-kilter, thrown, upset, confused, screwed, jilted, rejected, torqued, bajiggity, or—my favorites—verklempt or kerfuffled. And freaked out, because we thought we just saw a ghost.

Discrepancy Reduction: Those perturbations arriving from external sources (accidents, meteors, pandemics) are actually less familiar to us than the fissures in our own minds. Inconsistency bothers us: between two beliefs, two behaviors, a thought and a behavior, a current state and a desired goal. Discrepancy reduction can be a good thing or a bad—even evil—thing. Cognitive dissonance occurs when people rationalize, self-justify, self-deceive, even lie about their behavior. They even double their deceit to maintain a sense of consistency. Cigarette smokers rationalize their habits when faced with data showing that smoking kills: "They keep me from gaining weight." The tragedy of the mass suicide at the Peoples Temple in Jonestown occurred because its members made a series of ever-increasing commitments. After complying with small requests, they were initiated, left their homes, eventually gave up their property, and were later indoctrinated into a fake self-poisoning ritual to prove their faith. They had nothing left but their leader and their cause. Each previous commitment made the final one justifiable.

On the bright side, life's positive achievements are also discrepancy reductions. We start with an intention, a desired state of learning, accomplishment, or success; yet we know obstacles are deeply woven into the path toward the goal. In all human education, if we don't learn what we set out to, we will study more, pay closer attention, increase our grade or status. So much so that learning, knowledge, creativity, and wisdom have their own enduring and intrinsic motivation. We learn for the sake of learning. "Learning is its own exceeding, great reward," wrote humanistic essayist William Hazlitt. Similarly, all positive and moral behavior may be seen as arising from self-regulation and exercising an internal sense of control over the discrepancies, anxieties, and emotional interruptions that occur in life. But wait. Is it possible that all emotions are themselves the result of an Interruption?

Emotions (all of them): Most theories of emotion touch on the importance of how our human experience—and processing—of discrepancy and interruption leads to arousal in our ANS. The elegant theory of psychologist George Mandler focuses squarely on this discrepancy. Human beings have evolved through 1) our ability to detect a discrepancy between the world we expect and the world as it is; 2) quick response to the discrepancy through survival mechanisms that ignite changes in our body; 3) responding with the requisite level of arousal, activation, or energy; and 4) either staying still (immobilization), approaching, or avoiding as a way to enhance our well-being. Every emotion can be described through its level of intensity (the arousal caused by the Interruption), and its valence (the degree of neutral, positive, or negative feeling associated with approaching or avoiding). Other models and studies in the field of affective neuroscience are consistent with Mandler's model. This includes feelings associated with affiliation and social inclusion, such as empathy, joy, care, and adoration. Such feelings arise when we see others needing help or after they are helped or have achieved something. In other words, all emotions result from experiencing or resolving a perturbation in our own life, the life of others, or the social system we belong to. Even our emotional style appears due to how successful we are at anticipating and responding to interruptive events in our life.

Interruptions at Work: Fascinating research on Interruptions while we are working suggests that not all interruptions are bad for us. For example, interruptions by others can lead to poorer performance, whereas interrupting ourselves from time to time (taking breaks) can improve performance. However, the negative impact of others' interruptions can actually become positive. Again, context matters. It takes training and forethought to build the context. Interruptions may be useful when we first clarify a manager's expectations and manage boundaries between work and home. In addition, cultivating a *polychronic* style or attitude also helps. Individuals with a polychronic style work on multiple timeframes at once, view Interruptions as a positive, and generally have difficulty conforming to a consistent schedule. They sometimes even thrive on interruptions.

Technology and Interruption Overload: In fact, when it comes to having smartphones, multiple viewing screens, and switching between technologies, "polychrons" may do a lot better than "monochrons" (those who prefer singular clock-time and Routine). In other words, technology may be less disruptive for some than others. In one study of knowledge workers (people who "think for a living"), Chen and Karahanna (2018) assessed "interruption overload," or the extent to which they felt they had too many interruptions than they had the time, ability, or energy to deal with. The researchers studied when workers were interrupted by work when not at work. Phone interruptions contributed to overload more than text messaging. Both phone and text interruptions contributed to overload, but not email interruptions. Interruption overload also correlated with exhaustion and reduced performance. But here again, context matters. Techno-invasion was less hurtful for workers who used the interruptions to get closure on a task or those who forgot about work once the work day was over.

Synthesis

Perturbation depends on two things: continuity (or its illusion) and discontinuity (our good friend Chaos). My Jewish grandmother would always say, "People make plans, and God laughs." The above synopsis suggests no end to the human comedy. When life is seen as the unfurling of time's precious weave, wisdom reveals perturbation as one thread in that weave. Like the other threads, it pulls and tugs at the others. However, unlike other threads, this one tends to pull, stretch, and tear at things the most.

Remember that all Trajectories are objective and neutral, neither good nor bad in and of themselves. Life's Interruptions birth amazing things: the depth, intensity, and variety of emotions; the motivation to accomplish great things; inspiring testaments of resilience; innovation; and evolution itself. Everything is a function of external change. Seen in this way—from the broad and objective perspective of system perturbation—there are no such things as accidents. Alternatively, from Mark Twain: "Name the greatest of all inventors. Accident." Or, even better, "We interrupt this broadcast to bring you your life."

Other examples may drive home the value of Interruption into our routine-relishing brains. A "pattern interrupt" is a deconditioning technique used in hypnosis and neurolinguistic programming. A pattern interrupt helps us to break out of old addictive habits. Carlos Castaneda wrote about "the crack between the worlds" in Mexican Indian and Toltec shamanism. These parallel "worlds" represent the everyday reality of material objects (the *tonal*) and the more mysterious, unconscious, world where true power and spirit live (the *nagual*). Mystical experiences are the twilight, the transition into that crack between the worlds. And, as the Buddhist teacher Pema Chodron explains, reality is essentially groundless. The practice of accepting the groundless leads to transcending the world of pain and suffering.

In our Quest for Presence model, we place Interruption, disruption, and perturbation between Chaos and Time Shaping. Time Shaping bets on continuity, some belief that the present will unevenly flow into the future. We instinctively know that the future is not always a safe bet. It will always need some hedging. Technology keeps clipping and refining those hedges, yet weeds and blight come along. Acts of God just pop up. Time Shaping and Chaos keep dancing.

The other Trajectories help us along. The Interruption of an unhealthy Routine brings health. Many of life's disruptions can bring about a needed Transition. Accepting the Chaos of groundlessness awakens the soul and engenders compassion for all who suffer. No matter how much we Pace ourselves, time will always require some resetting, recovering, and re-visioning. The soul either begs for release, relishes the crumbling with awe, spontaneously jumps into the abyss, or embraces the dear, momentous feeling as a result of it all.

Contemplation (Q*fP* 4-9): Interruption

Interruptions, disruptions, and alterations occur within daily life and also across phases of our life story. Researchers label the daily interruptions as *hassles*; whereas life disruptors are termed a *life change unit* or *stressful life event*. Below are items I have adapted from research measures of daily hassles and stressful life events. Studies show that the more individuals experience these events, the more likely they will develop problems in life satisfaction and health, including increased risks for mental illness, disease, and death. However, studies also show that these problems are not inevitable and depend on how well we understand, adapt, and overcome.

This contemplation is designed to broaden your understanding of hassles and life events. As this is the last contemplation of the Trajectories, it also draws upon insights from all the other Trajectories and, as described in chapter 2, the dynamics of the entire mandala. Interruption is an integral part of the unfolding.

This contemplation has four parts. First, please note which and how many of the hassles and life events have occurred. Second, rate and reflect how well you have coped with or adjusted to them. Third, reflect on the role of the surrounding Trajectories as part of your experience and adjustment. Finally, journal and discuss Interruption in your responses.

Part 1: Hassles and Stressful Life Events

Check off all those hassles you have experienced in the past few days.

Financial concerns	Transportation/traffic	Dealing with technology
Health/medical concerns	Too many things to do	Media/social media
Concerns about weight	Dealing with spouse/partner	Home maintenance
Pain or anxiety	Misplacing or losing thing	Work related
Children	Physical appearance	Crime
Neighborhood issues	Physical safety	Dealing with addiction

Overall, how much have these hassles led you to feel that your time was "thrown off track" or you were otherwise irritated, stressed, or interrupted by them?

Not at all	0	1	2	3	4	5	6	7	8	9	10	Greatly

Check all of these life events that you have experienced in the past year.

Death of spouse/partner	Divorce	Separation from spouse or partner
Jail or violation of law	Death of close family member	Personal injury/illness
Marriage	Fired at work or job loss	Marital reconciliation
Retirement	Loss/decline of physical ability	Change in family health
Sex difficulties	Pregnancy or childbirth	Business readjustment
More arguing at home	Trouble with in-laws	Begin/end school/college
Living conditions change	Son or daughter leaving home	Change in line of work

Overall, how much have these hassles led you to feel that your time was "thrown off track" or you were otherwise irritated, stressed, or interrupted by them?

Not at all	0	1	2	3	4	5	6	7	8	9	10	Greatly

Part 2: Coping and Adjustment

- ✦ Overall, how well did you feel you coped with the daily hassles you listed or other recent ones that come to mind?
- ✦ Overall, how well did you feel you coped with the life stressors you listed or others that come to mind?
- ✦ How would you describe your overall ability to adjust as well as be resilient?

Part 3: The Surrounding Dance of Trajectories

The following questions ask you to look at hassles and stressful life events in context of the other Trajectories.

- ✦ **Interruption Influences Scheduling**: How much have you changed, had to change, or intentionally made an effort to alter your Schedules and Routines as a result of a) any of the hassles? b) any of the life events?
  - Does your life change as a result of Interruptions, or are these Interruptions just part of the fabric of your life?

- ✦ **Pacing Moderates Interruption**: How much has the Pace of your life either worsened or protected against the impact of a) any of the hassles? b) any of the life events?
  - How does the Pace of modern-day life (whether your own, from work, family, or culture) help with or keep you from working with difficult Interruptions? Is it possible that you speed up or slow down as a way to either escape your fear of them or otherwise conquer them?

CHAPTER 11

Dynamics and Origins of the Trajectories

In which Pooh, after all he has learned from Wise Old Owl, says "I learned the most from the storm." "How so?" asked Owl. "I used to think that finding honey was everything. Now, I see that sharing honey is everything." This brings a big smile and a wink from Owl, who looks up to see hundreds of bees smiling and winking back.

A single idea underlies the Trajectories: every day our lives fill up with opportunity to witness and take refuge in the amazing unfolding of life *as it happens*. This idea may seem either too simple, aspirational, or idealistic. It may run counter to everything you believe about life. I believe that the resistance to this approach lies in how we have evolved as a human species, how culture and civilization have trained our minds to think (in terms of space and not of time), and in our difficulty in adapting new insights from science—particularly neuroscience, quantum mechanics, and cosmology.

Most scientists accept that the evolution of our nervous system, particularly those circuits underlying our capacity to attend and focus, has led to an amazingly complex set of skills for a wide array of higher cognitive tasks: sustaining and allocating attention, focus, discernment, denoting, labeling, sorting, calculating, forecasting, executing, remembering, classifying, decision-making, strategizing, a wide array of ways to creatively combine the foregoing skills, and a whole lot more. As a result, the blurring effect of moment-to-moment changes in our environment has been significantly reduced. Indeed, all nervous systems evolve as a function of sensing the environment in order to make it less blurring and more navigable.

All of this is a good thing. We need to pay attention and get things done. At the same time as brains have evolved, so have society, culture, and civilization. Social and institutional norms and guidances have been created to help us pay attention. These norms help us learn to stay within the guardrails of our respective routines. We can productively contribute to those institutions and continue to prosper and flourish. Language plays the central role in all of this. You may have noticed that I threw "labeling" into the above list of higher cognitive skills. Labeling is often the king of the skill domain. If we don't label correctly, how would we communicate those norms and guidances to each other?

One major reason why I want you to learn the Trajectories is that we have been—for far too long—hyperfocused only on how to label the *contents and forms* of our experiences: the things, features, and details of our world. Labeling the content allows us to navigate, manage, and even subjugate the environment and social space of our lives. Specifically, most of us now know where we fit in our families and society, where we fit in the course of our lives, and how to potentially forecast how our lives should proceed over time (according to milestones, transitions, routines, and schedules).

As a result, we rarely attend to the *ongoing processes of how all these contents actually dance together*. We conquered the blur so completely that we are now blind to the processes of life itself.

> *We conquered the blur so completely that we are*
> *now blind to the processes of life itself.*

This is the cost of the information age, media bombardment, and the extraordinary access to technology. As a result, at a deep neurological and species level, we take time for granted. As a result, we are hurting the environment and life at an ever-increasing pace.

> In recent decades, the phrase or idiom "holding space" has been used by psychotherapists and mental health coaches to mean that one person really listens to and is present with another without judgment of that other person's emotions. In a parallel manner, we can talk about "holding time" or making more room for quality time in our lives. By seeing the qualities of time, we have more quality time. Interestingly, we have an increase in quality time when we hold space for each other.

In our story featuring Pooh and the Wise Old Owl, Pooh wants what he wants (honey), and he wants it now. So, he sees only the thorns that are in his way and not the roses. Out of fear and the need to survive, take control, and have power over things, we, too, may find ourselves focusing on only one part of life's equation.

The Trajectories are informed by three different lines of thought—*process philosophy*, *trialectics*, and *Living in Process*—which I learned from teachers in my own life. Perhaps by coincidence or by design, I had the privilege of studying with these teachers and borrowing from them. The purpose of the following sections is to give you a richer sense of the intricacies of these processes, to help you attend to the *ongoing processes of how all the Trajectories actually dance together*. I think the first thing to know is that the Trajectories can promote our well-being. They also influence each other. They obey a very specific logic of process and change. And together, they represent a neighborhood of energies.

How the Forces Promote Well-Being: Origins of the Routes or Trajectories

I believe that the ultimate purpose of the Trajectories (in and of themselves) is to inspire growth and evolution. When we touch into and honor the powerful life force they represent, we learn to thrive and manage our lifestyle in productive ways.

Routines manifest when Form and organization influence how and when we take action to shape our time. The repetition, ritual, or shared commonality that defines all Routine is a hallmark of organization that then functions to guide our behaviors. Ideally, this guidance leads to a thriving life.

Timing is a function of how Form and organization interrelate with, listen to, or embrace Nurturing Conditions. Attunement to the situation, taking mindful action, saying the "right" thing at the right time depends on a sense of order—conventions, social rules, honor, or diplomacy (see "Li" in Confucian thought). Ideally, as a result of Timing, new conditions arise that further nurture our consciousness and well-being in relationship to ourselves, others, and nature.

Rhythms manifest when Nurturing Conditions inform, influence, or temper the more chaotic and unpredictable aspects of life. With an honoring and acceptance of entropy, cycles of life and death, and the "other" or unknown, we introduce some Synchronization, give-and-take, and cadence to life. Ideally, as a result of Rhythm, we obtain a state of aliveness and engagement that would not be possible if we were just overwhelmed by Chaos or if there were no Chaos at all.

Transition is a function of how Nurturing Conditions influence, catalyze, or induce the current form or organization of a life, system, or entity to move from its current phase or status into a future phase or status. Ideally, this inducement leads to a deep connection to nature and the cosmos; we recognize that while all things are in Transition, an underlying pattern connects us all.

Transcendence occurs when Chaos influences the arising of Nurturing Conditions or impacts how things come into being to create conditions for the future. With honoring and acceptance of entropy and impermanence—that all things will pass—we simultaneously appreciate that time exists at different levels, even the idea that time does not exist at all.

Scheduling is the direct result of Time Shaping acting on the current or future form of time in our lives. By analogy, schedule (the verb) is to Time Shaping as schedule (the noun) is to Form. We observe, work with, and adjust our schedules (noun) by continually making acts of scheduling. Ideally, as a result of this back-and-forth process (create the Form of a schedule and adjust how we experience our time—Time Shaping), we do things that support health and well-being for ourselves and others.

Pacing is a function of how our actions and attempts at Time Shaping can actually temper, modify, or regulate the chaotic or unpredictable forces at work. Ideally, through Pacing, we neither do too much nor too little, find an evenness and regularity, and wake up to life in ways that would not be possible if we did not Pace ourselves.

Interruption or Perturbation manifests when chaotic or unpredictable forces impede, or thwart, an action or intended course of action. With honoring and acceptance of entropy and forces of impermanence—that some things may not go according to plans and intentions—we find ways to adjust, readjust, recover, learn, and grow.

The Dance

The Trajectories dance with each other. The following statements show how this dance works, how the Trajectories have a homeostatic relationship with each other. Over time, they balance each other out. Or, to be more accurate, our experience of time is a function of how these continually play off of each other.

1. **Transition and Disruption:** The different disruptions or Interruptions we experience in life soften through the eyes of Transition. That is, we accept life's problems to the degree we see how all things are perishable. In parallel fashion, without disruption (novelty, playfulness), life's transitions would become boring, endless, and overwhelming; that is, we can become apathetic, listless, and depressed.

2. **Routine and Rhythm:** Robotic and monotonous routines and habits become vitalizing dances when they are infused with a beat, tempo, or rhythm. That is, we enjoy life more when we can pivot, twirl, and do some juking and jiving with the dance routines society gives us. In parallel fashion, the order provided by Routine prevents excessive Rhythm, of things getting out of hand; that is, rhythm can mutate into a crazed mania, a frenzied disconnection from self, others, and nature.

3. **Timing and Pacing:** We experience Timing (right timing, perfect timing) as a gift to the degree we live a well-paced lifestyle. That is, life brings us needed inklings and insights only when we slow down just enough to appreciate them or speed up just enough to catch them. Otherwise, without Pacing, we may miss the gift of Timing altogether; time either loses meaning or we become shackled to time. In parallel fashion, without Timing, we would not know when to slow down or speed up. Our pace would be ever subject to disruptions and the whims of Chaos.

4. **Transcendence and Scheduling:** Without Transcendence, Scheduling can lead to a fixation on goals and material outcomes, exhaustion, burnout, disrupted rhythms, and missing out on life altogether. Taking time out of time (for example, for leisure and connection) prevents us from filling up our days with one activity and appointment after another. In a parallel manner, without Scheduling, Transcendence can lead to being ungrounded and "far out." The practice of Scheduling helps those who have experienced transcendental states from too much social withdrawal, being out of touch with reality, or a deterioration in mental status, delusion, or schizoid thought.

Influence (In-Flow-ence): Inner Paths and Outer Paths

One aspect of process philosophy, at least as I understand it, is that everything that happens is a simultaneous function of our experience of life as we are embedded within life and how life, operating separately from us, influences, affects, and impinges upon us. There is an inner path of awareness, of waking to our self as a whole person within this whole project of life. There is also an outer path of observing life objectively, as it is, whether or not we were here at all.

It is beyond the scope of this book, but metaphysics, philosophy, and religion also distinguish between *immanence* and *transcendence* (also discussed toward the end of chapter 7). Briefly, immanence refers to the idea that truth, knowledge, and God exist within all things and are inherent within them. In contrast, transcendence refers to the idea that truth, knowledge, and God exist beyond our experience and can only be estimated or hinted at but not directly known. A common way to understand this distinction is that God lives with and knows us directly, just as we can know God (a Being intimately available through direct contact), but also that God exists above and beyond us (an uninvolved and distant Being).

There is discussion among religious scholars about whether immanence and transcendence are diametrically opposed to each other or whether they are inextricably tied together. In our Quest for Presence, I believe that they influence each other all the time. Our Soulful Capacities are awakened when we tune into this influence. We become more accepting and present and more readily access states of Flow and Synchronicity. We are spiritual beings having a human experience. We are in the world, of the world, and above it all as well.

The Trajectories influence each other in ways that mimic the influence of transcendence and immanence. The Trajectories work along an outer path and an inner path (see diagram following). The outer path is a cycle that helps us to rise above life and most often involves having to surrender and awaken to a larger reality. The inner cycle helps us to embrace life; we are an integral part of our relationships with others, society, and family. The inner path often requires us to center, ground ourselves, and find harmony. Along these paths, the Trajectories influence each other. As we tune into and abide by this influence, we flow with life. Hence, their mutual influence can lead to "in-Flow-ence."

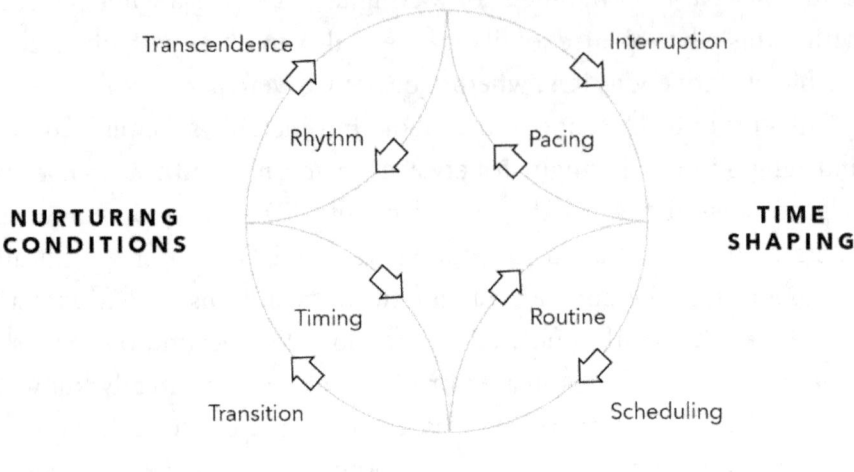

The Outer Path Toward Surrender and Awakening: This path is often initiated or catalyzed from a seemingly external moment, occasion, or event:

> → An Interruption occurs that unexpectedly throws us off course, thwarts our plans, or causes us to get lost or feel separate and apart from life and others (for example, a shock, confusion, bewilderment). →
>
> We attempt to reorganize by creating a sense of order in the future; we readjust our plans; we Schedule. →
>
> We realize that despite our Scheduling efforts (and sometimes because we learned from the past Interruption or disruption) that we are going through a phase or Transition and life is teaching us to adjust, gain insight, or let go. →
>
> However, even these efforts can fall short; we feel we have to step back even further. We need to get a sense of the bigger picture again and, ultimately, Transcend the struggle or difficulty inherent in the Interruption.

This entire experience can lead one to think that "something else is going on," or "there is a message here that I am not getting," or there is a feeling of brokenness, something else is calling one to see, learn, or become more.

The Inner Path toward Centering and Harmony: This path functions as a turning inward to the Routines, Rhythms, Pacings, and Timings of one's life. This turning inward may come in a number of ways.

→ We tune in to the season of our life, realize we have fallen out of Rhythm with others, become aware that we are moving too fast, or have an experience of poor Timing—a missed opportunity, saying or doing something at the wrong time. →

We adjust to this inward stirring by getting accustomed to and centered in Routine. →

We can then more easily Pace ourselves amid any new stressors that come our way or to the recurring or chronic problems that led us to turn inward in the first place. →

By Pacing ourselves, we are more apt to bring about harmony; we find ways to support the daily Rhythms of social interaction and the comings and goings of people in our lives. →

By supporting these Rhythms, we have more right Timing; things fall into place more readily. →

And such right Timing moves us forward to reinforce those Routines that bring about well-being. →

Unlike the outer path, where the Interruption comes from outside, here the turning inward is because of some stirring thought, an emotion, yearning, inkling, or intuition.

Trialectics: Process Logic of the Trajectories

Trialectics is a system of logic developed by Oscar Ichazo. This system stands in contrast to formal logic and dialectics in many respects. For our purposes, there are three important features of trialectics. These are: 1) change is inherent in the nature of reality; 2) change occurs because a system, structure, or person is attracted to a new potential or possible state; and 3) to move (Transition) from one structure or system to another, it is necessary to alter the first system's inherent ways of circulating energy—through an active force, an attractive force, and a function that will relate the system to its new configuration or state.

Briefly, the attractive force functions like a magnet and draws a system toward being in one of several potential new levels, functions, or configurations. For that movement to occur, the system must have an active force that acts upon, is receptive to, or is susceptible to the attractive force. As explained by Ford and Ford (1994): "Food is not attractive to someone who has just eaten, but it is to someone who is hungry; hunger is active, food is attractive. Things are attractive to people because they are 'active' with respect to these things; there is no attractive without an active."

The function is the process that relates the active and attractive to a future state result, which is often a new dynamic state of equilibrium, which itself becomes active and is subject to change. As explained by Horn (1984): "When a person feels hungry, he is in the attractive position and food is active. The function joining them will be the process of digestion and the result will be satisfaction. After this, the body becomes the active element while the feeling of satisfaction is attractive. The function connecting them is assimilation and the result is a satisfied body."

You can take a moment to trace all the various functions and results in the mandala diagram (on page 168). Doing so, you may get a sense that the whole system functions like an ongoing dance. Ironically, it is like "clockwork." However, it is important to keep in mind the duration of all these interactions. Sometimes, functions take longer to start and process before a result manifests. Other times, everything happens all at once. The mandala of Trajectories may be seen as a process that follows the laws of Trialectics.

See the table below, *The Trajectories as Both Functions and Results of Active and Attractive Forces,* which describes how each of the Trajectories is both a function and a result of an active and attractive Radiant Force. These functions are also described in some of the essays contained in each of the preceding chapters about the Trajectories.

For example, when the Radiant Force of Form is active and attracted to Time Shaping, Routine becomes the function that connects this active-attractive relationship and the result is Pacing. In behavior, this looks like those times when we know we need to, or already have, organized and structured our day or some tasks (Form) in order to accomplish some goal or achieve some outcome (Time Shaping). That is, when we create a Routine, a state of equilibrium results. This equilibrium brings a quality of Pacing to our series of actions. Alternatively, we take the necessary time (we pace ourselves) to complete each action as defined by the limits of the Routine.

THE TRAJECTORIES AS BOTH FUNCTIONS AND RESULTS OF ACTIVE AND ATTRACTIVE FORCES

ACTIVE	ATTRACTIVE	FUNCTION	RESULT
Form	Time Shaping	Routine	Pacing
Time Shaping	Chaos	Pacing	Rhythm
Chaos	Nurturing Conditions	Rhythm	Timing
Nurturing Conditions	Form	Timing	Routine
Time Shaping	Form	Scheduling	Transition
Form	Nurturing Conditions	Transition	Transcendence
Nurturing Conditions	Chaos	Transcendence	Interruption
Chaos	Form	Interruption	Scheduling

Think about any routine you have in your life (at home, at work, or at play). The routine itself has a Form that helps you to shape when and how much time you devote to the activity and subactivities of the routine. You know when to start the routine, how long it should take you, and what it will look and feel like to finish the routine. It is because of your knowledge of these boundaries or limits that make up the routine that you have the ability to pace yourself. You can speed up or slow down different subroutines or steps within the activity. As discussed in the Essay on Pacing, you know the limits so you can maintain homeostasis (a sense of balance or equilibrium) within the routine. Indeed, you develop a healthy Rhythm as a result.

See the following figure, *Examples of Trajectory Paths*, which further describes some examples of these relationships. The figure on the left shows when Nurturing Conditions are active. In this example, Transcendence is the function that connects Nurturing Conditions (active) to Chaos (attractive), with the result manifesting in Interruption. Also, Timing is the function that connects Nurturing Conditions (active) to Form (attractive), with the result manifesting in Routine. In this example, Routine is a result and Transcendence is a function. In the next example, where Form is active, these manifestations are flipped and Routine is a function and Transcendence a result.

Examples of Trajectory Paths

The figure on the right shows when Form is active. In this example, Routine is the function that connects Form (active) to Time Shaping (attractive), with the result manifesting in Pacing. Also, Transition is the function that connects Form (active) to Nurturing Conditions (attractive), with the result manifesting in Transcendence.

An important takeaway from these examples—and a core lesson of trialectics logic—is that a single phenomenon serves multiple roles when we are conscious of time as a process. There are times in our lives when our Routines (our habits, repetitions, rituals) give us identity, a sense of self, and the agency to pace our day (see chapter 3). There are other times, when these same routines become basic requirements to take action, where the timing and conditions of our lives bind us to a rigid course that is beyond our own will or any sense of self (see chapter 4).

Similarly, transcending time (timelessness, unity, seeing beyond our own time here) can break us open or break our hearts, propel us into a new future, a new version of ourselves; our life is interrupted, and we are not what we were before; we are altered (see chapter 10). But timelessness can also result from our attraction to a higher state of being, all the work we have done, the previous transitions, and the coming together of conditions that have nurtured our growth on a spiritual path (see chapter 7).

Trajectories as Our Friendly Neighborhood

Each Trajectory also has a sister, a mirror, and a counterpoint, as illustrated in the *Neighborhood of Trajectories* table.

NEIGHBORHOOD OF TRAJECTORIES

PRIMARY	SISTER	MIRROR	COUNTERPOINT
Routine	Scheduling	Transcendence	Rhythm
Pacing	Interruption	Transition	Timing
Rhythm	Transcendence	Scheduling	Routine
Timing	Transition	Interruption	Pacing
Scheduling	Routine	Rhythm	Transcendence
Transition	Timing	Pacing	Interruption
Transcendence	Rhythm	Routine	Scheduling
Interruption	Pacing	Timing	Transition

In addition to having influence on each other, each Trajectory also stands in some relationship to other trajectories in unique ways. Again, some of these relationships are described in the Portraits (essays) in the preceding chapters. Two examples, on Routine and Rhythm, are featured in the figure below.

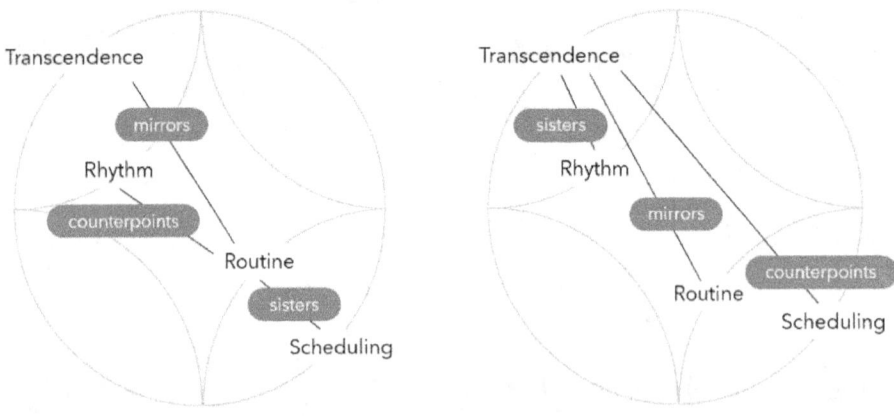

Routine: Routine and Scheduling work together as sisters. Our Routines facilitate Scheduling and our Schedules define our Routines. Routine mirrors Transcendence as expressed in the phrase, "As above, so below" or from Mahayana Buddhism, "There is no difference between suffering (samsara) and liberation (nirvana)." The idea is that the struggle to find Transcendence can itself be a source of suffering. Hence, we need only pay attention to our Routines, our ordinary lives, to find liberation there. This is also expressed in the Buddhist adage, "Chop wood, carry water" and in Christ's sermon (Matthew 6:25-34) to consider the birds, the flowers of the field, and the grass. Finally, Rhythm is the counterpoint to Routine. All the Rhythms of nature stem from day and night and wake to sleep. Without these Rhythms, there would be no anchor point for Routine. And yet, human beings have created Routines through ever-advancing technology that become unhinged from nature. This can go only so far without some backlash. To serve well-being, our Routines must find a natural Rhythm or entrain with Rhythms in nature (see the section "How the Forces Promote Well-Being: Origins of the Routes or Trajectories" on page 159).

Rhythm: Rhythm and Transcendence also collaborate as sisters: By letting go into the Rhythm (of life, music, dance, ritual, sex), we experience a real Transcendence of time altogether. By following a path of Transcendence, we tune into life's flow, the Tao, the Rhythm of nature's watercourse way. Rhythm in nature mirrors Scheduling in human activity. All of nature has its own Schedule, which we experience as Rhythm. The birds, bees, animals, flowers, and plants don't wake up in the morning and tell themselves, "I wonder what is on the schedule today!" And yet, they each have their own fairly well laid out schedules that come from deep oscillators in their nervous systems. In mirror-like fashion, human beings have schedules. Routine is the counterpoint or anchor to Rhythm, for without Routine, we may have no perception or appreciation of Rhythm. That is, we discern Rhythm only when we pay repeated or *routine* attention to the hummings and vibrations of life.

Contemplation (Q*f*P 4-10): The Mandala of the Trajectories, A Guided Visualization

Return for a minute to the story about Pooh and the Wise Old Owl. Imagine that both these characters live inside of you. They each represent different aspects of your nature. First, to get in touch with Pooh, ask yourself, "What is the honey I am wanting, craving, or attracted to in my life?" This can be anything ranging from career, love, or personal success, to education, meaning, travel, or spirituality. Get that image in your mind. Feel, sense, visualize what you want. Now, imagine what you have done, are doing, or will do along the Trajectory toward that pot of honey. This step is important. What have you done so far to get your honey? What will you do to get your honey? Feel, sense, and visualize all the activity involved. All of it. Fill up the movie with lots of activity, plot, circumstance, characters, challenges. Everything. Recall how it has all played out so far. Imagine how it may play out in the future.

Now, as you contemplate the entire moving image of your journey, reflect on what you have learned. Where are your past Routines and Schedules? What role do they play? What about, on one hand, the challenges and Interruptions and, on the other hand, those moments or efforts toward timelessness (Time Transcendence)? Continue like this. Where are the Transitions, the entraining with others (in Rhythm)? The Pacing? The Timing? Do your best to sense it all.

After a minute or two, shift your focus to get in touch with the Owl. He/She/It/Them. Notice that what you were actually doing above—visualizing yourself being Pooh—was activating the observant Owl. Just believe for a second or notice that there is a part of you that sees and witnesses the complete unfolding. Everything. You embody the blur as well as the focus. You embody the movement and the stillness. You embody scurrying about and staying in the nest. You are both embedded in the picture and also outside of it.

Take another moment. Sit with what it feels like in your body to be both of these qualities.

After you are done with this brief visualization, consider these prompts for discussion or journaling.

+ Create side-by-side lists of the benefits of being Owl, of being Pooh, and of being able to move back and forth between these two qualities or approaches.

+ Which of the Trajectories attracts, beckons, or calls to you most at this point in your day? Is it the Owl or Pooh or both who are attracted to that Trajectory?

+ Which of the Trajectories attracts, beckons, or calls to you most at this point in your life? Is it the Owl or Pooh or both who are attracted to that Trajectory?

+ Rank order the Trajectories in terms of which is the most compelling, interesting, and inspiring to you. Number one on the list should have all of these qualities. Number eight would be the least overall compelling, interesting, and inspiring to you.

+ Overall, what would you say is the greatest learning or insight you had from visiting the mandala of the Trajectories?

APPENDIX 1

Day Crafting Tool (Embracing the Trajectories)

This Appendix provides the Day Crafting Tool. The next Appendix provides sample profiles from individuals who have taken the Day Crafting Tool across a number of successive days.

Day Crafting is meant to guide you to practice healthy awareness of time, as well as help you develop wisdom about how time works in your life. The term "crafting" is used to suggest that we have some influence over what we pay attention to and how we respond to different qualities of time. To rescue time from clock prison requires seeing, noticing, attending, or witnessing the event of our day in the flow of time. Salience (what we pay attention to) is inherent in our awareness of time.

The following four steps are designed to help you practice healthy awareness of time. It is best to use Day Crafting at least three days in a row (ideally, seven days). Your rating reflects the degree to which the quality (**Bolded Italics**) is *salient, noticeable,* or *pronounced*. Keep track of which quality is more salient or pronounced on any given day. Note how these qualities change across time (either within or across a day).

STEP 1. Review Your Past Day
(best completed at the beginning or end of your day)

In the past day, the **Quality** of _____ was in the foreground, salient, noticeable, or pronounced.	Not at all	Sometimes	Often	Frequently
Routine | for example, I did the same routines as usual, experienced regularity or daily rituals, and kept events in order.	☐	☐	☐	☐
Scheduling | for example, I spent time prioritizing; I planned, worked with the calendar, and so was able to do things that needed getting done.	☐	☐	☐	☐
Transition | for example, some phase (in a project, work, relationship, family, my identity) in my life is either ending, beginning, or changing.	☐	☐	☐	☐
Timing | for example, key activities happened at the right time: work, play, communications, meetings, meals, travel, waking, sleeping, resting, other.	☐	☐	☐	☐
Rhythm | for example, my day had a natural rhythm for myself (wake, work, rest), with others (meet, leave), or with nature; things just felt synchronized.	☐	☐	☐	☐

Transcendence | for example, I paused or took time outside of time where I was not caught up in anything; I connected, relaxed, and let things unfold.	☐	☐	☐	☐
Interruption | for example, my day was filled with challenges, interruptions, or unforeseen events that took up my time in ways I had not planned.	☐	☐	☐	☐
Pacing | for example, my day had a relatively even or steady pace within events; things were well-paced (not too slow or fast) from event to event.	☐	☐	☐	☐

STEP 2. Bring Focus, Playfulness, and Learning to the Quality

Review the pattern of responses above. Notice if any area differed from (was more or less frequent) than others. Or, which area can you intuitively feel, play with, or learn from in the coming day? In the table below, select one area you need to embrace more, deepen your understanding of, or use to have more enjoyment of your happening life.

☐ Routine ☐ Scheduling ☐ Transition ☐ Timing
☐ Rhythm ☐ Transcendence ☐ Interruption ☐ Pacing

STEP 3. Select an Affirmation

Review the affirmations below. Select one affirmation from the area you selected above. Write it down, send it in an email, text yourself, or post it on social media. Practice repeating that affirmation during your day.

Routine	My daily routines nourish my growth and well-being.	I embrace the ordinary and simple things in life.
Scheduling	My schedule dances gracefully with the rhythm of the day.	Schedulers and to-do lists are a playground for my best self.
Transition	I witness the wonder of transition from dawn to dusk.	My story, filled with transitions, teaches me how to love.
Timing	My day unfolds with a right time for everything.	The curious timing of events brings wonder to my life.
Rhythm	My day has a vital rhythm of rest, work, and spontaneity.	My relationships have their own nurturing rhythm.
Transcendence	My day holds treasures, always waiting to be discovered.	I am part of, and contribute to, deeply meaningful work.
Interruption	Interruptions are presents for my greater presence.	What was once a hassle is now a source of wisdom.
Pacing	I effortlessly pace daily activities with vitality and ease.	I always come back to balance, not too fast or too slow.

STEP 4. Return to Step 1 for the Following Day

Over time, notice if you recycle the same affirmation or move from one affirmation to another. Do you need to practice more acceptance, presence, flow, or attunement to synchronicities in your life? Share your affirmations and pattern of responses with others, and talk about your favorite affirmation. What are your challenges? Insights? Discoveries?

APPENDIX 2

Day Crafting Tool (Sample Profiles)

This appendix presents sample Day Crafting profiles from four different individuals. This includes L.B. (male, age 23), P.L. (female, age 82), K.T. (female, age 66), A.F. (female, age 55), and A.F. (female, age 52). Each profile provides a graphic representation of the individual's ratings across a series of days and a total of ratings for each day, along with day of week, time of day, key affirmations, and their own key insights. In addition, "Areas to Consider" is provided as feedback to the individual. Everyone agreed to be interviewed about their profile, and we summarized the results of that interview in a narrative that precedes each profile. Note that A.F. completed the Day Crafting tool across two separate occasions more than 2.5 years apart.

In studying these profiles, we focus only on patterns *within* individuals rather than looking for consistent variations *across* individuals. Day Crafting is intended to help each person gain insight into their own style or pattern of *time weaving*. Each of us has a unique way of relating to our experience of time that is not anchored in clock-time only. Taken as a whole, the Quest for Presence series of books is intended to guide or help readers tap into this experience.

The sample profiles are offered here as an opportunity for you to reflect on your own experience and to encourage you to complete the Day Crafting Tool over a period of days, and at your own pace or cadence. You will note differences in how many days were completed and that days were sometimes skipped. As with other tools in QfP (Soulful Capacities in Book 2; The Attractions in Book 3), our intent is to help you make the ideas in the corresponding books come to life or have some practical application.

Day Crafting Profile for L.B., age 26

The Day Crafting profile for Luke B. shows that the most salient trajectories were *Scheduling* (21%) and *Routine* (19%), reflecting a strong preference for structure and planning. In contrast, *Transition* (5%), *Pacing* (9%), and *Interruption* (9%) were less prominent, indicating areas with more room for development or intentional focus.

Luke reflected that structure has always played a key role in his life, especially during periods of high demand. Looking back at the autumn when he used the tool—a time when he was interning part-time at two organizations while also attending university full time—he recalls working 4:00 a.m. to 11:00 p.m. days filled with class, work, and personal tasks. "Everything was scheduled down to the minute. It wasn't rigid in a negative way—it gave me energy and focus. But even small *Interruptions* could disrupt the flow."

Even now, Luke values *Routine* "My day starts with a plan. Whether I'm doing nonprofit work, freelance projects, or personal things, I'm more centered when I know what's ahead." However, he also acknowledges a subtle distinction between being flexible and enjoying flexibility. "I've learned how to be fluid—my role at work requires that—but liking fluidity is a different story. I still gravitate toward control and clarity."

A particularly insightful area of exploration for Luke was the lower salience of *Transition* and *Interruption*. Returning from travel or visiting his childhood home, for example, feels especially disorienting. "It's like I have to reinitiate my entire *Routine*. My adult life and childhood life are so different that it throws me off mentally and practically." These moments underscore how deeply his identity and sense of productivity are tied to structure—and how disruptions can feel like slipping out of sync. Interestingly, his ratings of *Rhythm* were inconsistent from day to day.

Still, Luke shows a growing awareness of the value in slowing down. He selected *Pacing* and *Interruption* as qualities to reflect on, even though they are not naturally central to his experience. "*Pacing* is hard for me. I'm always moving to the next thing. I don't like to slow down, but I'm starting to understand that I need to. Even when I'm interrupted, it can be difficult to stop and rethink my plan—but I'm learning that not all *Interruption* is negative."

He recalls a moment of growth when a job rejection led him to rethink his path: "It felt like a huge setback at the time, but looking back, it was the *Interruption* I needed. It reminded me that I could adapt. That life would go on." Interestingly, *Transcendence*—the ability to pause and connect with a bigger picture—was not a dominant theme, but Luke spoke of how it began to emerge in small ways. "On weekends during my student days, I'd let the day flow. That's when I'd feel that sense of beauty and reflection. I want to make space for that more often, even if it's just stopping to notice something small."

A review of Luke's data confirmed a consistent presence of *Scheduling* and *Routine*, but also an increasing openness to qualities like *Pacing* and *Transcendence*, especially when prompted by the Day Crafting tool. "Doing this process helped me be more present, even just a little. I started noticing when I slowed down and took things in instead of just checking boxes."

Today, he sees his relationship with time as more intentional. "I still prioritize structure—it's how I function—but I'm learning to integrate moments that aren't so planned. Small windows to breathe, to reflect, or to just *be*. That's new for me, and I want to keep working on it."

In summary, Luke B.'s Day Crafting journey highlights the importance of anchoring through structure, but also stretching into flexibility. He continues to value *Routine*, but with a growing recognition of the need for flow, space, and presence. "What stood out most to me is that even though my days will always involve planning, there's still room to grow. There's value in *Interruption*, beauty in *Pacing*, and a different kind of power in slowing down."

Day Crafting Profile
L.B. (Male, 23 years)

Season and Duration
Late October to Early November
8 days
5 skipped days

Typical Time of Day
Morning

Your Dominant Trajectories
Scheduling — Your days were well scheduled
Routine — Your days had consistent routine

AREAS TO CONSIDER (may need more attention)

Embrace moments when things naturally fall into place, allowing change to unfold with ease and trust (transition). Align your timing with intentional daily habits to cultivate both stability and efficiency (pacing). Recognize moments when interruptions lead to unexpected insights or necessary breaks (interruption).

Pacing
Interruption
Transcendence
Rhythm
Timing
Transition
Scheduling
Routine

AFFIRMATIONS (per your own selection)

 Pacing: *I effortlessly pace daily activities with vitality*

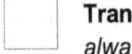 **Transcendence:** *My day holds treasures, always waiting to be discovered*

 Interruption: *What was once a hassle is now a source of wisdom.*

YOUR KEY INSIGHT

"Monday felt like the weekend because I was still at 'home-home.' I have found, with age, that when I go back to where I grew up, I fall into an abyss separate from reality. So, when I come back to reality, I have to re-initiate routines and scheduling."

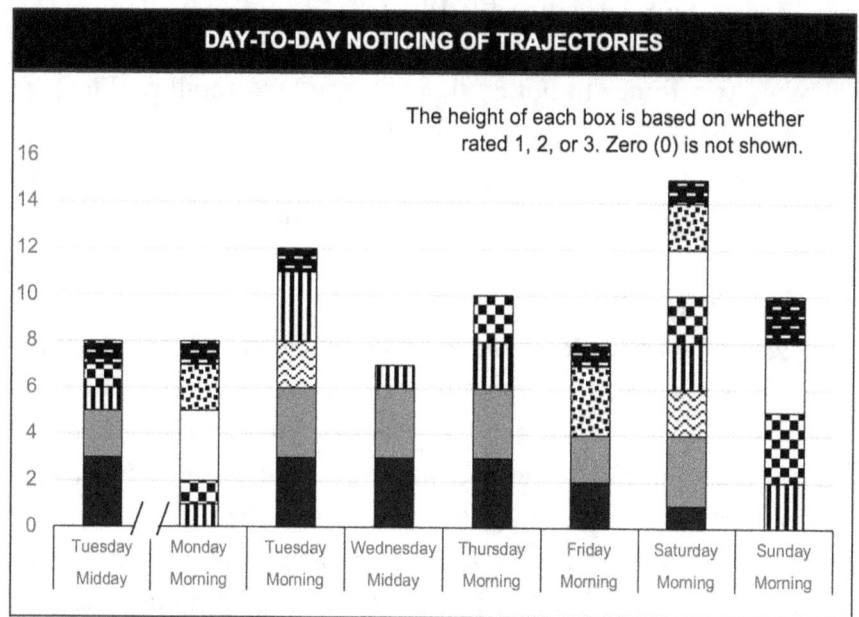

Most days had some degree of **Scheduling** and **Routine**. Many days had some **Timing**. There was a general fluctuation (down-up-down-up) in noticing. There were not any noticeable differences based on time of day (Morning versus Midday).

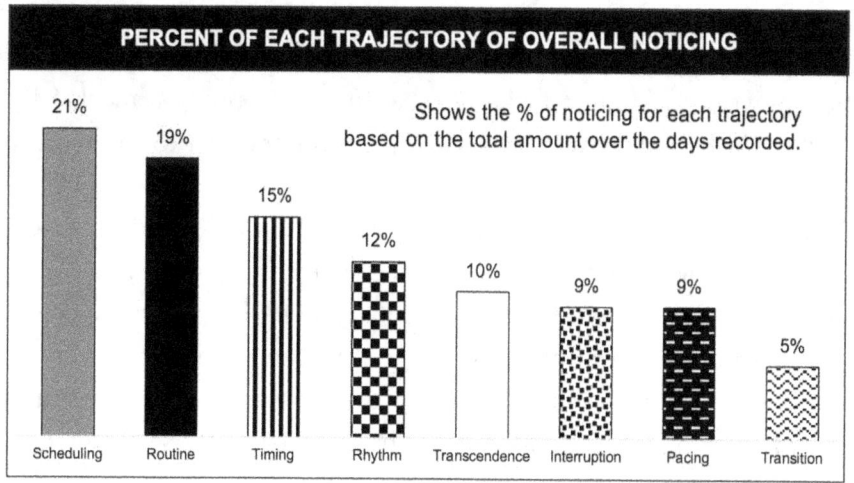

Scheduling made up (21%) of overall noticing, followed by **Routine** (19%), **Timing** (15%), and **Transition** was the lowest (5%).

APPENDIX 2   183

Day Crafting Profile for P.L., age 82

There are two things to notice about Penny L.'s overall profile. First, she had overall higher levels of noticing on most days. That is, 24 is the highest score on any given day for noticing (a rating of 3 for each of the eight trajectories). Following Day 1, the remaining four days had a total of 16. Second, she completed the profile at the same time (evening) every day, which is consistent with her favored aphorism on *Routine* ("My daily *Routines* nourish my growth and well-being.")

Overall, it's clear how much the radiant force of Form (structure, *Scheduling*, *Routine*) and the trajectory of *Rhythm* shape her days. Her highest trajectories were *Scheduling* (21%), *Routine* (18%), and *Rhythm* (16%). These suggest that she moves through the day with intention, relying on well-established patterns and a steady flow of activity. That's not to say her days are rigid—she appears to leave space for spontaneity and connection (see *Transcendence* below)—and finds peace and purpose in maintaining a sense of order.

Penny reflected, "I've come to appreciate the grounding power of structure—not just having things scheduled, but knowing what kind of day I want to shape. When I start my morning with Scripture and then move into kitchen tasks like baking or prepping a meal, I feel both anchored and available—to God, to others, and to the work of the day."

Compared to other trajectories, *Interruption* (7%) and *Transition* (11%) were less central to her experience during this week. That doesn't mean the days were free from change, but Penny seems to have developed a comfort with small shifts and adaptations. "*Interruptions* do happen—like a neighbor dropping by, or a conversation going longer than planned—but I don't experience those moments as disruptions. More often, they feel like invitations."

Transcendence (15%) stood out more than she expected. Initially uncertain about how to define it, Penny came to recognize how often she was pulled toward things beyond herself. Whether listening to someone share a burden, setting aside plans to care for a friend, or simply taking time in the garden to be still—these quiet, meaningful pauses were a consistent thread. "There was one afternoon when I was mentally worn out, but I still felt drawn to show up for someone else. That choice didn't come from pressure—it came from a sense of purpose."

Pacing (12%) and *Timing* (14%) were also present in subtle but important ways. Penny often thinks about the *Rhythm* of the day—not just when something will happen, but how it will feel. "For me, *Pacing* isn't about going slow or fast—it's about being in step. There are moments when I move quickly and others when I slow down, but I'm always trying to stay connected to what matters."

While *Transition* wasn't especially high in her profile, Penny seems to live with a quiet awareness of movement—from one task to another, or from one season of life to the next. "I don't always mark those shifts with ceremony, but I try to notice them. Whether it's the change in the weather or the way the house feels different at the end of the day, I find meaning in those small *Transition*s."

Looking back, her week reveals how all these trajectories weave together. Penny's days are not dramatic, but they are meaningful—full of purpose, quiet decisions, and care. As she put it, "I didn't expect a 'regular' week to reveal so much—but it turns out that the way I spend my time says a lot about what I value. Even the most ordinary moments can carry a kind of grace."

Day Crafting Profile

P.L. (Female, Age 82)

Season and Duration
Mid May
5 days

Typical Time of Day
Evening

Your Dominant Trajectory
Scheduling
Your days had consistent scheduling

AREAS TO CONSIDER (may need more attention)

Embrace moments when things naturally fall into place, allowing change to unfold with ease and trust (transition). Recognize moments when interruptions that lead to unexpected insights or necessary breaks (interruption) may also be opportunities for transcendence or "rising above" (as you said).

AFFIRMATIONS (per your own selection)

Pattern	Category
	Pacing
	Interruption
	Transcendence
	Rhythm
	Timing
	Transition
	Scheduling
	Routine

 Routine: *My daily routines nourish my growth and well-being.*

YOUR KEY INSIGHT

"I chose 'transcendence' to mean 'rising above.' I tried to help someone who will be 100 years old in October, who is in rehab for a broken leg and wants me to be his power of attorney. I'm not comfortable with that, but I did make some phone calls on his behalf. I had a friend over for dinner who had a plumbing problem that had flooded her house. (I'm washing the sheets on the guest bed in case she needs to stay here overnight.) Neither of these things was on my to-do list, so of course I set aside things I had planned to do (mostly work in the yard) to help them. I am very tired and am looking forward to a good night's sleep."

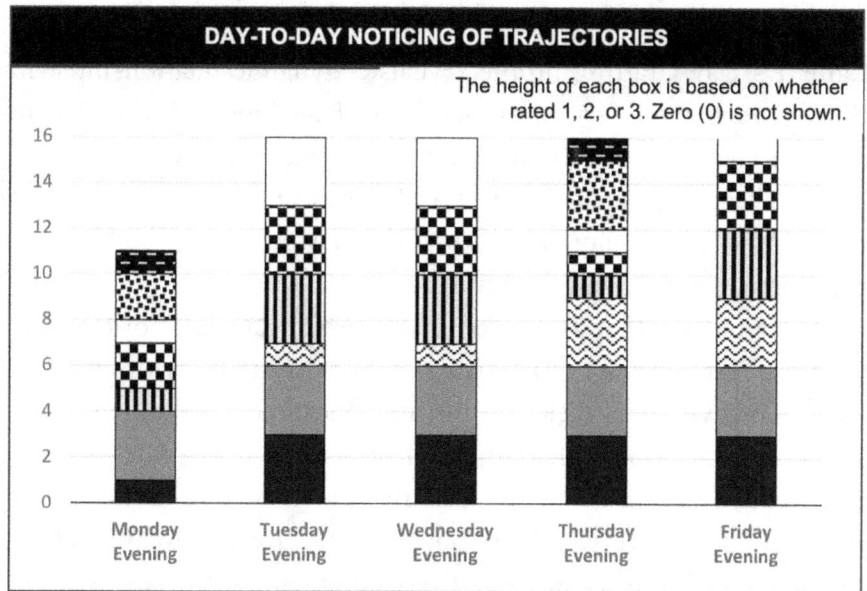

Most days had some degree of **Scheduling and Routine.** Many days had some **Rhythm.** There was a general fluctuation (down-up-down-up) in noticing. There were not any notable differences based on time of day.

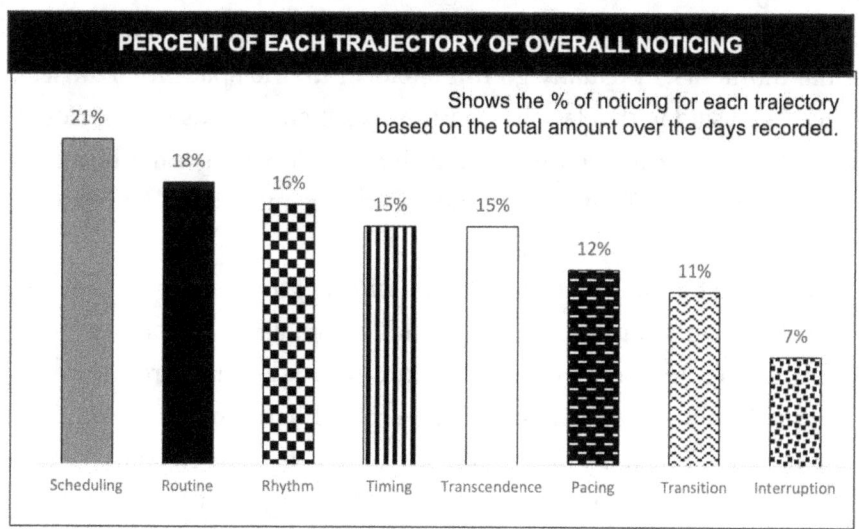

Scheduling made up (21%) of overall noticing, followed by **Routine** (18%), and **Interruption** was the lowest (7%).

Day Crafting Profile for K.T., age 66

Katie T.'s Day Crafting profile reveals a dynamic relationship with time—one shaped most prominently by *Transition* (16%) and *Transcendence* (15%), with *Rhythm* and *Interruption* closely behind (11% each). These trajectories suggest a life lived in constant motion, not necessarily chaotic, but rich with shifts between responsibilities and the search for grounding meaning.

Katie reflects that *Transition* is a near-constant part of her daily *Rhythm*. "I'm always in *Transition*—things come up with family or work. I'm switching back and forth all the time," she noted. These shifts aren't always subtle, either. "If something happens, everything else stops. That's just how it goes." In fact, she described how *Interruptions* can often trigger *Transitions*, saying, "*Interruptions* break the *Rhythm*, which pushes me into *Transition* mode. It throws things off and makes it hard to plan."

Despite the steady movement between tasks and roles, Katie still finds ways to reach for something deeper. *Transcendence*, the second most noticed trajectory in her profile, came through in small, intentional moments. "I usually go in the closet to find space for *Transcendence*," she said with a laugh—yet the statement reveals how seriously she values space to reconnect with herself. Morning time became a window for that. "That's when I write, create, and edit. It's quiet and a time I can work at my own pace."

When asked about *Rhythm* and *Interruption*—each making up 11% of her noticing—Katie acknowledged that she doesn't naturally follow a strict tempo. "I don't like structure. Schedules are the devil," she joked. "This isn't just about the week I filled out the chart. That's how my days normally are." Still, she noted that her capacity to handle disruptions has changed over time. "*Interruptions* and *Transitions* have gotten easier. I've learned to pause and ask, 'Do I need to deal with this right now?'"

This awareness extended to the kind of *Transitions* that require mental shifts—especially those involving creativity. "Switching from something creative to something technical can be abrupt and kills the flow," she said. "It's hard to get back into it once you're pulled away." Yet, she also pointed to resilience. "I've gotten better at switching tasks. I've learned how to handle it."

Scheduling (7%) and *Pacing* (3%) were the least noticed trajectories in Katie's profile—which was unsurprising to her given her preference for flexibility. "I prefer fluid *Scheduling*," she explained. "Weekdays, weekends—it doesn't matter. I just don't like structure." Her approach to time tends to follow an internal logic more than a formal plan, and she expressed a desire for days that flow more naturally, "like a wave … ebb and flow."

The affirmations she selected—focused on *Timing*, *Transcendence*, and *Interruption*—offered a helpful lens. "I think I've come to acknowledge that *Interruption*s will happen. I just try to find a way to flow around them instead of resisting." This mindset aligned with her key insight from the exercise: the importance of navigating rather than reacting to life's disruptions.

Reflecting on the shape of the chart, Katie didn't see a clear pattern in the rise and fall of trajectory intensity across days. "Nothing really stood out about the high or low points," she said. "*Transition* is just a big part of my day—I juggle a lot of balls."

Looking ahead, she expressed a desire to deepen her experience of *Transcendence* and *Rhythm*. "I want to work on incorporating more of that in my daily life. I'm not sure how to describe it—but I want more of that wave-like flow … more fluid and *Rhythm*ic living."

Finally, Katie shared that the process of completing the Day Crafting exercise itself brought valuable perspective. "It woke me up to look at things. I don't usually pay attention to this on a day-to-day basis. Seeing the balance laid out helped me reflect on where I am—and where I want to be."

Day Crafting Profile
K.T. (Female, Age 66)

Season and Duration
Mid May
5 days
2 days skipped

Typical Time of Day
Morning

Your Dominant Trajectory
Transition
Your days had consistent transition

AREAS TO CONSIDER (may need more attention)

Treat your schedule like a commitment to yourself—block out time not just for work, but also for rest, reflection, and the things that refuel you (scheduling). Align your timing with intentional daily habits to cultivate both stability and efficiency (pacing). Recognize moments when interruptions lead to unexpected insights or necessary breaks (interruption).

AFFIRMATIONS (per your own selection)

Timing: *My day unfolds with a right time for everything.*

Transcendence: *I am part of, and contribute to, deeply meaningful work.*

Interruption: *Interruptions are presents for my greater presence.*

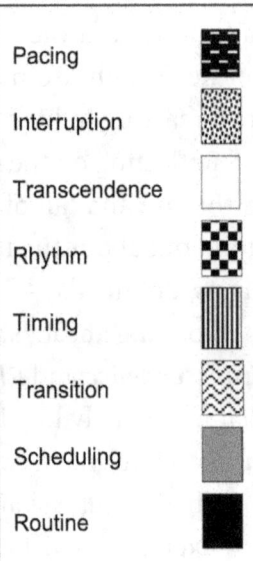

Pacing
Interruption
Transcendence
Rhythm
Timing
Transition
Scheduling
Routine

YOUR KEY INSIGHT

"I need to accept interruptions as part of life and navigate around or through them instead of resisting."

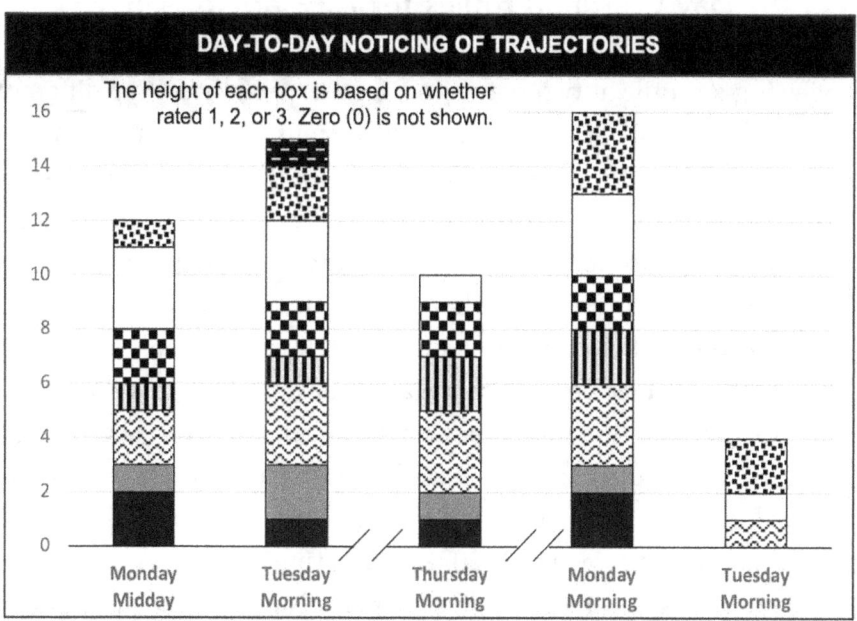

Most days had some degree of **Transition and Transcendence**. Many days had some **Rhythm** and **Interruption**. There was a general fluctuation (down-up-down-up) in noticing. There were not any notable differences based on time of day.

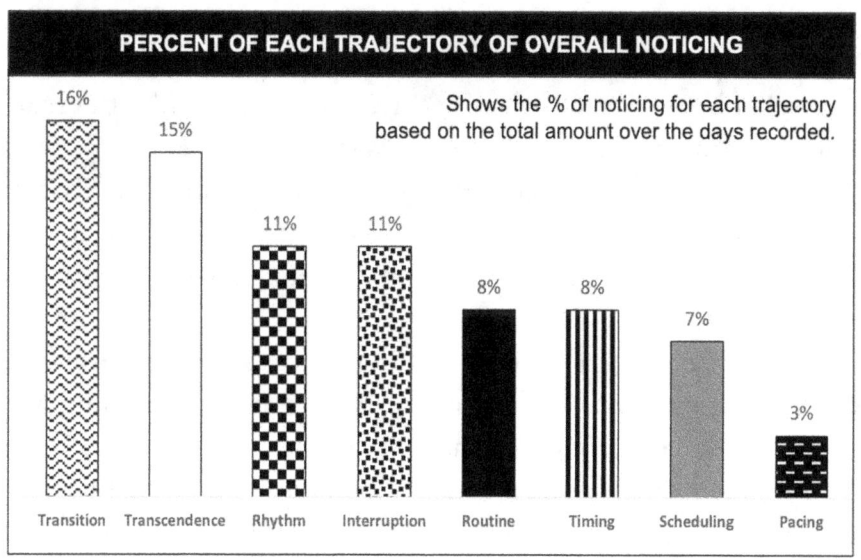

Transition made up (16%) of overall noticing, followed by **Transcendence** (15%), and **Pacing** was the lowest (3%).

Day Crafting Profiles for A.F., age 52–55

Reviewing a profile at two points in time—especially during different phases of life—can produce important insights. The greatest change in the current profile was an increase in **Rhythm** and a decrease in **Routine**. These two trajectories are viewed as Counterpoints in the "Friendly Neighborhood" view (see Chapter 11), which means that they co-occur less often than other pairs of trajectories but that, when experienced together, can enrich our sense of whole time.

Annie F. reflected that a major reason for this change was a shift in priorities. Because she was somewhat stuck in a **Routine**, she decided to significantly reduce her workload by setting aside Fridays for more personal development. "Looking back at how my relationship with time has shifted between fall 2022 and spring 2025, I can see some clear patterns—both in how I lived my days and in how I responded to the survey. The differences say a lot about what was going on in my life and what I was prioritizing."

As a mother of a teenager, Annie previously needed to have more structure, but because of this, she also had to deal with continual **Interruptions** due to changes in her teenager's own dynamic schedule with school, sports, and friends. "In 2022, qualities like **Interruption** and **Routine** stood out. My days were highly structured, but not always in a way that felt grounding. There was a constant sense of being pulled in different directions, and even though I planned carefully, it didn't always translate into flow. I often felt like I was reacting to the day rather than shaping it."

With her teenager's growing independence, Annie's shift toward **Rhythm** came about as an intention to have more grounding and vitality. However, throughout the 2.5-year period, the trajectory of **Transition** remained the most salient for Annie., "By 2025, those patterns had shifted. **Rhythm** became more prominent in my responses. I think that reflects a conscious effort I made to move away from being overscheduled and overstretched. I started valuing fluidity more than fixed **Routines**—trying to simplify, focus on fewer things, and allow for more space between obligations." This shift was itself a *Transition* for Annie. "That change didn't happen overnight, but over time, I began to prioritize the feeling of *how* I was moving through the day, not just *what* I was getting done."

In the "Neighborhood of Trajectories," *Transcendence* has less of a relationship with Annie's predominant trajectories of *Transition* and *Timing*. Because she focused more on dealing with unhealthy *Routines* and wanted to have more vitality, *Transcendence* was not as salient. "Interestingly, *Transcendence* remained relatively low across both years. I think that speaks to how challenging it is for me to truly pause or disconnect. I tend to stay busy, and while I recognize the value of quiet moments, they don't come naturally. Still, I've started to carve out brief windows—especially in the mornings—to reflect and set intentions, even if it's just for a few minutes."

A review of Annie's daily chart showed that in both time periods, she always noticed *Pacing*. However, *Pacing* meant different things across the two periods. "The theme of *Pacing* emerged in a new way. I used to move quickly from task to task, often without taking a breath. By 2025, I was more aware of how important it is to slow down—mentally, emotionally, and physically. That awareness came from experience: burnout, shifting priorities, and the realization that I needed to be more present, not just productive."

Finally, Annie comments on the general takeaways from the exercise. "Overall, I can see real growth between these two points in time. I may not have mastered every trajectory, but I've become more intentional. More focused on what matters. And more willing to let go of what doesn't."

Day Crafting Profile

This is the first of two profiles completed over 2 years apart

A.F. (Female, Age 52)

Season and Duration
Late October & Early November
4 days
1 day skipped

Typical Time of Day
Midday and Afternoon

Your Dominant Trajectory
Transition
Your days had consistent transition

AREAS TO CONSIDER (may need more attention)

Welcome the moments when life aligns effortlessly—trusting in the natural unfolding of change (transcendence). Align your timing with intentional daily habits to cultivate both stability and efficiency (pacing). Recognize moments when interruptions lead to unexpected insights or necessary breaks (interruption).

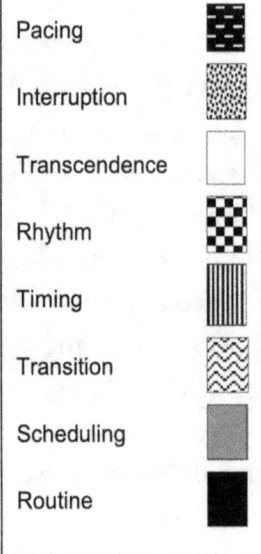

Pacing
Interruption
Transcendence
Rhythm
Timing
Transition
Scheduling
Routine

AFFIRMATIONS (per your own selection)

 Transition: *My story, filled with transitions, teaches me how to love.*

 Rhythm: *My day has a vital rhythm of rest, work, and spontaneity.*

 Transcendence: *My day holds treasures, always waiting to be discovered.*

YOUR KEY INSIGHT

"Interruptions will always happen. Being aware of this and going with the flow makes for a less stressful experience."

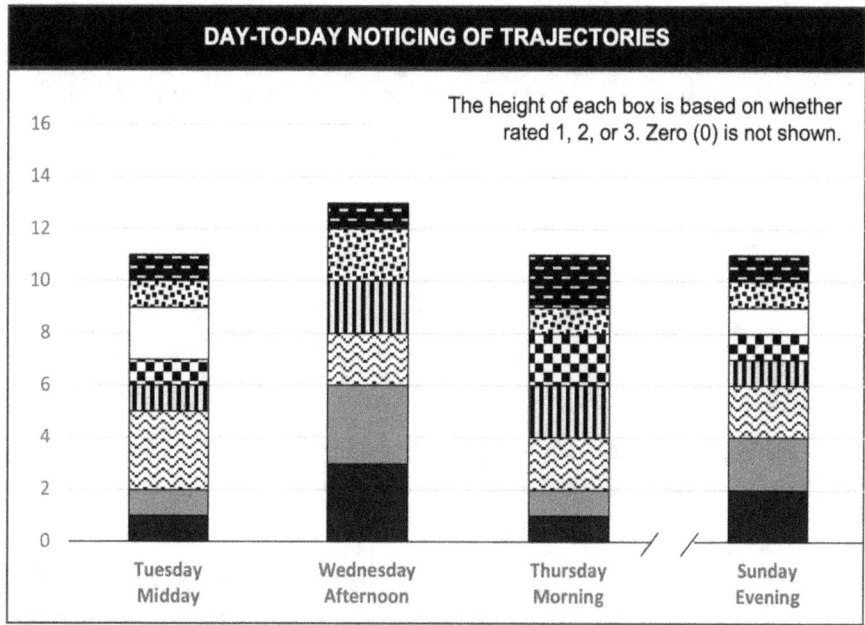

Most days had some degree of **Transition, Routine, and Scheduling.** Many days had some **Timing**. There was a general fluctuation (down-up-down-up) in noticing. There were not any notable differences based on time of day.

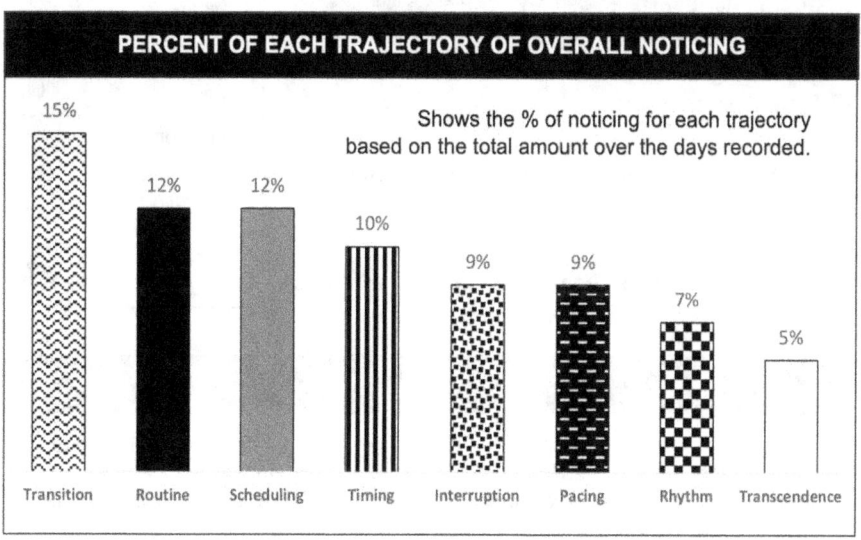

Transition made up (15%) of overall noticing, followed by **Routine** and **Scheduling** (12%), **Timing** (10%), and **Transcendence** was the lowest (5%).

Day Crafting Profile

This is the second of two profiles completed over 2 years apart

A.F. (Female, Age 52)

Season and Duration: Early April, 4 days

Typical Time of Day: Evening and Afternoon

Your Dominant Trajectory: Transition — Your days had consistent transition

AREAS TO CONSIDER (may need more attention)

Ground yourself in steady daily habits that create clarity and sustainable flow (pacing). Stay open to interruptions as invitations for pause, redirection, or unexpected insight (interruption). Trust the moments when effort gives way to ease, and change unfolds through something greater than planning alone (transcendence).

Legend:
- Pacing
- Interruption
- Transcendence
- Rhythm
- Timing
- Transition
- Scheduling
- Routine

AFFIRMATIONS (per your own selection)

 Pacing: *I always come back to balance, not too fast or too slow.*

 Rhythm: *My day has a vital rhythm of rest, work, and spontaneity.*

 Transcendence: *I am part of, and contribute to, deeply meaningful work.*

YOUR KEY INSIGHT

"I am part of and contribute to meaningful work" is the affirmation I chose. I have to remind myself of this because I am so busy. I coach many people, write articles on a variety of topics, and volunteer quite often. I try to help people to see the power of being resilient and the value of healthy coping. I love the work I do. I am doing a lot of great things for society and a large part of my work is managing and caring for my family and they are thriving. I need to remind myself of all of my meaningful work and get less caught up in the day-to-day."

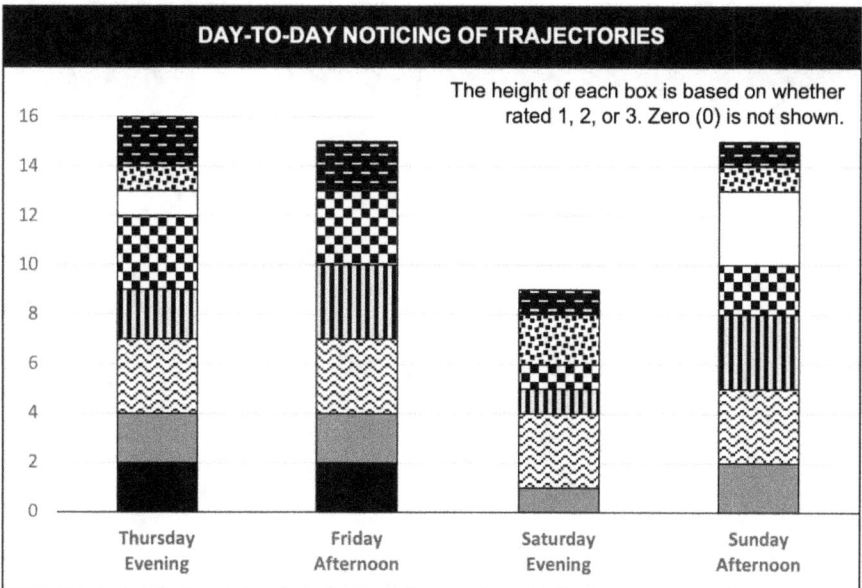

Most days had some degree of **Transition, Timing, and Rhythm**. Many days had some **Scheduling**. There was a steady decline and then increase towards the end of the week in noticing. There were not any notable differences based on time of day.

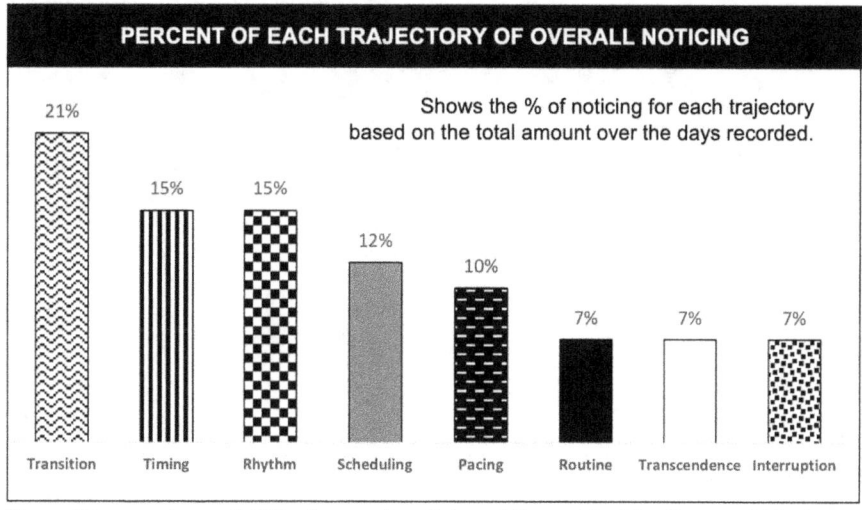

Transition made up (21%) of overall noticing, followed by **Rhythm** and **Timing** (15%), **Scheduling** (12%), and **Transcendence, Routine**, and **Interruption** were the lowest (7%).

Key Terms

Attraction (as a term used in trialectics, see below, and different from Attractions (Capitalized A, see below). In trialectics, attraction is a fundamental part of all processes. The axiom of attraction in trialectics states: "Process occurs in accordance with the attraction of material manifestation points at different levels." Everything is attracted to vibrate or resonate at a higher or lower level by virtue of its attraction to existing at another level of manifestation. Each Trajectory manifests as an attraction from one Radiant Force to another.

Attractions. *(see QfP Book 3)*. The nine Attractions are aspects of our personality and represent personal tendencies that each individual has toward one or more of the four Radiant Forces. Attractions show us how our particular attitudes, moods, motives, and strengths move (pull, draw, invite) us from our current state of being to a deeper, more essential or soulful state, one that is more in touch with the Radiant Forces. The nine attractions are Challenging/Catalyzing, Intending/Time Shaping, Coordinating/Engineering, Centering/Organizing, Discerning/Negotiating, Potentiating/Nurturing, Crafting, Opening/Innovating, and Synthesizing/Integrating. [Note: Attraction, as used in Book 4, differs from the Attractions as described in Book 3. See above definition of Attraction for use in Book 4. A key difference is that the Attractions (Book 3) represent our personal tendencies toward the Radiant Forces, whereas trajectories emerge as one Radiant Force is attracted to another (Book 4)].

Contemplation. The Quest for Presence series encourages readers to embrace contemplation as an active state of being. While the word *contemplation* is a noun, it refers to the act of looking thoughtfully at something for a long time. The devices and exercises at the end of each chapter are named "Contemplations" because they are intended to awaken and activate your mind to engage with the material experientially.

Mandala. A mandala is both an image and a principle. As an image, it has been defined by *Random House Webster's Collegiate Dictionary* (1992) as having a "concentric configuration of geometric shapes, each of which contains an image or attribute of a deity." The mandala originates from Buddhist and Hindu philosophy as a schematized representation of the cosmos. The spiritual and philosophical aspects of mandalas are overlooked, often due to commercial representations. In the Quest for Presence series, the mandala principle refers to the idea of orderly chaos; that everything we experience has interdependence—a center has its fringe and vice versa.

Radiant Forces. The fundamental or deep source of the precious weave of time and discussed in depth in *QfP Book 1*. The forces are specifically forces of time; that is, everything that happens and that we experience as happening emerges or unfolds through the activity of these forces. Each Radiant Force is itself energy and strength with the potential to move things, influence, and provide power, ultimately causing our experience to unfold. Our experience of time's flow (moving from past to present to future) also depends upon the operation of each force and the influence of each one on each other. These forces exist independently of our experience, but we would not have experience without them.

Soulful Capacity (see *QfP Book 2*). A Soulful Capacity refers to our innate and ever-present ability to experience the precious weave and the operation of the Radiant Forces, especially as those forces manifest in the Treasures of this happening life. The Quest for Presence series identifies four such capacities: Acceptance, Presence, Flow, and Synchronicity. They are soulful because they come from and help us touch into a more enduring, essential, and transcendent experience of our journey in this life.

Trajectories. A Trajectory is the path followed by an object moving under the action of a given force or set of forces. In the Quest for Presence series, the Trajectories refer to eight ways we experience time in our day-to-day life. Each Trajectory (seen on the "surface" of the map) emerges through the interplay of the Radiant Forces (the deeper process). Each Trajectory is the surface manifestation of these four Radiant Forces at work. Trajectories include Routines, Scheduling, Timing, Transitions, coordinating (entraining) Rhythms, Transcending Time, Interruptions, and Pacing.

Trialectics. Trialectics is a system of logic developed by Oscar Ichazo to account for change and time as part of logic. Mutation, change, transition, movement, transformation, process, operations are all words for the same concept. The model of the Trajectories described in this book may be seen through the lens and logic of trialectics.

Bibliographic References for the Essays

References for Essay on Routine

Alheit, P. (1994). Everyday time and life time: On the problems of healing contradictory experiences of time. *Time & Society, 3*(3), 305–319. https://doi.org/10.1177/0961463X94003003004

Aurelius, Marcus. (2011). *Meditations: With selected correspondence* (R. Hard, Trans.). Oxford World's Classics. https://www.amazon.com/Meditations-selected-correspondence-Oxford-Classics-ebook/dp/B006QV7YN8/ref=sr_1_3? (Original work published 1634).

Baer, J. C., & Martinez, C. D. (2006). Child maltreatment and insecure attachment: A meta-analysis. *Journal of Reproductive and Infant Psychology, 24*(3), 187–197. https://doi.org/10.1080/02646830600821231

Becker, L. C. (2017). *A new stoicism: Revised edition*. Princeton University Press.

Bernthal, J. C. (2016). *Queering Agatha Christie*. Palgrave Macmillan.

Bradford, K. (2014). *Life hacks: Any procedure or action that solves a problem, simplifies a task, reduces frustration, etc. in one's everyday life*. Adams Media.

Brand, B. L., Armstrong, J. G., & Loewenstein, R. J. (2006). Psychological assessment of patients with dissociative identity disorder. *Psychiatric Clinics of North America, 29*(1), 145–168. https://doi.org/10.1016/j.psc.2005.10.014

Carvalho, F. G., de Souza, C. M., & Hidalgo, M. P. L. (2018). Work routines moderate the association between eveningness and poor psychological well-being. *PLoS ONE, 13*(4), e0195078. https://doi.org/10.1371/journal.pone.0195078

Chopik, W. J., & Grimm, K. J. (2019). Longitudinal changes and historic differences in narcissism from adolescence to older adulthood. *Psychology and Aging, 34*(8), 1109–1123. https://doi.org/10.1037/pag0000379

Cipriani, R. (2013). The many faces of social time: A sociological approach. *Time & Society, 22*(1), 5–30. https://doi.org/10.1177/0961463X12473948

Clear, J. (2018). *Atomic habits: Tiny changes, remarkable results: An easy & proven way to build good habits & break bad ones*. Penguin Group.

Curran, T., & Hill, A. P. (2019). Perfectionism is increasing over time: A meta-analysis of birth cohort differences from 1989 to 2016. *Psychological Bulletin, 145*(4), 410–429. https://doi.org/10.1037/bul0000138

Daily Stoic: Ancient Wisdom for Everyday Life (n.d.). *Routine is everything*. Retrieved January 28, 2020, from https://dailystoic.com/routine-is-everything/

Duhigg, C. (2012). *The power of habit: Why we do what we do in life and business*. Random House.

Epictetus, & Lebell, S. (2004). *The art of living: The classical manual on virtue, happiness, and effectiveness*. HarperOne.

Fiese, B. H. (2007). Routines and rituals: Opportunities for participation in family health. *OTJR: Occupational Therapy Journal of Research, 27*(1_suppl), 41S–49S. https://doi.org/10.1177/15394492070270S106

Fisher, C. (2015, December 3). *Retaining the soul of stoicism*. Traditional Stoicism. http://www.traditionalstoicism.com/retaining-the-soul-of-stoicism/

Hale, L., Berger, L. M., LeBourgeois, M. K., & Brooks-Gunn, J. (2011). A longitudinal study of preschoolers' language-based bedtime routines, sleep duration, and well-being. *Journal of Family Psychology, 25*(3), 423–433. https://doi.org/10.1037/a0023564

Hamamura, T., Johnson, C. A., & Stankovic, M. (2020). Narcissism over time in Australia and Canada: A cross-temporal meta-analysis. *Personality and Individual Differences, 155*(4), Article 109707. https://doi.org/10.1016/j.paid.2019.109707

Holiday, R. (2014). *The obstacle is the way: The timeless art of turning trials into triumph*. Portfolio / Penguin.

Holiday, R. (2016). *Ego is the enemy*. Portfolio / Penguin.

Holmes, H. (2015). Self-time: The importance of temporal experience within practice. *Time & Society, 27*(2), 176–194. https://doi.org/10.1177/0961463X15596461

Koome, F., Hocking, C., & Sutton, D. (2012). Why routines matter: The nature and meaning of family routines in the context of adolescent mental illness. *Journal of Occupational Science, 19*(4), 312–325. https://doi.org/10.1080/14427591.2012.718245

Le Bas, G. A., Youssef, G. J., Macdonald, J. A., Rossen, L., Teague, S. J., Kothe, E. J., McIntosh, J. E., Olsson, C. A., & Hutchinson, D. M. (2020). The role of antenatal and postnatal maternal bonding in infant development: A systematic review and meta-analysis. *Social Development, 29*(1), 3–20. https://doi.org/10.1111/sode.12392

Madigan, S., Atkinson, L., Laurin, K., & Benoit, D. (2013). Attachment and internalizing behavior in early childhood: A meta-analysis. *Developmental Psychology, 49*(4), 672–689. https://doi.org/10.1037/a0028793

Moore, K. (2019). *Wellbeing and aspirational culture*. Springer Nature Switzerland AG.

Morley, T. E., & Moran, G. (2011). The origins of cognitive vulnerability in early childhood: Mechanisms linking early attachment to later depression. *Clinical Psychology Review, 31*(7), 1071–1082. https://doi.org/10.1016/j.cpr.2011.06.006

Norman, A. (2014). *Agatha Christie: The disappearing novelist*. Fonthill Media.

Pathak, H. P., & Bajaj, A. (2013). Agatha Christie: A life narrative. *Dialogue: A Journal Devoted to Literary Appreciation, 9*(02), 21–31.

Pigliucci, M. (2017). *How to be a stoic: Ancient wisdom for modern living.* Ebury Publishing.

Shoham, H. (2020). It is about time: Birthdays as modern rites of temporality. *Time & Society, 30*(1), 78–99. https://doi.org/10.1177/0961463X20955094

Southerton, D. (2012). Habits, routines and temporalities of consumption: From individual behaviours to the reproduction of everyday practices. *Time & Society, 22*(3), 335–355. https://doi.org/10.1177/0961463X12464228

Suggitt, C. (2018). Five record-breaking book facts for National Bookshop Day. Guinness World Records (online). https://www.guinnessworldrecords.com/news/2018/10/5-page-turning-book-facts

Tichelman, E. (2020). *Mother-to-infant bonding: Determinants and impact on child development: Challenges for maternal health care* [Doctoral dissertation, University of Groningen]. https://doi.org/10.33612/diss.132367897

Twenge, J. M., & Foster, J. D. (2010). Birth cohort increases in narcissistic personality traits among American college students, 1982–2009. *Social Psychological and Personality Science, 1*(1), 99–106. https://doi.org/10.1177/1948550609355719

Usunier, J.-C., & Valette-Florence, P. (2007). The Time Styles Scale: A review of developments and replications over 15 years. *Time & Society, 16*(2–3), 333–366. https://doi.org/10.1177/0961463X07080272

van Fenema, P. C., & Räisänen, C. (2005). Invisible social infrastructures to facilitate time-pressed distributed organizing. *Time & Society, 14*(2–3), 341–360. https://doi.org/10.1177/0961463X05055144

Vihalemm, T., & Harro-Loit, H. (2018). Measuring society's temporal synchronization via days of importance. *Time & Society, 28*(4), 1333–1362. https://doi.org/10.1177/0961463X17752555

Wenley, R. M. (1924). *Stoicism and its influence.* Marshall Jones Company.

Wetzel, E., Brown, A., Hill, P. L., Chung, J. M., Robins, R. W., & Roberts, B. W. (2017). The narcissism epidemic is dead; long live the narcissism epidemic. *Psychological Science, 28*(12), 1833–1847. https://doi.org/10.1177/0956797617724208

Whiting, K., & Konstantakos, L. (2018, April 17). *Life-hack stoicism—is it worth it?* The Partially Examined Life. https://partiallyexaminedlife.com/2018/04/17/life-hack-stoicism-is-it-worth-it/

Zerubavel, E. (1985). *Hidden rhythms: Schedules and calendars in social life.* University of California Press.

References for Essay on Timing

Behm, D. G., & Carter, T. B. (2020). Effect of exercise-related factors on the perception of time. *Frontiers in Physiology, 11*, 770. https://doi.org/10.3389/fphys.2020.00770

Benau, E. M., & Atchley, R. A. (2020). Time flies faster when you're feeling blue: Sad mood induction accelerates the perception of time in a temporal judgment task. *Cognitive Processing, 21*(3), 479-491. https://doi.org/10.1007/s10339-020-00966-8

Bennett, B. (2018). *Being diplomatic: Book six in the life mastery course*. Published by eBookIt.com.

Berger, W. (2018). T*he book of beautiful questions: The powerful questions that will help you decide, create, connect, and lead*. Bloomsbury Publishing.

BibleGateway (n. d.). https://www.biblegateway.com/passage/?search=Ecclesiastes%203&version=GNV

Boniwell, I. (2006). *Satisfaction with time use and its relationship with subjective well-being* [Doctoral thesis, The Open University]. Open Research Online. https://doi.org/10.21954/ou.ro.0000e971

Bowen, F. E., Rostami, M., & Steel, P. (2010). Timing is everything: A meta-analysis of the relationships between organizational performance and innovation. *Journal of Business Research, 63*(11), 1179–1185. https://doi.org/10.1016/j.jbusres.2009.10.014

Cardassilaris, N. R. (2019). *From nature to the ideal: A cross-disciplinary study of ancient Greek kairos, circa 3000-146 BCE* [Unpublished doctoral dissertation, Ball State University].

Chaput, J.-P., Dutil, C., Featherstone, R., Ross, R., Giangregorio, L., Saunders, T. J., Janssen, I., Poitras, V. J., Kho, M. E., Ross-White, A., Zankar, S., & Carrier, J. (2020). Sleep timing, sleep consistency, and health in adults: A systematic review. *Applied Physiology, Nutrition, and Metabolism, 45*(10 (Suppl. 2)), S232–S247. https://doi.org/10.1139/apnm-2020-0032

Cooper, B. B. (2018, February 28). *The daily routines of 7 famous entrepreneurs and how to design your own master routine*. Buffer. https://buffer.com/resources/daily-schedule/

Cooren, F., Fox, S., Robichaud, D., & Talih, N. (2005). Arguments for a plurified view of the social world: Spacing and timing as hybrid achievements. *Time & Society, 14*(2–3), 265–282. https://doi.org/10.1177/0961463X05055138

Elchardus, M., & Smits, W. (2006). The persistence of the standardized life cycle. *Time & Society, 15*(2–3), 303–326. https://doi.org/10.1177/0961463X06066944

Eliade, M. (1991). *Images and symbols: Studies in religious symbolism*. Princeton University Press.

Gelang, M. (2013). Kairos, the rhytm of timing. In J. H. Hoogstad & B. S. Pedersen (Eds.), *Off Beat* (pp. 89–101). https://doi.org/10.1163/9789401208871_007

Gram-Hanssen, K., Christensen, T. H., Madsen, L. V., & do Carmo, C. (2019). Sequence of practices in personal and societal rhythms—Showering as a case. *Time & Society, 29*(1), 256–281. https://doi.org/10.1177/0961463X18820749

Grondin, S. (2010). Timing and time perception: A review of recent behavioral and neuroscience findings and theoretical directions. *Attention, Perception, & Psychophysics, 72*, 561–582. https://doi.org/10.3758/APP.72.3.561

Ham, J., van Schendel, J., Koldijk, S., & Demerouti, E. (2017). Finding kairos: The influence of context-based timing on compliance with well-being triggers. In L. Gamberini, A. Spagnolli, G. Jacucci, B. Blankertz, & J. Freeman (Eds.), *International workshop on symbiotic interaction* (pp. 89–101). Springer, Cham. https://doi.org/10.1007/978-3-319-57753-1_8

Kelman, H. (1969). Kairos: The auspicious moment. *The American Journal of Psychoanalysis, 29*, 59–83. https://doi.org/10.1007/BF01872669

Metcalfe, A. (2006). 'It was the right time to do it': Moving house, the life-course and *kairos*. *Mobilities, 1*(2), 243–260. https://doi.org/10.1080/17450100600726621

Miller, D. F. (1993). Political time: The problem of timing and chance. *Time & Society, 2*(2), 179–197. https://doi.org/10.1177/0961463X93002002003

Okakura, Kakuzō (1906). *The book of tea*. Mint.

Peary, A. (2016). The role of mindfulness in *kairos*. *Rhetoric Review, 35*(1), 22–34. https://doi.org/10.1080/07350198.2016.1107825

Ren, F., Kwan, M.-P., & Schwanen, T. (2013). Investigating the temporal dynamics of internet activities. *Time & Society, 22*(2), 186–215. https://doi.org/10.1177/0961463X11421359

Smith, J. E. (1969, January 1) Time, times, and the 'right time'; *Chronos* and *Kairos*. *The Monist, 53*(1), 1–13. https://doi.org/10.5840/monist196953115

Smollan, R. K., Sayers, J. G., & Matheny, J. A. (2010). Emotional responses to the speed, frequency and timing of organizational change. *Time & Society, 19*(1), 28–53. https://doi.org/10.1177/0961463X09354435

Stavenhagen, W. K., & Dougherty, T. R. (2019). Contemplation as kairotic composure. *Across the Disciplines, 16*(1), 66–78. http://wac.colostate.edu/docs/atd/contemplative/stavenhagen_dougherty2019.pdf

What is the meaning of the Greek word kairos? (n.d.). Got Questions. Retrieved February 6, 2021, from https://www.gotquestions.org/kairos-meaning.html

References for Essay on Rhythm

Albrecht, U. (2012). Timing to perfection: The biology of central and peripheral circadian clocks. *Neuron, 74*(2), 246–260. https://doi.org/10.1016/j.neuron.2012.04.006

Andrew. (2015, April 6). *Shifting your clock: Shift work and the circadian clock*. ADBScience. https://adbscience.com/2015/04/06/shifting-your-clock/

Apter-Levi, Y., Zagoory-Sharon, O., & Feldman, R. (2014). Oxytocin and vasopressin support distinct configurations of social synchrony. *Brain Research, 1580*, 124–132. https://doi.org/10.1016/j.brainres.2013.10.052

Au, J., & Reece, J. (2017). The relationship between chronotype and depressive symptoms: A meta-analysis. *Journal of Affective Disorders, 218*, 93–104. https://doi.org/10.1016/j.jad.2017.04.021

Barnett, J. E. (1999). *Time's pendulum: From sundials to atomic clocks, the fascinating history of timekeeping and how our discoveries changed the world*. Harcourt Brace & Company.

Baron, K. G., & Reid, K. J. (2014). Circadian misalignment and health. *International Review of Psychiatry, 26*(2), 139–154. https://doi.org/10.3109/09540261.2014.911149

Blume, C., Lechinger, J., Santhi, N., del Giudice, R., Gnjezda, M.-T., Pichler, G., Scarpatetti, M., Donis, J., Michitsch, G., & Schabus, M. (2017). Significance of circadian rhythms in severely brain-injured patients: A clue to consciousness? *Neurology, 88*(20), 1933–1941. https://doi.org/10.1212/WNL.0000000000003942

Buijs, F. N., León-Mercado, L., Guzmán-Ruiz, M., Guerrero-Vargas, N. N., Romo-Nava, F., & Buijs, R. M. (2016). The circadian system: A regulatory feedback network of periphery and brain. *Physiology (Bethesda, Md.), 31*(3), 170–181. https://doi.org/10.1152/physiol.00037.2015

Cho, Y., Ryu, S. H., Lee, B. R., Kim, K. H., Lee, E., & Choi, J. (2015). Effects of artificial light at night on human health: A literature review of observational and experimental studies applied to exposure assessment. *Chronobiology International, 32*(9), 1294–1310. https://doi.org/10.3109/07420528.2015.1073158

Coomans, C. P., Lucassen, E. A., Kooijman, S., Fifel, K., Deboer, T., Rensen, P. C. N., Michel, S., & Meijer, J. H. (2015). Plasticity of circadian clocks and consequences for metabolism. *Diabetes, Obesity and Metabolism, 17*(S1), 65–75. https://doi.org/10.1111/dom.12513

Csernus, V., & Mess, B. (2003). Biorhythms and pineal gland. *Neuroendocrinology Letters, 24*(6), 404–411.

Damm, L., Varoqui, D., De Cock, V. C., Dalla Bella, S., & Bardy, B. (2020). Why do we move to the beat? A multi-scale approach, from physical principles to brain dynamics. *Neuroscience & Biobehavioral Reviews, 112*, 553–584. https://doi.org/10.1016/j.neubiorev.2019.12.024

Ehret, S., Roth, S., Zimmermann, S. U., Selter, A., & Thomaschke, R. (2020). Feeling time in nature: The influence of directed and undirected attention on time awareness. *Applied Cognitive Psychology, 34*(3), 737–746. https://doi.org/10.1002/acp.3664

Fogelin, L. (2007). The archaeology of religious ritual. *Annual Review of Anthropology, 36*, 55–71. https://doi.org/10.1146/annurev.anthro.36.081406.094425

Forger, D. B. (2017). *Biological clocks, rhythms, and oscillations: The theory of biological timekeeping.* The MIT Press.

Gobert, F., Luauté, J., Raverot, V., Cotton, F., Dailler, F., Claustrat, B., Perrin, F., & Gronfier, C. (2019). Is circadian rhythmicity a prerequisite to coma recovery? Circadian recovery concomitant to cognitive improvement in two comatose patients. *Journal of Pineal Research, 66*(3), e12555. https://doi.org/10.1111/jpi.12555

Guido, M. E., Carpentieri, A. R., & Garbarino-Pico, E. (2002). Circadian phototransduction and the regulation of biological rhythms. *Neurochemical Research, 27*, 1473–1489. https://doi.org/10.1023%2FA%3A1021696321391

Hines, T. M. (1998). Comprehensive review of biorhythm theory. *Psychological Reports, 83*(1), 19–64. https://doi.org/10.2466/pr0.1998.83.1.19

Hittle, B. M., & Gillespie, G. L. (2018). Identifying shift worker chronotype: Implications for health. *Industrial Health, 56*(6), 512–523. https://doi.org/10.2486/indhealth.2018-0018

Hood, S., & Amir, S. (2017). Neurodegeneration and the circadian clock. *Frontiers in Aging Neuroscience, 9*, 170. https://doi.org/10.3389/fnagi.2017.00170

Hughes, A. T. L., & Piggins, H. D. (2014). Disruption of daily rhythms in gene expression: The importance of being synchronised. *BioEssays, 36*(7), 644–648. https://doi.org/10.1002/bies.201400043

Julien, D., Brault, M., Chartrand, É., & Bégin, J. (2000). Immediacy behaviours and synchrony in satisfied and dissatisfied couples. *Canadian Journal of Behavioural Science,* 32(2), 84–90. https://doi.org/10.1037/h0087103

Kohsaka, A., & Bass, J. (2007). A sense of time: How molecular clocks organize metabolism. *Trends in Endocrinology & Metabolism,* 18(1), 4–11. https://doi.org/10.1016/j.tem.2006.11.005

Kriegsfeld, L. J., & Silver, R. (2006). The regulation of neuroendocrine function: Timing is everything. *Hormones and Behavior,* 49(5), 557–574. https://doi.org/10.1016/j.yhbeh.2005.12.011

Li, Z., & Yang, Q. (2018). Systems and synthetic biology approaches in understanding biological oscillators. *Quantitative Biology,* 6(1), 1–14. https://doi.org/10.1007/s40484-017-0120-7

Lipnevich, A. A., Credè, M., Hahn, E., Spinath, F. M., Roberts, R. D., & Preckel, F. (2017). How distinctive are morningness and eveningness from the Big Five factors of personality? A meta-analytic investigation. *Journal of Personality and Social Psychology,* 112(3), 491–509. https://doi.org/10.1037/pspp0000099

Merica, H., & Fortune, R. D. (2011). The Neuronal Transition Probability (NTP) Model for the dynamic progression of non-REM sleep EEG: The role of the suprachiasmatic nucleus. *PLoS ONE,* 6(8), e23593. https://doi.org/10.1371/journal.pone.0023593

Mertel, I., Pavlov, Y. G., Barner, C., Müller, F., Diekelmann, S., & Kotchoubey, B. (2020). Sleep in disorders of consciousness: Behavioral and polysomnographic recording. *medRxiv,* 1–28. https://doi.org/10.1101/2020.05.21.20106807

Morehart, C. T. (2017). Ritual time: The struggle to pinpoint the temporality of ritual practice using archaeobotanical data. In M. P. Sayre & M. C. Bruno (Eds.), *Social perspectives on ancient lives from paleoethnobotanical data* (pp. 145–158). Springer.

Murnane, E. L., Abdullah, S., Matthews, M., Choudhury, T., & Gay, G. (2015). Social (media) jet lag: How usage of social technology can modulate and reflect circadian rhythms. In *Proceedings of the 2015 ACM International Joint Conference on Pervasive and Ubiquitous Computing* (pp. 843–854). Association for Computing Machinery. https://doi.org/10.1145/2750858.2807522

Prieto, P. D., Díaz-Morales, J. F., Barreno, C. E., Mateo, M. J. C., & Randler, C. (2012). Morningness-eveningness and health-related quality of life among adolescents. *The Spanish Journal of Psychology,* 15(2), 613–623. http://dx.doi.org/10.5209/rev_SJOP.2012.v15.n2.38872

Randler, C. (2008). Morningness–eveningness and satisfaction with life. *Social Indicators Research,* 86, 297–302. https://doi.org/10.1007/s11205-007-9139-x

Renfrew, C. (2007). The archaeology of ritual, of cult, and of religion. In E. Kyriakidis (Ed.), *The archaeology of ritual* (pp. 109–122). Cotsen Institute of Archaeology, UCLA.

Rijo-Ferreira, F., & Takahashi, J. S. (2019). Genomics of circadian rhythms in health and disease. *Genome Medicine,* 11, Article 82. https://doi.org/10.1186/s13073-019-0704-0

Roenneberg, T., Wirz-Justice, A., & Merrow, M. (2003). Life between clocks: Daily temporal patterns of human chronotypes. *Journal of Biological Rhythms,* 18(1), 80–90. https://doi.org/10.1177/0748730402239679

Saxbe, D., & Repetti, R. L. (2010). For better or worse? Coregulation of couples' cortisol levels and mood states. *Journal of Personality and Social Psychology, 98*(1), 92–103. https://doi.org/10.1037/a0016959

Silver, R., & Kriegsfeld, L. J. (2014). Circadian rhythms have broad implications for understanding brain and behavior. *European Journal of Neuroscience, 39*(11), 1866–1880. https://doi.org/10.1111/ejn.12593

Stevens, R. G., Brainard, G. C., Blask, D. E., Lockley, S. W., & Motta, M. E. (2014). Breast cancer and circadian disruption from electric lighting in the modern world. *CA: A Cancer Journal for Clinicians, 64*(3), 207–218. https://doi.org/10.3322/caac.21218

Tandon, A., Kaur, P., Dhir, A., & Mäntymäki, M. (2020). Sleepless due to social media? Investigating problematic sleep due to social media and social media sleep hygiene. *Computers in Human Behavior, 113*, Article 106487. https://doi.org/10.1016/j.chb.2020.106487

Thorn, L., Hucklebridge, F., Esgate, A., Evans, P., & Clow, A. (2004). The effect of dawn simulation on the cortisol response to awakening in healthy participants. *Psychoneuroendocrinology, 29*(7), 925–930. https://doi.org/10.1016/j.psyneuen.2003.08.005

Ujma, P. P., Baudson, T. G., Bódizs, R., & Dresler, M. (2020). The relationship between chronotype and intelligence: The importance of work timing. *Scientific Reports, 10*, Article 7105. https://doi.org/10.1038/s41598-020-62917-9

Woods, H. C., & Scott, H. (2016). #Sleepyteens: Social media use in adolescence is associated with poor sleep quality, anxiety, depression and low self-esteem. *Journal of Adolescence, 51*(1), 41–49. https://doi.org/10.1016/j.adolescence.2016.05.008

Yoon, H., Choi, S. H., Kim, S. K., Kwon, H. B., Oh, S. M., Choi, J.-W., Lee, Y. J., Jeong, D.-U., & Park, K. S. (2019). Human heart rhythms synchronize while co-sleeping. *Frontiers in Physiology, 10*, 190. https://doi.org/10.3389/fphys.2019.00190

Yuan, X., Zhu, C., Wang, M., Mo, F., Du, W., & Ma, X. (2018). Night shift work increases the risks of multiple primary cancers in women: A systematic review and meta-analysis of 61 articles. *Cancer Epidemiology, Biomarkers & Prevention, 27*(1), 25–40. https://doi.org/10.1158/1055-9965.EPI-17-0221

Zelinski, E. L., Deibel, S. H., & McDonald, R. J. (2014). The trouble with circadian clock dysfunction: Multiple deleterious effects on the brain and body. *Neuroscience & Biobehavioral Reviews, 40*, 80–101. https://doi.org/10.1016/j.neubiorev.2014.01.007

References for Essay on Transition

Alam, M. J. (2015). Soliloquies in Hamlet: Necessary or unnecessary in the context of the play. *International Journal of Novel Research in Interdisciplinary Studies, 2*(3), 1–10.

Arendzen, J. (1909). Gnosticism. In *The Catholic Encyclopedia*. Robert Appleton Company. Retrieved March 3, 2021 from: http://www.newadvent.org/cathen/06592a.htm

Armstrong, T. (2012, August 17). *The transitional object: A half-way house for identity formation*. American Institute for Learning and Human Development. https://www.institute4learning.com/2012/08/17/the-transitional-object-a-half-way-house-for-identity-formation/

Ashenhurst, J. (2025, January 28). *What's a transition state?* Master Organic Chemistry. https://www.masterorganicchemistry.com/2010/11/03/whats-a-transition-state/

Bartlett, R. A., & Hauck, D. W. (2009). *Real alchemy: A primer of practical alchemy*. Ibis.

Bennett, J. B. (2000). *Time and intimacy: A new science of personal relationships*. Taylor & Francis.

Boggs, C. L., Watt, W. B., & Ehrlich, P. R. (Eds.) (2003). *Butterflies: Ecology and evolution taking flight*. University of Chicago Press.

Campbell, J. (2008). *The hero with a thousand faces*. New World Library.

Chodron, T. (2009, September 5). Contemplating impermanence. In *The four seals of Buddhism*. Bhikshuni Thubten Chodron. https://thubtenchodron.org/2009/09/conditioned-phenomena-change/

CNRS. (2013, December 16). When will Earth lose its oceans? ScienceDaily. https://www.sciencedaily.com/releases/2013/12/131216142310.htm

Dash, R. K. (2014). Applying the Alchemical Transformation Model (ATM) to study the Bhagavad Gita. *Language in India*, 14(12), 701–717.

Dowden, B. (n.d.). Time. Internet Encyclopedia of Philosophy. Retrieved March 1, 2021, from https://iep.utm.edu/time/

Eisenberg, J. D., & Finlayson, M. A. (2017). A simpler and more generalizable story detector using verb and character features. In *Proceedings of the 2017 Conference on Empirical Methods in Natural Language Processing* (pp. 2708–2715). Association for Computational Linguistics. http://dx.doi.org/10.18653/v1/D17-1287

Flammer, C., & Bansal, P. (2017). Does a long-term orientation create value? Evidence from a regression discontinuity. *Strategic Management Journal*, 38(9), 1827–1847. https://doi.org/10.1002/smj.2629

Gavetti, G., & Rivkin, J. W. (2007). On the origin of strategy: Action and cognition over time. *Organization Science*, 18(3), 420–439. https://doi.org/10.1287/orsc.1070.0282

Gilby, T., Coomaraswamy, A. K., & Tollast, R. (1933). Maha-Pralaya and last judgment. *Blackfriars*, 14(159), 494–497. https://doi.org/10.1111/j.1741-2005.1933.tb01898.x

Guarino, B. (2018, January 30). This chemist is unlocking the secrets of alchemy. *The Washington Post*. https://www.washingtonpost.com/news/speaking-of-science/wp/2018/01/30/this-chemist-is-unlocking-the-secrets-of-alchemy/

Harding, S., & Margulis, L. (2009). Water Gaia: 3.5 thousand million years of wetness on planet Earth. In E. Crist & H. B. Rinker (Eds.), *Gaia in turmoil: Climate change, biodepletion, and earth ethics in an age of crisis*. The MIT Press. https://doi.org/10.7551/mitpress/7845.001.0001

Irvine, I. (2008). *Jung, alchemy and the technique of active imagination*. Mercurius Press.

Jung, C. G., Adler, G. (Ed.), & Hull, R. F. C. (Trans.) (1968). *Psychology and alchemy*. Princeton University Press.

Maslow, A. H. (1943). A theory of human motivation. *Psychological Review*, 50(4), 370–396. https://doi.org/10.1037/h0054346

Telos. (n.d.). Philosophy Terms. Retrieved March 1, 2021, from https://philosophyterms.com/telos/

Trafton, A. (2019, December 16). *Chemists glimpse the fleeting "transition state" of a reaction.* MIT News. https://news.mit.edu/2019/chemists-transition-state-reaction-1216

van Tienoven, T. P. (2019). A multitude of natural, social and individual time. *Time & Society, 28*(3), 971–994. https://doi.org/10.1177/0961463X17752554

Wilber, K. (2000). *Integral psychology: Consciousness, spirit, psychology, therapy.* Shambhala Publications.

Wilson, A., & Robinson, N. M. T. (2002). Transitional objects and transitional phenomena. In M. Hersen, W. Sledge, A. M. Gross, J. Kay, B. Rounsavile, & W. W. Tryon (Eds.), *Encyclopedia of Psychotherapy* (pp. 861–866). Elsevier Science.

Yang, C.-C., Brown, B. B., & Braun, M. T. (2014). From Facebook to cell calls: Layers of electronic intimacy in college students' interpersonal relationships. *New Media & Society, 16*(1), 5–23. https://doi.org/10.1177%2F1461444812472486

References for Essay on Transcendence (Timelessness, Time Transcendence)

Amaro, A. (2020). Time and timelessness. *Mindfulness in Practice, 12,* 1298–1300. https://doi.org/10.1007/s12671-020-01531-2

Bashew, J. (Director). (2009). *Eckhart Tolle: Awakening in the now* [DVD]. Sounds True.

de Graaf, J., Wann, D., & Naylor, T. H. (2014). *Affluenza: How overconsumption is killing us—and how to fight back* (3rd ed.). Berrett-Koehler Publishers.

Eger, E. E. (2018). *The choice: Embrace the possible.* Scribner.

Frankl, V. E. (2006). *Man's search for meaning.* Beacon Press.

"Gate, gate, paragate, parasamgate" #1. (n.d.) White Lotus Judith Ragir. Retrieved March 26, 2021, from https://www.judithragir.org/2014/11/gate-gate-paragate-parasamgate-1/

Heschel, A. J. (2005). *The Sabbath.* Farrar Straus Giroux.

Huffington, M. (2011, May 25). *For what profits a man if he gains the whole world but loses his own soul.* Huffpost. Retrieved March 26, 2021, from https://www.huffpost.com/entry/for-what-profits-a-man-if_b_98783

Jonas-Simpson, C. (2010). Awakening to space consciousness and timeless transcendent presence. *Nursing Science Quarterly, 23*(3), 195–200. https://doi.org/10.1177/0894318410371848

Koltko-Rivera, M. E. (2006). Rediscovering the later version of Maslow's Hierarchy of Needs: Self-transcendence and opportunities for theory, research, and unification. *Review of General Psychology, 10*(4), 302–317. https://doi.org/10.1037%2F1089-2680.10.4.302

Lopez, D. S. (2008). *What's in a mantra?* Tricycle. Retrieved March 26, 2021, from https://tricycle.org/magazine/whats-mantra/

Mainemelis, C., & Dionysiou, D. D. (2015). Play, flow, and timelessness. In C. E. Shalley, M. A. Hitt, & J. Zhou (Eds.), *The Oxford Handbook of Creativity, Innovation,* and Entrepreneurship (pp. 121–140), Oxford Library of Psychology. https://doi.org/10.1093/oxfordhb/9780199927678.013.0006

Myss, C. (2003). *Sacred contracts: Awakening your divine potential*. Harmony.

Myss, C. (n.d.). *Appendix: A gallery of archetypes*. https://www.myss.com/free-resources/sacred-contracts-and-your-archetypes/appendix-a-gallery-of-archtypes/

Pike, N. C. (2002). *God and timelessness*. Wipf and Stock Publishers.

Pitch, A. S. (2015). *Our crime was being Jewish: Hundreds of holocaust survivors tell their stories*. Skyhorse.

Sharew, B. (2020, November 21). *The misconception that poor people are happier*. Borgen Magazine. Retrieved March 26, 2021, from https://www.borgenmagazine.com/poor-people-are-happier/

Smith, T. W. (2006). The national spiritual transformation study. *Journal for the Scientific Study of Religion, 45*(2), 283–296. https://doi.org/10.1111/j.1468-5906.2006.00306.x

Tolle, E. (2003). *Stillness speaks*. New World Library.

Tolle, E. (2005). *A new earth: Awakening to your life's purpose*. Penguin Life.

Tolle, E. (2008). *Oneness with all life: Inspirational selections from a new earth*. Penguin Life.

Whitbourne, S. K. (2020, February 15). *The emotional ups and downs in the lives of the depressed*. Psychology Today. Retrieved March 27, 2021, from https://www.psychologytoday.com/us/blog/fulfillment-any-age/202002/the-emotional-ups-and-downs-in-the-lives-the-depressed

References for Essay on Schedule

Aeon, B., Faber, A., & Panaccio, A. (2021). Does time management work? A meta-analysis. *PloS ONE, 16*(1), e0245066. https://doi.org/10.1371/journal.pone.0245066

Azar, S., & Zafer, S. (2013). Confirmatory factor analysis of time management behavior scale: Evidence from Pakistan. *Interdisciplinary Journal of Contemporary Research in Business, 4*(12), 946–959.

Bond, M. J., & Feather, N. T. (1988). Some correlates of structure and purpose in the use of time. *Journal of Personality and Social Psychology, 55*(2), 321–329. https://doi.org/10.1037/0022-3514.55.2.321

Boniwell, I. (2005). Beyond time management: How the latest research on time perspective and perceived time use can assist clients with time-related concerns. *International Journal of Evidence Based Coaching and Mentoring, 3*(2), 61–74. https://psycnet.apa.org/record/2007-06305-006

Bowles, T. V. (2018). Motivation to the past, present, and future: Time orientation and disorientation before therapy. *Australian Psychologist, 53*(3), 223–235. https://doi.org/10.1111/ap.12289

Britton, B. K., & Tesser, A. (1991). Effects of time-management practices on college grades. *Journal of Educational Psychology, 83*(3), 405–410. https://doi.org/10.1037/0022-0663.83.3.405

Chatzitheochari, S., & Arber, S. (2009). Lack of sleep, work and the long hours culture: Evidence from the UK Time Use Survey. *Work, Employment and Society*, 23(1), 30–48. https://doi.org/10.1177%2F0950017008099776

Claessens, B. J. C., van Eerde, W., Rutte, C. G., & Roe, R. A. (2007). A review of the time management literature. *Personnel Review*, 36(2), 255–276. https://doi.org/10.1108/00483480710726136

Gregg, M. (2018). *Counterproductive: Time management in the knowledge economy*. Duke University Press.

Häfner, A., Stock, A., & Oberst, V. (2015). Decreasing students' stress through time management training: An intervention study. *European Journal of Psychology of Education*, 30, 81–94. https://doi.org/10.1007/s10212-014-0229-2

Häfner, A., Stock, A., Pinneker, L., & Ströhle, S. (2013). Stress prevention through a time management training intervention: An experimental study. *Educational Psychology*, 34(3), 403–416. https://doi.org/10.1080/01443410.2013.785065

Holman, D., Johnson, S., & O'Connor, E. (2018). Stress management interventions: Improving subjective psychological well-being in the workplace. In E. Diener, S. Oishi, & L. Tay (Eds.), *Handbook of well-being*. DEF Publishers.

Jo, I.-H., Kim, D., & Yoon, M. (2015). Constructing proxy variables to measure adult learners' time management strategies in LMS. *Educational Technology & Society*, 18(3), 214–225. www.jstor.org/stable/jeductechsoci.18.3.214

Joireman, J., Shaffer, M. J., Balliet, D., & Strathman, A. (2012). Promotion orientation explains why future-oriented people exercise and eat healthy: Evidence from the two-factor Consideration of Future Consequences-14 Scale. *Personality and Social Psychology Bulletin*, 38(10), 1272–1287. https://doi.org/10.1177/0146167212449362

Kanigel, R. (2005). *The one best way: Frederick Winslow Taylor and the enigma of efficiency*. The MIT Press.

Kazakina, E. (2013). Time perspective of older adults: Research and clinical practice. In M. P. Paixão, J. T. da Silva, V. Ortuño, & P. Cordeiro (Eds.), *International Studies in Time Perspective*. Coimbra University Press.

Kazakina, E. (2015). The uncharted territory: Time perspective research meets clinical practice. Temporal focus in psychotherapy across adulthood and old age. In M. Stolarski, N. Fieulaine, & W. van Beek (Eds.), *Time Perspective Theory; Review, Research and Application*, 499–516. Springer, Cham. https://doi.org/10.1007/978-3-319-07368-2_32

Kooij, D. T. A. M., Kanfer, R., Betts, M., & Rudolph, C. W. (2018). Future time perspective: A systematic review and meta-analysis. *Journal of Applied Psychology*, 103(8), 867–893. https://doi.org/10.1037/apl0000306

Macan, T. H. (1994). Time management: Test of a process model. *Journal of Applied Psychology*, 79(3), 381–391. https://doi.org/10.1037/0021-9010.79.3.381

Milfont, T. L., Wilson, J., & Diniz, P. (2012). Time perspective and environmental engagement: A meta-analysis. *International Journal of Psychology*, 47(5), 325–334. https://doi.org/10.1080/00207594.2011.647029

Milner, A., Witt, K., LaMontagne, A. D., & Niedhammer, I. (2018). Psychosocial job stressors and suicidality: A meta-analysis and systematic review. *Occupational and Environmental Medicine, 75*(4), 245–253. http://dx.doi.org/10.1136/oemed-2017-104531

Mirzania, A., Firoozi, M., & Saberi, A. (2022). The efficacy of time perspective therapy in reducing symptoms of post-traumatic stress, anxiety, and depression in females with breast cancer. *International Journal of Cancer Management, 14*(12). https://doi.org/10.5812/ijcm.112915

Petrocelli, J. V. (2003). Factor validation of the Consideration of Future Consequences Scale: Evidence for a short version. *The Journal of Social Psychology, 143*(4), 405–413. https://doi.org/10.1080/00224540309598453

Pfeffer, J., (2018). *Dying for a paycheck*. Harper Business.

Pfeffer, J., & Carney, D. R. (2018). The economic evaluation of time can cause stress. *Academy of Management Discoveries, 4*(1), 74–93. https://doi.org/10.5465/amd.2016.0017

Rapp, A. A., Bachrach, D. G., & Rapp, T. L. (2013). The influence of time management skill on the curvilinear relationship between organizational citizenship behavior and task performance. *Journal of Applied Psychology, 98*(4), 668–677. https://doi.org/10.1037/a0031733

Rappange, D. R., Brouwer, W. B. F., & van Exel, N. J. A. (2009). Back to the Consideration of Future Consequences Scale: Time to reconsider? *The Journal of Social Psychology, 149*(5), 562–584. https://doi.org/10.1080/00224540903232324

Sobol-Kwapińska, M., Jankowski, T., Przepiorka, A., Oinyshi, I., Sorokowski, P., & Zimbardo, P. (2018). What is the structure of time? A study on time perspective in the United States, Poland, and Nigeria. *Frontiers in Psychology, 9*, Article 2078. https://doi.org/10.3389/fpsyg.2018.02078

Sohn, S. Y., Rees, P., Wildridge, B., Kalk, N. J., & Carter, B. (2019). Prevalence of problematic smartphone usage and associated mental health outcomes amongst children and young people: A systematic review, meta-analysis and GRADE of the evidence. *BMC Psychiatry, 19*, Article 356. https://doi.org/10.1186/s12888-019-2350-x

Strathman, A., Gleicher, F., Boninger, D. S., & Edwards, C. S. (1994). The consideration of future consequences: Weighing immediate and distant outcomes of behavior. *Journal of Personality and Social Psychology, 66*(4), 742–752. https://doi.org/10.1037/0022-3514.66.4.742

Vagni, G. (2020). The social stratification of time use patterns. *The British Journal of Sociology, 71*(4), 658–679. https://doi.org/10.1111/1468-4446.12759

wangcynt. (2013, April 26). A slice of time: An exploration of temporal capital and its relationships to economics, culture, and society in a technological and digital age. *Gnovis Journal*. https://gnovisjournal.georgetown.edu/journal/a-slice-of-time-an-exploration-of-temporal-capital-and-its-relationships-to-economics-culture-and-society-in-a-technological-and-digital-age/#

Widyanto, L., Griffiths, M. D., & Brunsden, V. (2011). A psychometric comparison of the Internet Addiction Test, the Internet-Related Problem Scale, and self-diagnosis. *Cyberpsychology, Behavior, and Social Networking, 14*(3), 141–149. https://doi.org/10.1089/cyber.2010.0151

Yonkers, V. (2015). Mobile technology and social identity. In Z. Yan (Ed.), *Encyclopedia of Mobile Phone Behavior* (pp. 719–731). IGI Global Scientific Publishing.

Zhang, J. W., Howell, R. T., & Bowerman, T. (2013). Validating a brief measure of the Zimbardo Time Perspective Inventory. *Time & Society*, 22(3), 391–409. https://doi.org/10.1177%2F0961463X12441174

Zimbardo, P. G., & Boyd, J. N. (2008). *The time paradox: The new psychology of time that will change your life*. Atria Books.

Zimbardo, P. G., & Boyd, J. N. (2015). Putting time in perspective: A valid, reliable individual-differences metric. In M. Stolarski, N. Fieulaine, & W. van Beek (Eds.), *Time Perspective Theory; Review, Research and Application* (pp. 17–55). Springer, Cham. https://doi.org/10.1007/978-3-319-07368-2_2

References for Essay on Pacing

Barbiero, S., Aimo, A., Castiglione, V., Giannoni, A., Vergaro, G., Passino, C., & Emdin, M. (2018). Healthy hearts at hectic pace: From daily life stress to abnormal cardiomyocyte function and arrhythmias. *European Journal of Preventive Cardiology*, 25(13), 1419–1430. https://doi.org/10.1177/2047487318790614

Bettencourt, L. M. A., Lobo, J., Helbing, D., Kühnert, C., & West, G. B. (2007). Growth, innovation, scaling, and the pace of life in cities. *Proceedings of the National Academy of Sciences*, 104(17), 7301–7306. https://doi.org/10.1073/pnas.0610172104

Bick, A., Brüggemann, B., & Fuchs-Schündeln, N. (2019). Hours worked in Europe and the United States: New data, new answers. *The Scandinavian Journal of Economics*, 121(4), 1381–1416. https://doi.org/10.1111/sjoe.12344

Borritz, M., Bültmann, U., Rugulies, R., Christensen, K. B., Villadsen, E., & Kristensen, T. S. (2005). Psychosocial work characteristics as predictors for burnout: Findings from 3-year follow up of the PUMA study. *Journal of Occupational and Environmental Medicine*, 47(10), 1015–1025. https://psycnet.apa.org/doi/10.1097/01.jom.0000175155.50789.98

Campos, M. (2017, November 22). *Heart rate variability: A new way to track well-being*. Harvard Health Publishing. https://www.health.harvard.edu/blog/heart-rate-variability-new-way-track-well-2017112212789

Chalmers, J. A., Quintana, D. S., Abbott, M. J.-A., & Kemp, A. H. (2014). Anxiety disorders are associated with reduced heart rate variability: A meta-analysis. *Frontiers in Psychiatry*, 5, 80. https://doi.org/10.3389/fpsyt.2014.00080

Colvile, R. (2016). *The great acceleration: How the world is getting faster, faster*. Bloomsbury Publishing.

de Sampaio Barros, M. F., Araújo-Moreira, F. M., Trevelin, L. C., & Radel, R. (2018). Flow experience and the mobilization of attentional resources. *Cognitive, Affective, & Behavioral Neuroscience*, 18, 810–823. https://doi.org/10.3758/s13415-018-0606-4

Eller, N. H., Netterstrøm, B., Gyntelberg, F., Kristensen, T. S., Nielsen, F., Steptoe, A., & Theorell, T. (2009). Work-related psychosocial factors and the development of ischemic heart disease: A systematic review. *Cardiology in Review*, 17(2), 83–97. https://doi.org/10.1097/CRD.0b013e318198c8e9

Honoré, C. (2010). *In praise of slow: How a worldwide movement is challenging the cult of speed*. Orion.

Kim, H.-G., Cheon, E.-J., Bai, D.-S., Lee, Y. H., & Koo, B.-H. (2018). Stress and heart rate variability: A meta-analysis and review of the literature. *Psychiatry Investigation, 15*(3), 235–245. https://dx.doi.org/10.30773%2Fpi.2017.08.17

Kristensen, M. L. (2018). Mindfulness and resonance in an era of acceleration: A critical inquiry. *Journal of Management, Spirituality & Religion, 15*(2), 178–195. https://doi.org/10.1080/14766086.2017.1418413

Kristensen, T. S., Bjorner, J. B., Christensen, K. B., & Borg, V. (2004). The distinction between work pace and working hours in the measurement of quantitative demands at work. *Work & Stress, 18*(4), 305–322. https://doi.org/10.1080/02678370412331314005

Kuslapuu, K. (2009). *The impact of cultural values and societal factors on the pace of life and on the relationship between work and leisure in the United States, western Europe and Estonia: A comparative analysis* [Master's Thesis, University of Tartu]. https://dspace.ut.ee/server/api/core/bitstreams/babca836-04cb-4628-85b5-bae7b65e758f/content

Levine, R.V. (n.d.) *Time and culture*. NOBA. Retrieved January 5, 2021, from https://nobaproject.com/modules/time-and-culture

Maynard, K. (n.d.) *The slow office: A new anti-striving approach after the pandemic*. WorkTech Academy. Retrieved January 5, 2021, from https://www.worktechacademy.com/the-slow-office-a-new-anti-striving-approach-after-the-pandemic/ [exclusive content; https://www.worktechacademy.com/?p=7664]

McCarthy, N. (2017, June 26). *American workers get the short end on vacation days*. Forbes. https://www.forbes.com/sites/niallmccarthy/2017/06/26/american-workers-have-a-miserable-vacation-allowance-infographic/?sh=4a08df62126d

McGrath, P., & Sharpley, R. (2017) Slow travel and tourism: New concept or new label? In M. Clancy (Ed.), *Slow Tourism, Food and Cities* (pp. 49–62). Taylor & Francis.

Moen, P., Kelly, E. L., & Lam, J. (2013). Healthy work revisited: Do changes in time strain predict well-being? *Journal of Occupational Health Psychology, 18*(2), 157–172. https://doi.org/10.1037/a0031804

Moss, D. (2004). Heart rate variability and biofeedback. *Psychophysiology Today: The Magazine for Mind-Body Medicine, 1*, 4–11. https://www.researchgate.net/publication/259560433_Heart_rate_variability_and_biofeedback

Neuheimer, A. B. (2019). The pace of life: Time, temperature, and a biological theory of relativity. *bioRxiv*. 1–24. https://doi.org/10.1101/609446

Riley, J. C. (2005). The timing and pace of health transitions around the world. *Population and Development Review, 31*(4), 741–764. https://doi.org/10.1111/j.1728-4457.2005.00096.x

Rosa, H. (2013). *Social acceleration: A new theory of modernity*. Columbia University Press.

Schmitt, D. P. (2008). Evolutionary perspectives on romantic attachment and culture: How ecological stressors influence dismissing orientations across genders and geographies. *Cross-Cultural Research, 42*(3), 220–247. https://doi.org/10.1177%2F1069397108317485

Sullivan, O., & Gershuny, J. (2017). Speed-up society? Evidence from the UK 2000 and 2015 Time Use Diary Surveys. *Sociology, 52*(1), 20–38. https://doi.org/10.1177%2F0038038517712914

Vostal, F. (2014). Towards a social theory of acceleration: Time, modernity, critique. *European Journal of Social Sciences, 52*(2), 235–249. https://doi.org/10.4000/ress.2893

Wajcman, J. (2016). Pressed for time: The digital transformation of everyday life. *Sociologisk Forskning, 53*(2), 193–198. https://www.jstor.org/stable/24899037

Williams, S. J. (2014). The sociology of sleep and the measure of social acceleration: A rejoinder to Hsu. *Time & Society, 23*(3), 309–316. https://doi.org/10.1177%2F0961463X14536483

References for Essay on Interruption

Addas, S., & Pinsonneault, A. (2018). Theorizing the multilevel effects of interruptions and the role of communication technology. *Journal of the Association for Information Systems, 19*(11), 1097–1129. https://doi.org/10.17705/1jais.00521

Asselmann, E., Wittchen, H.-U., Lieb, R., & Beesdo-Baum, K. (2017). A 10-year prospective-longitudinal study of daily hassles and incident psychopathology among adolescents and young adults: Interactions with gender, perceived coping efficacy, and negative life events. *Social Psychiatry and Psychiatric Epidemiology, 52*, 1353–1362. https://doi.org/10.1007/s00127-017-1436-3

Beeftink, F., van Eerde, W., & Rutte, C. G. (2008). The effect of interruptions and breaks on insight and impasses: Do you need a break right now? *Creativity Research Journal, 20*(4), 358–364. https://doi.org/10.1080/10400410802391314

Berscheid, E. (1991). The Emotion-in-Relationships Model: Reflections and update. In W. Kessen, A. Ortony, & F. I. M. Craik (Eds.), *Memories, thoughts, and emotions: Essays in honor of George Mandler* (pp. 323–335). Lawrence Erlbaum Associates, Inc.

Brand, R., Timme, S., & Nosrat, S. (2020). When pandemic hits: Exercise frequency and subjective well-being during COVID-19 pandemic. *Frontiers in Psychology, 11*, Article 570567. https://doi.org/10.3389/fpsyg.2020.570567

Burger, J. M., & Arkin, R. M. (1980). Prediction, control, and learned helplessness. *Journal of Personality and Social Psychology, 38*(3), 482–491. https://psycnet.apa.org/doi/10.1037/0022-3514.38.3.482

Carver, C. S., & Scheier, M. F. (2012). *Attention and self-regulation: A control-theory approach to human behavior*. Springer Science & Business Media.

Chen, A., & Karahanna, E. (2018). Life interrupted: The effects of technology-mediated work interruptions on work and nonwork outcomes. *MIS Quarterly, 42*(4), 1023–1042. https://doi.org/10.25300/MISQ/2018/13631

Chmitorz, A., Kurth, K., Mey, L. K., Wenzel, M., Lieb, K., Tüscher, O., ... & Kalisch, R. (2020). Assessment of microstressors in adults: Questionnaire development and ecological validation of the Mainz Inventory of Microstressors. *JMIR Mental Health, 7*(2), e14566. https://doi.org/10.2196/14566

Clark, M. E., & Hirschman, R. (1990). Effects of paced respiration on anxiety reduction in a clinical population. *Biofeedback and Self-Regulation, 15,* 273–284. https://doi.org/10.1007/BF01011109

Counted, V., Pargament, K. I., Bechara, A. O., Joynt, S., & Cowden, R. G. (2020). Hope and well-being in vulnerable contexts during the COVID-19 pandemic: Does religious coping matter? *The Journal of Positive Psychology, 17*(1), 70–81. https://doi.org/10.1080/17439760.2020.1832247

Domeny, M. (2020). *Thrown off script: Turn interruptions into opportunities and thrive in the unexpected.* Author Academy Elite.

Fullana, M. A., Hidalgo-Mazzei, D., Vieta, E., & Radua, J. (2020). Coping behaviors associated with decreased anxiety and depressive symptoms during the COVID-19 pandemic and lockdown. *Journal of Affective Disorders, 275,* 80–81. https://doi.org/10.1016/j.jad.2020.06.027

Gollwitzer, P. M. (1993). Goal achievement: The role of intentions. *European Review of Social Psychology, 4*(1), 141–185. https://doi.org/10.1080/14792779343000059

Grondin, S., Mendoza-Duran, E., & Rioux, P.-A. (2020). Pandemic, quarantine, and psychological time. *Frontiers in Psychology, 11,* Article 581036. https://dx.doi.org/10.3389%2Ffpsyg.2020.581036

Henagan, S. (2020). *Breathe again: Choosing to believe there's more when life has left you broken.* Thomas Nelson.

Holmes, T. H., & Rahe, R. H. (1967). The social readjustment rating scale. *Journal of Psychosomatic Research 11*(2), 213–218. https://doi.org/10.1016/0022-3999(67)90010-4

Hunter, E. M., Clark, M. A., & Carlson, D. S. (2017). Violating work-family boundaries: Reactions to interruptions at work and home. *Journal of Management, 45*(3), 1284–1308. https://doi.org/10.1177%2F0149206317702221

Kanner, A. D., Coyne, J. C., Schaefer, C., & Lazarus, R. S. (1981). Comparison of two modes of stress measurement: Daily hassles and uplifts versus major life events. *Journal of Behavioral Medicine, 4*(1), 1–39.

Kaufman-Scarborough, C., & Lindquist, J. D. (1999). Time management and polychronicity: Comparisons, contrasts, and insights for the workplace. *Journal of Managerial Psychology, 14*(3/4), 288–312. https://doi.org/10.1108/02683949910263819

Lin, T. T. C. (2019). Why do people watch multiscreen videos and use dual screening? Investigating users' polychronicity, media multitasking motivation, and media repertoire. *International Journal of Human–Computer Interaction, 35*(18), 1672–1680. https://doi.org/10.1080/10447318.2018.1561813

Lund, K., Argentzell, E., Bejerholm, U., & Eklund, M. (2019). Breaking a cycle of perceived failure: The process of making changes toward a more balanced lifestyle. *Australian Occupational Therapy Journal, 66*(5), 627–636. https://doi.org/10.1111/1440-1630.12604

Mandler, G., & Watson, D. L. (1966). Anxiety and the interruption of behavior. In C. D. Spielberger (Ed.), *Anxiety and Behavior* (pp. 263–288). Academic Press. https://doi.org/10.1016/C2013-0-12378-1

Mandler, G. (1975). *Mind and emotion*. Robert E. Krieger Publishing Company.

Mandler, G. (1997). *Human nature explored*. Oxford University Press.

Moore, R. (2018). *Understanding Jonestown and Peoples Temple*. Praeger.

Myers, R. A., McCarthy, M. C., Whitlatch, A., & Parikh, P. J. (2016). Differentiating between detrimental and beneficial interruptions: A mixed-methods study. *BMJ Quality & Safety*, 25(11), 881–888.

Noone, P. A. (2017). The Holmes–Rahe Stress Inventory. *Occupational Medicine*, 67(7), 581–582. https://doi.org/10.1093/occmed/kqx099

Osherow, N. (1988). Making sense of the nonsensical: An analysis of Jonestown. In E. Aronson (Ed.), *Readings about the social animal* (5th ed., pp. 68–86). W. H. Freeman.

Pachler, D., Kuonath, A., Specht, J., Kennecke, S., Agthe, M., & Frey, D. (2018). Workflow interruptions and employee work outcomes: The moderating role of polychronicity. *Journal of Occupational Health Psychology*, 23(3), 417–427. https://doi.org/10.1037/ocp0000094

Payne, P., & Crane-Godreau, M. A. (2015). The preparatory set: A novel approach to understanding stress, trauma, and the bodymind therapies. *Frontiers in Human Neuroscience*, 9, Article 178. https://doi.org/10.3389/fnhum.2015.00178

Porges, S. W., & Dana, D. A. (Eds.). (2018). *Clinical applications of the polyvagal theory: The emergence of polyvagal-informed therapies*. W. W. Norton & Company.

Shanahan, L., Steinhoff, A., Bechtiger, L., Murray, A. L., Nivette, A., Hepp, U., Ribeaud, D., & Eisner, M. (2022). Emotional distress in young adults during the COVID-19 pandemic: Evidence of risk and resilience from a longitudinal cohort study. *Psychological Medicine*, 52(5), 824–833. https://doi.org/10.1017/S003329172000241X

Stets, J. E. (2005). Examining emotions in identity theory. *Social Psychology Quarterly*, 68(1), 39–56. https://doi.org/10.1177/019027250506800104

Thiede, K. W., Anderson, M. C. M., & Therriault, D. (2003). Accuracy of metacognitive monitoring affects learning of texts. *Journal of Educational Psychology*, 95(1), 66–73. https://doi.org/10.1037/0022-0663.95.1.66

Wigert, B., & Agrawal, S. (2018, July 12). *Employee burnout, part 1: The 5 main causes*. Gallup. https://www.gallup.com/workplace/237059/employee-burnout-part-main-causes.aspx

Wood, W., Quinn, J. M., & Kashy, D. A. (2002). Habits in everyday life: Thought, emotion, and action. *Journal of Personality and Social Psychology*, 83(6), 1281–1297. https://doi.org/10.1037/0022-3514.83.6.1281

Research Notes

About Book 4

(page 4) **The Spiritual Life of Children.** Research on childhood spirituality is replete with examples and findings that suggest children have an easy grasp of concepts and ideas that transcend time. In their study of almost 370 children (ages 7 to 11), Moore and colleagues (2016) concluded: "Children were also able to engage with concepts of the divine being omnipresent. That is, they perceived the transcendent as having supernatural qualities that go beyond time and space." The experience of wonder—more likely in childhood—may be the best way to understand how time and spirituality are connected. Consider this quote from L'Ecuyer (2014): "the wondering attitude is to consider this thing 'as if for the first time,' as well as 'as if for the last time.'" This "first-time and last-time" together perspective in childhood might presage the adult attitude of a balanced time perspective, where we can embrace the past, present, and future together as one whole. Research suggests that a balanced time perspective may not only be important for optimal well-being in adults (Boniwell & Zimbardo, 2015), but may also help children grow from adversity and trauma (Gökkaya, Yurdalan, & Çıvgın, 2025). Book 5 of the QfP collection (*The Treasures*) views wonder (awe) as one of many Treasures that, despite one's age, may be responsible for a flourishing life (Wolbert, de Ruyter, & Schinkel, 2021).

Boniwell, I., & Zimbardo, P. G. (2015). Balancing time perspective in pursuit of optimal functioning. In S. Joseph (Ed.), *Positive psychology in practice: Promoting human flourishing in work, health, education, and everyday life*, (pp. 223–236). John Wiley & Sons, Inc.

Coles, R. (1990). *The spiritual life of children*. Houghton Mifflin.

Gökkaya, F., Yurdalan, F., & Çıvgın, U. (2025). Does time perspective affect the association between childhood traumas and post-traumatic growth? *Current Psychology, 44*, 1527–1540.

Hyde, B. (2008). *Children and spirituality: Searching for meaning and connectedness.* Jessica Kingsley Publishers.

L'Ecuyer, C. (2014). The wonder approach to learning. *Frontiers in Human Neuroscience, 8*, 764.

Moore, K., Gomez-Garibello, C., Bosacki, S., & Talwar, V. (2016). Children's spiritual lives: The development of a children's spirituality measure. *Religions, 7*(8), 95.

Moriarty, M. W. (2008). Children's experience of time, and how it may shape their personal and spiritual narrative. *Journal of Religious Education, 56*(1), 52–57.

Wolbert, L., de Ruyter, D., & Schinkel, A. (2021). The flourishing child. *Journal of Philosophy of Education, 55*(4–5), 698–709.

Chapter 2

(page 20) **Mandala Art and Meditation.** Many proven methods reduce distractibility and increase Presence. Most of these provide, both figuratively and metaphorically, a circle with a center to focus on as your attention moves from the center to the periphery and back again. The word "mandala" means circle (Sanskrit). A mandala is both a visual representation and, in Buddhism and Hinduism, a symbol of cosmological forces. There are coloring books and self-help guides that teach individuals to draw many types of concentrically organized pictures. The image shown at the beginning of this book displays different features of the Quest for Presence model (e.g., four Radiant Forces, four Soulful Capacities, eight Trajectories) as a mandala. Research suggests that mandala drawing and meditation can help individuals with attention deficit disorder or high distractibility. Consider the first four concepts highlighted in these end notes: wonder, mandala, trajectory, and blur. A mandala may help us center our attention and potentially embrace the blur—the busyness, juggling, and distractibility of life.

As a finished work of art, a mandala is also iconography, a stable image, a representation fixed on a single dimension. As such, it cannot capture the changing multi-layered dynamics of time in our daily life. However, the *process* of making a mandala requires the careful (mindful) creation, delineating, and drawing of lines and arcs. Mandala-making is a traditional ritual in Tibetan Buddhism and a real-time immersive experience of actively creating (enacting) arcs. Per the next Note, *a Trajectory is the arc followed by an object moving under the action of given forces*. This book assumes that each day of our whole, happening life is an immersion of many Trajectories. Each day is a mandala, an opportunity to experience another Treasure (see Book 5), and just how coherent and harmonious it all is. That is something to meditate on.

Cairncross, M., & Miller, C. J. (2020). The effectiveness of mindfulness-based therapies for ADHD: A meta-analytic review. *Journal of Attention Disorders, 24*(5), 627–643.

Davis, J. (2016). The primordial mandalas and east and west: Jungian and Tibetan Buddhist approaches to healing and transformation. *NeuroQuantology, 14*(2), 242–254.

Levinson, D. B., Stoll, E. L., Kindy, S. D., Merry, H. L., & Davidson, R. J. (2014). A mind you can count on: Validating breath counting as a behavioral measure of mindfulness. *Frontiers in Psychology, 5,* Article 1202.

Shankar, R., & Amir, R. (2020). The effectiveness of mandala colouring therapy in increasing year 3 pupils' focus during the initial lesson. *Creative Education, 11,* 581–595.

Smitheman-Brown, V., & Church, R. P. (1996). Mandala drawing: Facilitating creative growth in children with ADD or ADHD. *Art Therapy: Journal of the American Art Therapy Association, 13*(4), 252–260.

(page 20) Trajectory definition. Given this book's title, more discussion of a definition is called for. The definition of trajectory (see previous note) on page 20 was adapted from Merriam-Webster's Collegiate Dictionary. (n.d.). *Trajectory*. Retrieved July 21, 2022, from https://unabridged.merriam-webster.com/collegiate/trajectory.

An alternate definition from an earlier Merriam-Webster's Collegiate Dictionary (1996) reads:

> 1: the curve that a body (as a planet or comet in its orbit or a rocket) describes in space
>
> 2: a path, progression, or line of development resembling a physical trajectory

The reference to force ("under the action of given forces") in the 2022 definition is a key difference of special relevance to QfP as it entails a sense of movement, change, and direction. We are not talking about a curve or line on a single three-dimensional plane. A trajectory comes and goes, fades, is impermanent. Like time, a trajectory is not palpable, concrete, something you can get your hands around. Shooting stars, dashing fireflies, fireworks, and the swoop of a handheld light wand—examples of trajectories privileged by the night and the naked eye—only come into being because of a given force and our presence. Paper airplanes, the arrow released from the bow, and the bullet from the gun's chamber demonstrate how successively greater levels of force match our inability to detect an arc at all.

The eight temporal phenomena described in this book are not labeled as features, qualities, or elements. They are Trajectories. They arc—they jump across the gaps of our day—due to the interplay of Radiant Forces (*QfP Book 1*), which can be discerned through and even influenced by our own Soulful Capacities (Book 2), and which we are attracted to (Book 3). In our task to develop a healthy relationship to time beyond clock-time, it helps to contemplate and discern these Trajectories, their nature, flow, salience, and presence. They are more like fireflies and paper airplanes than planets, comets, and rockets. Like fireflies, they have their own internal light. Like flying paper airplanes, we can bring some of our own force to their launch and then watch them as they take flight. This can be momentous (another Treasure).

(page 22) Embracing the Blur. The topics of the previous end notes—seeing the big picture, reducing distractibility, gaining more definition, discernment—might suggest that the goal of Presence work is to achieve more clarity and comprehension. This is true at one level and at certain points in our evolution. At other times, confusion is a good thing. We need both. Consider this quote from the 13th century Sufi poet, Jalāl al-Dīn Muḥammad Rūmī, "God turns you from one feeling to another and teaches by means of opposites so that you will have two wings to fly, not one."

A full study of the blur requires a transdisciplinary approach, beyond the scope of the QfP collection. It will likely entail bringing together insights from quantum physics (following Rovelli's work); studies from the neurosciences that assess temporality, time perception; and "dysfunctions" in time perception in schizophrenia, attention deficit hyperactivity disorder (ADHD), other mental health diagnoses, and the visual arts. In keeping with the spiritual sciences, we can look to mystical writings about time as an illusion. Regarding neural time-scales, readers should see Wolff and colleagues (2022) and their application to schizophrenia (e.g., Northoff et al., 2021). Problems in time perception have been identified in ADHD (Weissenberger et al., 2021), psychosis (Ueda, Maruo, & Sumiyoshi, 2018), and depression (Thönes & Oberfeld, 2015). These and many other studies suggest that the subjective experience of time is quite idiosyncratic and subject to multiple distortions. Of course, modern physics has validated that time is relative. Regarding the mystical idea that time is an illusion, there are hundreds of esoteric references, including the idea of time as "watery" in Jewish mysticism (Morray-Jones, 2021). There is even research that examines qualitative data from individuals who have had "Time Expansion Experiences" or TEEs. Taylor (2022) studied both dramatic and less intense experiences of TEEs and found several participants reporting experiences of blur.

Two visual metaphors may help make sense of how blurriness and our experience of time are inter-related. First, some artistic photographers use blurred, overlapped, or extended time exposures for creative time-distorting purposes. These photographs are featured in the book, *Vanishing Presence* (Parry-Janis et al., 1989) with essays that discuss how blurred images in old daguerreotypes, once viewed as errors, conveyed the limits of technology in capturing human presence. In post-modern photography, time exposures and juxtapositions are designed deliberately to disorient the viewer into recognizing that time is not fixed. Second, I show students an hourglass with sand pouring from the top to the bottom globe. I ask them to imagine that the top globe is the past (relatively full and fixed) and the bottom is the future (relatively empty but with potential). In both cases, it is easy to distinguish the grains of sand at rest. Then I show a close-up of the sand pouring through the center-point and call that the present. Sand pouring is happening now, at the center-point. Students cannot distinguish particles; due to the rate of pour, the moving sand appears as a blur. Both metaphors show that in the moment of happening which may be most considered as the present, the world is truly blurry.

CBS News (2006, June 22). *Study: 'Time' Is Most Often Used Noun.* https://www.cbsnews.com/news/study-time-is-most-often-used-noun/.

Morray-Jones, C. R. A. (2021). *A transparent illusion: The dangerous vision of water in Hekhalot Mysticism. A source-critical and tradition-historical inquiry.* Brill.

Northoff, G., Sandsten, K. E., Nordgaard, J., Kjaer, T. W., & Parnas, J. (2021). The self and its prolonged intrinsic neural timescale in schizophrenia. *Schizophrenia Bulletin, 47*(1), 170–179.

Parry-Janis, E., Kozloff, M., Weinberg, A. D., & Friedman, M. (1989). *Vanishing Presence.* Minneapolis: Walker Art Center, and Rizzoli, 1989. Published in conjunction with the exhibition of the same name. Available from Internet Archive (https://archive.org/details/vanishingpresenc0000parr) and Amazon (https://www.amazon.com/Vanishing-Presence-Eugenia-Parry-Janis/dp/0847810070) as of May, 2025.

Rovelli, C. (2019). *The Order of Time*. Penguin.

Taylor, S. (2020). When seconds turn into minutes: Time expansion experiences in altered states of consciousness. *Journal of Humanistic Psychology, 62*(2), 208–232.

Thönes, S., & Oberfeld, D. (2015). Time perception in depression: A meta-analysis. *Journal of Affective Disorders, 175*, 359–372.

Ueda, N., Maruo, K., & Sumiyoshi, T. (2018). Positive symptoms and time perception in schizophrenia: A meta-analysis. *Schizophrenia Research: Cognition, 13*, 3–6.

Weissenberger, S., Schonova, K., Büttiker, P., Fazio, R., Vnukova, M., Stefano, G. B., & Ptacek, R. (2021). Time perception is a focal symptom of attention-deficit/hyperactivity disorder in adults. *Medical Science Monitor: International Medical Journal of Experimental and Clinical Research, 27*, e933766.

Wolff, A., Berberian, N., Golesorkhi, M., Gomez-Pilar, J., Zilio, F., Northoff, G. (2022). Intrinsic neural timescales: Temporal integration and segregation. *Trends in Cognitive Sciences, 26*(2), 159–173.

(page 23) The quote from Carlo Rovelli is from *The Order of Time,* pages 211–212.

Rovelli, C. (2019). *The Order of Time*. Penguin.

Rovelli's work is also available in audiobook, eloquently narrated by the British actor, Benedict Cumberbatch. Rovelli, C. (2018). *The Order of Time* (B. Cumberbatch, Narrator). Penguin Audio.

As a follow up to the previous end note, our experience of the blur, of things falling outside the frame, lands not only in the cognitive realm. Bewilderment, confusion, alarm, anxiety, uncertainty, amazement, or surprise may signal our touching the blur. We do not expect to live our lives in an ongoing state of such feelings. Yet, for most of us as adults, when these emotional intrusions occur, we typically have worked out a way to manage them. In a parallel manner, culture has given us instruments for framing time—clocks, calendars, watches, smartphones—that shore up a sense of order, direction, and security. We have been rescued from the blur. As Rovelli explains, these instruments are artifacts of culture that do an amazing job of helping us get along. Much of daily life is about when, how, and why we notice what time it is (clock-time) and have attendant feelings or intentions (e.g., relaxation, anxiety, need to wake up, speed up, slow down, make a call, stop). An alternative view, to appreciate rather than control the blur, offers one way out of time pressures and prisons (workloads, burnout, hectic pace). Instead of noticing the clock, notice some Trajectory; for example, the Transitions ("in between" times), the coming together of Rhythms (the timings when things align). A central hypothesis of this book is that, by doing so, you will become more present to your happening life and less stuck in clock-time.

Chapter 3

(page 38) *Atomic Habits* and *Life Hacks*. From the QfP perspective, these two books are more recent examples of how the popular topic of "time management" has played out in our society. Ultimately, they are about making the most of our day and time by how we manage routines and for self-improvement. These books represent a new twist to time management by introducing simpler or "bite-size" techniques and tips to help us get through one moment or challenge to the next and, ideally, stay focused on a goal (which is the intention of Time Shaping). As of 2025, the book *Atomic Habits* has been ranked #2 on Amazon's best-seller list and has been there for almost seven years. It can be worth reading through the 10,000+ reviews on Amazon. Clearly, the book has helped many people. Paradoxically, many reviewers lament that it is "repetitive" and "obvious"—two hallmarks of Routine itself. I appreciate one reviewer who called the book "productivity porn." Nonetheless, Routine is a foundational Trajectory in life and one that has been most written about in the self-help literature. Also, see Duhigg.

Bradford, K. (2014). *Life hacks: Any procedure or action that solves a problem, simplifies a task, reduces frustration, etc. in one's everyday life.* Adams Media.

Clear, J. (2018). *Atomic habits: An easy & proven way to build good habits & break bad ones: Tiny changes, remarkable results.* Avery.

Duhigg, C. (2012). *The power of habit: Why we do what we do in life and business.* Random House.

(page 39) Hidden Rhythms.

Zerubavel, E. (1985). *Hidden rhythms: Schedules and calendars in social life.* University of California Press.

By its title, Zerubavel's book appears to address the Trajectory of Rhythm (see chapter 5) and it equally applies to Routine because of the subtitle. Highly recommended and well-cited in the academic literature, Zerubavel's work is typically cited or approached as a way of understanding time as *structure*, rather than time as a *resource* or *process* (Blagoev et al., 2024). The emphasis on structure, within the essay on Routine, is consistent with this view. However, the four principles he describes (sequence, duration, location, recurrence) are ultimately about promoting the resources provided by societal synchronization and rhythm entrainment. A quantitative time-diary study by Kim (2023), drawing from Zerubavel, demonstrates that such social synchrony predicts life satisfaction and health, but not daily mood. The study, based on 26,091 respondents with recorded 52,182 diaries over a year, yields interesting insights that point to influence of time of day and day of week as important influences on mood. The inextricable *process* relationship between the Trajectories is one takeaway from this scholarship. We need routines so that we have the vitality of synchrony and, in complementary fashion, social synchrony motivates and encourages us to work, play, and bond together by setting up routines. As explained in Chapter 11 and Trialectics (see end note for page 164), Routine emerges because at some point previous conditions—most often, conditions of social synchrony—were attractive toward the creation of some form or stability. This attraction was experienced as a right timing or a sense of fitness or alignment, and a subsequent desire to preserve that fitness.

Blagoev, B., Hernes, T., Kunisch, S., & Schultz, M. (2024). Time as a research lens: A conceptual review and research agenda. *Journal of Management, 50*(6), 2152–2196.

Kim, S. (2023). Doing things when others do: Temporal synchrony and subjective wellbeing. *Time & Society, 33*(1), 48–68.

(pages 40–41) Language-based bedtime routines. Many studies demonstrate the importance of establishing routines for childhood well-being. Reading stories (Hale et al., 2011) is one example. New studies suggest that the use of touchscreens and videos as substitutes (rather than supplements) for lullabies can be detrimental to children's well-being. Bedtime routines are just one nexus point where families synchronize for whole-time immersion and well-being (see previous note). A study of shared reading in families (Hall, 2024) showed that while reading often was a signal for approaching bedtime, it equally functioned to support "togetherness" and parents' desire to support their child's growth, what Hall describes as the "normative tendency to situate children as future beings." Again, we see the relationship between three Trajectories: Routine, Rhythm Entrainment, and Transition. The transition to bedtime foreshadows (and even shapes) how families work toward the larger transition of childhood to adulthood.

Brooks, W. (2016). Putting lullabies to bed: The effects of screened presentations on lullaby practices. *Australian Journal of Music Education, 50*(2), 83–97.

Cheung, C. H. M., Bedford, R., De Urabain, I. R. S., Karmiloff-Smith, A., & Smith, T. J. (2017). Daily touchscreen use in infants and toddlers is associated with reduced sleep and delayed sleep onset. *Scientific Reports, 7*, Article 46104.

Hale, L., Berger, L. M., LeBourgeois, M. K., & Brooks-Gunn, J. (2011). A longitudinal study of preschoolers' language-based bedtime routines, sleep duration, and well-being. *Journal of Family Psychology, 25*(3), 423–433.

Hall, M. (2024). 'It's sharing a point in time': The temporal dimensions of shared reading in families. *British Journal of Sociology of Education, 45*(7–8), 1025–1041.

Chapter 4

(page 49) Timing of Life Transitions. Research suggests that the life cycle of every individual follows a certain normative sequence with relatively strict milestones of Transition. This sequence is both an overlay and an influence on our experience about time in life, through life, and toward the end of life. Some typical milestones in Western society include the following secular events, which can vary or be supplemented by religious rituals (for example, Bat Mitzvah, confirmation): entering formal education, first sexual intercourse, obtaining first driver's license, achieving voting age, first work experience, financial autonomy, end of formal schooling, cohabitation, marriage, first child, purchase of a house, last child, middle age, retirement. Compelling research suggests that people believe there is an "ideal age" for these events. Elchardus and Smits (2006) found that as each event passes, individuals experience less of an "open future," and life becomes progressively more determined. They conclude that despite cultural messages, one can choose one's life course, an "ideal life course still exists, which is characterized by an unambiguous sequential order and a surprisingly strict timing of the transitions." In other words, within a certain age window, *when* certain transition events happen in our life is never random. Instead, the timing of these events occurs because human beings (either consciously but mostly intuitively through culture) know that their life is moving toward an inevitable end.

The "open future" of Chaos is drawing us to those conditions that allow us to entrain with each other and get on with the work and the play of life. One study found that "on time" transitions (when one leaves home, gets married, and becomes a parent) is associated with great subjective well-being (Johnson et al., 2021). However, gender, education, and race play a role. Another study found that women see the start and end of middle age as occurring later in life than do men and health is greater for women who show postponement of middle age and increases in perceived control of their lives over time (Toothman & Barrett, 2011). As the essay on Timing suggests, the "ability to choose" when something happens is integral to the definition of Timing. However, the sociological studies cited in this note (and others) indicate that choice varies significantly according to status, gender, and other factors that form society.

Elchardus, M., & Smits, W. (2006). The persistence of the standardized life cycle. *Time & Society, 15*(2–3), 303–326.

Johnson, M. D., Galambos, N. L., & Krahn, H. J. (2021). Family context, life transitions, and subjective well-being from age 18 to 50 years. *Developmental Psychology, 57*(11), 1968–1980.

Pink, D. H. (2018). *When: The scientific secrets of perfect timing*. Riverhead Books.

Toothman, E. L., & Barrett, A. E. (2011). Mapping midlife: An examination of social factors shaping conceptions of the timing of middle age. *Advances in Life Course Research, 16*(3), 99–111.

Chapter 5

(page 71) **Conformal Cyclic Cosmology.** The idea behind the CCC is that our universe is just one stage in a potentially infinite cycle of cosmic extinction (cf. *Chaos*) and rebirth (cf. *Nurturing Conditions*). The greatest cosmological Rhythm operates beyond our imagination and current measurements. The universe births, grows, dies, and is reborn again in an endless cycle. The proposal by Penrose of the CCC is neither philosophical nor New Age musings but instead is derived from precise mathematical formulations in the fields of cosmology and relativity. Based on this view, all matter eventually decays and is converted into light or other forms of energy as the universe expands. This decay allows for the smooth transition between aeons and avoids the need for a sudden re-creation of matter (Wikipedia, 2025). The chapter on Transition offers a parallel perspective from ancient Hindu Vedic cosmology with the concept of *Pralaya* or dissolution, reabsorption, destruction, and annihilation. Nurturing Conditions is the receptacle for both complete and total Transition (impermanence) and complete and total Rhythm (conformal cyclic cosmology).

Cartlidge, E. (2018, August 21). *New evidence for cyclic universe claimed by Roger Penrose and colleagues*. Physics World. https://physicsworld.com/a/new-evidence-for-cyclic-universe-claimed-by-roger-penrose-and-colleagues/

Markwell, O., & Stevens, C. (2023). Toward fixing a framework for conformal cyclic cosmology. *General Relativity and Gravitation, 55*, 93.

Penrose, R. (2020). *Black Holes, Cosmology, and Space-Time Singularities*. Available online: https://www.nobelprize.org/prizes/physics/2020/penrose/lecture/ (accessed on 23 May 2025).

Wikipedia (2025, May). Conformal Cyclic Cosmology. https://en.wikipedia.org/wiki/Conformal_cyclic_cosmology (accessed on 23 May 2025).

Chapter 6

(page 85) Liminality and Response to Adversity and Recovery. Addictive processes (whether attachment to substances like alcohol or opioids or to processes like sex and power) play an important role in our understanding of Presence: the move from darkness and confusion to clarity and direction. The addict succumbs to the impulse and attitude expressed as "I want what I want and I want it now." Time compresses and imprisons them. Several studies document how former and recovering addicts go through Transitions that give them wisdom into a more relaxed understanding of time (e.g., Davies & Filippopoulos, 2015; Erdos et al., 2009). The Transition from hopelessness to optimism and from seeing the illness as a problem to seeing it as a growth opportunity (cf. post-traumatic growth) speaks to a more process-oriented and less fixed view of time. Recovery is a liminal process (Schaef, 1999). The addict must cross a threshold. The concept of threshold was examined fully in the prelude to this QfP collection (*The Connoisseur of Time: An Invitation to Presence*) and can help bring together many ideas in the current chapter. This quote from Kirst (2023) echoes the experience of many in recovery:

> *A liminal period gives us time and space to make a transition. It's a state of being neither here nor there, perhaps dissolved like a cocooned creature, a period of chaos and disorientation, of being faced with the unholy and sacred experience of the unknown. Somewhere before or within this process lies the threshold moment, perhaps barely notable in all the ambiguity and muck.*

Andresen, R., Caputi, P., & Oades, L. (2006). Stages of recovery instrument: Development of a measure of recovery from serious mental illness. *The Australian & New Zealand Journal of Psychiatry, 40*(11–12), 972–980. https://doi.org/10.1080/j.1440-1614.2006.01921.x

Ashenshurt, J. (2021, March 27). *What's a transition state?* Master Organic Chemistry. https://www.masterorganicchemistry.com/2010/11/03/whats-a-transition-state/

Davies, S., & Filippopoulos, P. C. (2015). Changes in psychological time perspective during residential addiction treatment: A mixed-methods study. *Journal of Groups in Addiction & Recovery, 10*(3), 249–270.

Erdos, M. B., Gabor, K., & Brettner, Z. (2009). It's High Time ... Time experience of drug-dependent persons in recovery. *Journal of Groups in Addiction & Recovery*, 4(3), 202–218.

Kirst, P. F. (2023). Thresholds and liminality. *Psychological Perspectives*, 66(2), 147–151.

Metzner, R. (1980). Ten classical metaphors of self-transformation. *Journal of Transpersonal Psychology*, 12(1), 47–62. https://www.semanticscholar.org/paper/TEN-CLASSICAL-METAPHORS-OF-SELF-TRANSFORMATION-Metzner/de2446be25f84558ad6e5b2797e32b0ed3050d0b

Schaef, A. W. (1999). *Living in process: Basic truths for living the path of the soul*. Wellspring/Ballantine.

Chapter 7

(page 101) Connection & Unity: Transcendence with and without Reference to God. Some self-report measures of transcendence reference God (including Gomez & Fisher, 2003) while others do not (Levenson et al., 2005). Half of the items in the Daily Spiritual Experience Scale reference God (I feel God's presence) and half do not (I experience a connection to all of life) (Underwood & Teresi, 2002). Maslow (1969) provides thirty-five definitions of transcendence, and not even one references "God" per se but rather God-like points of view. A more recent model defines "self-transcendent experiences" (STEs) as generalized reductions of self-centeredness and selfish motivations, fading self-boundaries, and a sense of unity (Yaden et al., 2017). Compared with the research just cited, one study about transcendence, receiving the most citations by others, has nothing to do with spirituality. Liberman and Trope (2008) see transcendence of the "here and now" as a cognitive construal of events that are psychologically distant. Human beings have the capacity to transcend through their ability to engage in abstract thinking about things and events that are far. The farther away they are, the more abstract, and the more likely they will have meaning.

Gomez, R., & Fisher, J. W. (2003). Domains of spiritual well-being and development and validation of the Spiritual Well-Being Questionnaire. *Personality and Individual Differences*, 35(8), 1975–1991. https://doi.org/10.1016/S0191-8869(03)00045-X

Levenson, M. R., Jennings, P. A., Aldwin, C. M., & Shiraishi, R. W. (2005). Self-transcendence: Conceptualization and measurement. *The International Journal of Aging and Human Development*, 60(2), 127–143. https://doi.org/10.2190/XRXM-FYRA-7U0X-GRC0

Liberman, N., & Trope, Y. (2008). The psychology of transcending the here and now. *Science*, 322(5905), 1201–1205. https://doi.org/10.1126/science.1161958

Maslow, A. H. (1969). Various meanings of transcendence. *Journal of Transpersonal Psychology*, 1, 56–66. https://www.atpweb.org/jtparchive/trps-01-69-01-056.pdf

Underwood, L. G., & Teresi, J. A. (2002). The daily spiritual experience scale: Development, theoretical description, reliability, exploratory factor analysis, and preliminary construct validity using health-related data. *Annals of Behavioral Medicine, 24*(1), 22–33. https://doi.org/10.1207/S15324796ABM2401_04

Yaden, D. B., Haidt, J., Hood, Jr., R. W., Vago, D. R., & Newberg, A. B. (2017). The varieties of self-transcendent experience. *Review of General Psychology, 21*(2), 143–160.

Chapter 8

(page 114) Karōshi. This chapter on Scheduling may be framed as a commentary on the benefits of having an expansive or positive (non-fatalistic) future time perspective, one that is fueled by intentionality and the need and desire to make the most of one's whole-time (live, work, play; see next Note), and the costs of time compression and not having such a perspective. Studies show that thoughts of suicide correlate with a lack of, or fatalistic, future time-perspective in high school and college students (Laghi et al., 2009; Wang et al., 2024). As referenced in Chapter 11, Scheduling serves as a mirror to Rhythm Entrainment; it brings the vitality of social synchrony into our lives. Without it, and when we suffer from over-scheduling, the future is not only bleak: there is no future. In 2019, Japan's Ministry of Health defined karōshi as the sudden death of an employee who works more than 80 to 100 hours of overtime a month. A recent government report showed nearly a quarter of Japanese companies had employees who worked those hours.

Caputo, I. (2019, January 10). Japan's shrinking labor force is finding new ways to fight karōshi—'Death by overwork'. *The World (PRI).* https://www.pri.org/stories/2019-01-10/japan-s-shrinking-labor-force-finding-new-ways-fight-kar-shi-death-overwork

Laghi, F., Baiocco, R., D'Alessio, M., & Gurrieri, G. (2009). Suicidal ideation and time perspective in high school students. *The Journal of the Association of European Psychiatrists, 24*(1), 41–46.

Wang, L., Xian, X., Hu, J., Liu, M., Cao, Y., Dai, W., ... & Ye, M. (2024). The relationship between future time perspective and suicide ideation in college students: Multiple mediating effects of anxiety and depression. *Heliyon, 10*(17), e36564

(pages 114–115) Leisure time. Compared with the previous endnote, leisure time is an opportunity to escape both scheduling and schedules. There is a whole research literature devoted to the study of leisure time. There are two research journals: *Leisure Studies* (since 1982) and the *Journal of Leisure Research* (since 1969), both published by Taylor & Francis. The three types of leisure time are described by Kraaykamp and colleagues (2009) and how, when, and how much "recreationalists" schedule their time has received extensive study. For example, a balanced time perspective is associated with a more positive leisure experience with others and also when alone (García & Ruiz, 2015). My organization (Organizational Wellness & Learning Systems) consulted on a project where we were given survey data on stress and leisure time on 76,000 employees from almost 100 companies. Participants were asked "Do you spend at least 5 hours of relaxation or recreational time together with your family each week?" and responded yes or no. Employees answering yes had significantly lower levels of both work stress and home stress.

Bennett, J. (2011). *Research utilization of a behavioral risk audit* [unpublished report]. Available from the author.

Broome, K., & Bennett, J. (2010). *Stress at and away from work: An ICAS White Paper.* Available from the author.

García, J. A., & Ruiz, B. (2015). Exploring the role of time perspective in leisure choices: What about the balanced time perspective? *Journal of Leisure Research, 47*(5), 515–537.

Kraaykamp, G., van Gils, W., & van der Lippe, T. (2009). Working status and leisure: An analysis of the trade-off between solitary and social time. *Time & Society, 18*(2–3), 264–283. https://doi.org/10.1177/0961463X09337845

Chapter 9

(pages 134–137) Cultural pace. Many studies examine international differences in time-orientation and cultural pace. In one study comparing time-orientation across twenty-four countries, the United States was among the highest in future-orientation and lowest in present-orientation, compared with New Zealand with the opposite pattern.

Ferrari, J. R., Díaz-Morales, J. F., O'Callaghan, J., Díaz, K., & Argumedo, D. (2007). Frequent behavioral delay tendencies by adults: International prevalence rates of chronic procrastination. *Journal of Cross-Cultural Psychology, 38*(4), 458–464. https://doi.org/10.1177/0022022107302314

Levine, R. V., & Norenzayan, A. (1999). The pace of life in 31 countries. *Journal of Cross-Cultural Psychology, 30*(2), 178–205. https://doi.org/10.1177/0022022199030002003

Morewedge, C. K., Preston, J., & Wegner, D. M. (2007). Timescale bias in the attribution of mind. *Journal of Personality and Social Psychology, 93*(1), 1–11. https://doi.org/10.1037/0022-3514.93.1.1

Sircova, A., van de Vijver, F. J. R., Osin, E., Milfont, T. L., Fieulaine, N., Kislali-Erginbilgic, A., & Zimbardo, P. G. (2015). Time perspective profiles of cultures. In M. Stolarski, N. Fieulaine, & W. van Beek (Eds.), *Time perspective theory; review, research and application* (pp. 169–187). Springer, Cham. https://doi.org/10.1007/978-3-319-07368-2_11

(page 135) Acceleration, Time Urgency, and Slowing Growth. Several studies suggest coronary-prone behavior (heart disease or heart attack) is influenced by time urgency (e.g., Gallacher et al., 2003) and that employees are experiencing greater job demands because of acceleration in technology, social change, and pace of life (Ulferts et al., 2013). These and other studies show that Pacing, like all the Trajectories, is multidimensional and, because of cultural factors, not entirely within our control. As a counterpoint to these ideas, Dorling (2020) offers very compelling evidence that, from a broader geopolitical and demographic perspective, most things are showing gradual deceleration within their increased growth; something he calls "slowing growth." In his book, Dorling makes the case that "slowdown means the end of rampant capitalism" and that "slowdown gives us time to worry more about one another and less about what we will ourselves receive in the future." It is worth comparing Dorling's book (titled *Slowdown*) with Gleick's book (titled *Faster*), which—on the surface—appear to contradict each other. Either way, they are both about the phenomena of Pace and Pacing and how humans struggle to understand and master this fundamental Trajectory.

Dorling, D. (2020). *Slowdown: The end of the great acceleration—and why it's good for the planet, the economy, and our lives*. Yale University Press.

Friedman, M., & Rosenman, R. H. (1959). Association of specific overt behavior pattern with blood and cardiovascular findings: Blood cholesterol level, blood clotting time, incidence of arcus senilis, and clinical coronary artery disease. *Journal of the American Medical Association, 169*(12), 1286–1296. https://doi.org/10.1001/jama.1959.03000290012005

Gallacher, J. E. J., Sweetnam, P. M., Yarnell, J. W. G., Elwood, P. C., & Stansfeld, S. A. (2003). Is type A behavior really a trigger for coronary heart disease events? *Psychosomatic Medicine, 65*(3), 339–346. https://doi.org/10.1097/01.psy.0000041608.55974.A8

Gleick, J. (1999). *Faster: The acceleration of just about everything*. Pantheon.

Jenkins, C. D., Rosenman, R. H., & Zyzanski, S. J. (1974). Prediction of clinical coronary heart disease by a test for the coronary-prone behavior pattern. *The New England Journal of Medicine, 290*(23), 1271–1275. https://doi.org/10.1056/NEJM197406062902301

Ulferts, H., Korunka, C., & Kubicek, B. (2013). Acceleration in working life: An empirical test of a sociological framework. *Time & Society, 22*(2), 161–185. https://doi.org/10.1177/0961463X12471006

(page 137) The Slow Movement. Pace, culture, and meaning in life may be intertwined. It is not clear how much the Slow Movement is only an ideology of meaningfulness adopted by small groups of individuals or whether it has reached anything like a viable social movement. The essay on Pace describes some of these efforts and additional references. Readers interested in the Slow Movement may wish to visit the Long Now Foundation (https://longnow.org/) with many projects and talks dedicated to fostering long-term thinking and slowing down. Through both personal (and contemplative) experience of nature and time and an intellectual review of the impact of industrial time on modern life, O'Dell (2024) wrestles with ways to find a pace that brings meaning and purpose. Hectic and fast paced cultures can be disorienting and require us to have a more paced perspective to stay healthy (see Sica et al., 2024). The entire QfP collection is dedicated to contemplation, which could not happen without some slowing down.

Berg, M., & Seeber, B. K. (2016). *The slow professor: Challenging the culture of speed in the academy*. University of Toronto Press.

Clancy, M. (Ed.). (2017). *Slow tourism, food and cities: Pace and the search for the "good life."* Routledge.

Odell, J. (2024). *Saving time: Discovering a life beyond productivity culture.* Random House Trade Paperbacks.

Sica, L. S., Parola, A., De Rosa, B., Sommantico, M., Fenizia, E., Postiglione, J., ... & Parrello, S. (2024). Meaning matters: A person-centered investigation of meaning in life, future time perspective, and well-being in young adults. *Journal for Person-Oriented Research, 10*(2), 104–116.

Wexler, M. N., Oberlander, J., & Shankar, A. (2017). The slow food movement: A 'big tent' ideology. *Journal of Ideology, 37*(1), Article 1. https://scholarcommons.sc.edu/ji/vol37/iss1/1

(page 137) Anxiety and Time Perspective. Several studies suggest that anxiety is related to a negative future time perspective (for example: Usually, I do not know how I will be able to fulfill my goals in life). This negative outlook on the future is also associated with sleep problems (Rönnlund & Carelli, 2018). The essay on Pace describes the importance of Pace for maintaining homeostasis and healthy, regular sleep patterns. It seems that one's orientation to the future may impact how one paces one's life.

Åström, E., Wiberg, B., Sircova, A., Wiberg, M., & Carelli, M. G. (2014). Insights into features of anxiety through multiple aspects of psychological time. *Journal of Integrative Psychology and Therapeutics, 2*, Article 3. http://umu.diva-portal.org/smash/record.jsf?pid=diva2%3A756436&dswid=6891

Carelli, M. G., Wiberg, B., & Åström, E. (2015). Broadening the TP profile: Future negative time perspective. In M. Stolarski, N. Fieulaine, & W. van Beek (Eds.), *Time perspective theory; Review, research and application* (pp. 87–97). Springer, Cham. https://doi.org/10.1007/978-3-319-07368-2_5

Rönnlund, M., & Carelli, M. G. (2018). Time perspective biases are associated with poor sleep quality, daytime sleepiness, and lower levels of subjective well-being among older adults. *Frontiers in Psychology, 9*, Article 1356. https://doi.org/10.3389/fpsyg.2018.01356

Chapter 10

(page 145) Grief unmakes and remakes the self. Of all emotions, grief is likely the most accurate barometer of life disruption or Interruption and brings us to a deeper understanding of time. Several essays in this book discuss the self. For example, Routines and subroutines help one preserve an identity. The self goes through many development changes as part of our contemplation of Transition. In contrast, grief response to loss or trauma has a profound influence on self-concept. At first, one loses self-clarity but, by working through emotions, a newly defined self can emerge.

Boelen, P. A. (2017). Self-identity after bereavement: Reduced self-clarity and loss-centrality in emotional problems after the death of a loved one. *The Journal of Nervous and Mental Disease, 205*(5), 405–408. https://doi.org/10.1097/NMD.0000000000000660

Ellingsen, S., Moi, A. L., Gjengedal, E., Flinterud, S. I., Natvik, E., Råheim, M., ... & Sekse, R. J. T. (2021). "Finding oneself after critical illness": Voices from the remission society. *Medicine, Health Care and Philosophy, 24*, 35–44. https://doi.org/10.1007/s11019-020-09979-8

Meekings, S. (2018). Writing through loss: The rise of grief narratives through the lens of Linville's Self-complexity Theory. *Life Writing, 16*(3), 413–427. https://doi.org/10.1080/14484528.2018.1537048

(page 144) Complex Trajectories after grief. As we contemplate Interruption, it may provide some sense of order and organization to believe that grief occurs in specified stages, as was theorized by Elisabeth Kübler-Ross (1969). Her model points to five stages of grief: denial and isolation, anger, bargaining, depression, and acceptance. It is interesting that her last stage of Acceptance is the first of the Soulful Capacities described in Book 2 of QfP. Very often, we require great loss before we cultivate Acceptance but, importantly, we need not always struggle through multiple phases to get there (Hall, 2011).

Hall, C. (2011). Beyond Kübler-Ross: Recent developments in our understanding of grief and bereavement. *InPsych: The Bulletin of the Australian Psychological Society Ltd., 33*(6), 8. https://psychology.org.au/for-members/publications/inpsych/2011/dec/beyond-kubler-ross-recent-developments-in-our-und

Kübler-Ross, E. (1969). *On death and dying*. Macmillan.

(page 149) Affective Neuroscience. Readers who are interested in the field of affective neuroscience might want to search for writings on polyvagal theory and the work of Stephen Porges and Deborah Dana. Examples are provided below.

Porges, S. W. (2022). Polyvagal theory: A science of safety. *Frontiers in Integrative Neuroscience, 16*, 871227.

Porges, S. W., & Dana, D. (Eds.). (2018). *Clinical applications of the polyvagal theory: The emergence of polyvagal-informed therapies* (Norton Series on Interpersonal Neurobiology). W. W. Norton & Company.

Chapter 11

(page 159) Process Philosophy, Trialectics, and Living in Process. In writing this book, it became clear how much my earlier studies and mentors influenced my understanding of process-oriented views of time and temporal dynamics. The first of these, process philosophy, I learned from Dr. Robert Neville in 1972. Dr. Neville taught me about the work of Alfred North Whitehead and other process philosophers. Process philosophers hold that reality is essentially and always dynamic and becoming, as opposed to a view of reality as essentially about being and made up of static entities that persist or endure. Process theism, articulated by Whitehead and Charles Hartshorne, views God as more dynamic, changeable, and existing in creative relationship to things (human beings) than God as eternal, unchangeable, and abstract. In addition to studying with Neville, I had the chance to dine once with

Dr. Hartshorne, not knowing how much his ideas would influence me. Trialectics, described in more detail in a research note for chapter 11, was developed by Oscar Ichazo and taught to me through the Arica® 40-day training in 1975. Living in Process, developed by Anne Wilson Schaef, is an approach to living life fully and in deep connection to oneself, others, and nature, and with an abiding and ever-learning relationship to intimacy and spirituality. Schaef sees the Living in Process system as based in native and earth-loving cultures and distinct from the addictive system that is often the predominant modern culture that fosters addiction to substances (alcohol, sugar, drugs) and processes (sex, pornography, gambling, power). I had the good fortune to study with Schaef from 1990 to 1993.

Hartshorne, C. (1948). *The divine relativity: A social conception of God*. Yale University Press.

Neville, R. C. (1980). *Creativity and God: A challenge to process theology*. Seabury Press.

Schaef, A. W. (1992). *Beyond therapy, beyond science: A new model for healing the whole person*. HarperCollins.

Seibt, J. (2020). "Process Philosophy" in Edward N. Zalta (Ed.), *The Stanford Encyclopedia of Philosophy* (Summer 2020 Edition). https://plato.stanford.edu/archives/sum2020/entries/process-philosophy/

Whitehead, A. N. (1925). *Science and the modern world*. Macmillan.

Whitehead, A. N. (1933). *Adventures of ideas*. Macmillan.

(page 160) Li in Confucianism. The concept of Li in Confucian philosophy is defined at different levels. Most often, it is translated as referring to proper social conduct, rituals, rites, and abiding by social norms. Ultimately, Li is about principle and living by principle to preserve order among people. At another level, Li transcends mere politeness and ritual and refers to being in tune or in touch with nature and the cosmic order of things. From the QfP perspective, I understand Timing to represent the connection between the Form of mindful or heedful social relations and Nurturing Conditions: the growth or nurturance of those relations to evolve in ways that support the most positive or highest and best outcomes. To read more about Li, see these authors.

Encyclopedia Britannica (2019). li. In *Encyclopedia Britannica*. https://www.britannica.com/topic/li-Chinese-philosophy

Krummel, J. W. M. (2010). Transcendent or immanent? Significance and history of li in Confucianism. *Journal of Chinese Philosophy*, 37(3), 417–437.

Shun, K.-L. (1993). Jen and Li in the "Analects". *Philosophy East and West*, 43(3), 457–479.

The Spiritual Life (n.d.). *Li in Confucianism*. In *The Spiritual Life*. Retrieved 2021, from https://slife.org/li-confucianism/

(page 161) **The Dance and the Neighborhood of the Trajectories.** To better understand and experience this dance, as described in the next sections, readers may wish to first complete the exercise in Appendix 1, the "Day Crafting Tool," over a period of several days. Keep track of which quality is more salient or pronounced on any given day. Note how these qualities change across time (either within or across a day). Over time, you may see patterns that reflect the Dance and the Neighborhood. Reading the previous chapters (from 3-Routine to 10-Interruption) may enhance this perception. This book is an invitation to cultivate an attitude of curiosity toward time outside of clock-time. Chapter 11, specifically, hypothesizes that the distinct qualities of time we experience in daily life co-occur, and continually interact with, define, support, and enhance each other. As a hypothesis, the chapter is more intellectual than would afford direct experience. Unfortunately, the more we think about time, the less we might experience it. The ideas of sister, mirror, and counterpoint are meant to serve as pointers to *experience* time more deeply or expansively (over time) if not more directly (in the moment). Further clarifications and examples are below.

- *Sister* refers to the idea that two Trajectories collaborate, complement, and influence each other in a dynamic dance that makes each more noticeable or salient. Scheduling leads to the creation of Routine and honoring Routine requires Scheduling. Pace moderates Interruption and Interruption requires Pace. The ongoing immersion into Rhythm (Entrainment) often brings about Transcendence and after experiencing Transcendence we are required to "come back to the reality" of living (synchronizing with others) in society.

- *Mirror* refers to the idea that two Trajectories are opposite to, reflect, or serve as a negative image of each other. We are less likely to fully experience Transition when our Pace is off (too fast or too slow) and, as a sort of mirror, the less paced we are, the less likely we can navigate Transition. Life's interruptions rarely occur at just the right time (Timing) and the experience of perfect Timing is also (by definition) not an Interruption, and more of a coming together (coherence).

- *Counterpoint* refers to the idea that two Trajectories co-occur and create a type of complexity or texture to our experience of time's flow. We can hold both together at the same time which leads to developing a sense of whole-time. The chapter explains Routine as the counterpoint to Rhythm; we are more likely to feel the rich vitality of life when both occur at the same time. Transcendence is the counterpoint to Schedule in the experience of "being in the world but not of the world." We embrace the scheduling required of daily life without getting attached to the outcome. As we age, and cultivate wisdom, our sense of perfect Timing is enriched during times of both fast (dense, hectic) or slow (prolonged) Pace. It is possible to experience Flow, Synchronicity, and meaning even when life is the most chaotic.

(page 165) **Function and Result.** The use of the Terms "function" and "result" for each Trajectory is based on a theory of logic called "Trialectics" which is also described in the next note. For now, just imagine that everything happening in your life—a thought, emotion, act, event, or occasion—both (1) functions to bring about (directly or indirectly) some result in the future of your life; and (2) is itself the result of some previous function. In other words, everything is both a consequence of and contributor to the changing process of your life. This is very different from the typical understanding of change embodied in the quote "one cannot step into the same river twice because it is not the same river and not the same person." In the model of Trialectics, time is not a passive stream that we enter. Instead, all moments of time function to either increase or decrease our enlightenment from, and presence to, the stream altogether.

(page 165) **Trialectics.** There are many facets to trialectics theory as developed by Oscar Ichazo (1976, 1982), and I provide key references below for any reader wishing to pursue serious study. The core element or feature of trialectics is a "material manifestation point: or MMP." This is any identifiable state, at a given time, of a system (people, groups of people, objects, plants, animals, thoughts, emotions, ideas, and so on). Any one MMP inevitably mutates into another MMP. As a system of logic, trialectics has three axioms or laws: (1) Mutation. There is a mutation from one MMP to another MMP (for example, mutation is completed when inner equilibrium has been achieved); (2) Circulation. Inside of everything there is the seed of its apparent opposite. The equilibrium between the two oppositions depends on the balanced circulation energy (meaning there are no random accidents, only the process of circulation); and (3) Attraction. The perpetual motion of all creation is because of the interchange of energy between MMPs and there is, therefore, an inherent attraction to either a higher or lower MMP (for example, higher MMPs are constrained or conformed by a smaller number of factors or elements).

Bahm, A. J. (1984, September). An overview of *Trialectics* within applications to psychology and public policy [Review of the book *Trialectics: Toward a practical logic of unity*, by R. E. Horn (Ed.)]. *Systems Research*, *(1)*3, 205. Wiley Online Library. https://onlinelibrary.wiley.com/toc/10991735/1984/1/3

Ford, J. D., & Ford, L. W. (1994). Logics of identity, contradiction, and attraction in change. *The Academy of Management Review*, *19*(4), 756–785. https://doi.org/10.2307/258744

Horn, R. (1984). *Traps of traditional logic and dialectics*. (Lexington Institute Monograph No. 84-102). Retrieved July 21, 2022 from https://citeseerx.ist.psu.edu

Ichazo, O. (1976). *The human process for enlightenment and freedom: A series of five lectures*. Arica Institute.

Ichazo, O. (1982). *Between metaphysics and protoanalysis: A theory for analyzing the human psyche*. Arica Institute Press.

Trialetics. (2009, October 29; 11:06) In P2P Foundation Wiki. https://wiki.p2pfoundation.net/index.php?title=Trialectics&action=history

Acknowledgments

This is the tale of two journeys: My own story and also the story of the Quest for Presence collection itself. Throughout the books in the Q*f*P collection, I acknowledge many teachers, friends, and family for their contribution to my story. For those personal acknowledgements, I direct readers to the books, especially chapter 7 in Book 3.

But the story of this entire Quest for Presence—the many who helped birth it, and its many phases—all began with several opportunities to share early ideas. Thanks to Dr. Steve Duck, Lawrence Erlbaum Press published *Time and Intimacy: A New Science of Personal Relationships* in 2000. These were research and academic ideas. I yearned to have more practical conversations and started searching. I was first graced with the open arms of the C. G. Jung Society of North Texas (thank you, Maureen Lumley), Unity Church of Dallas and also of Fort Worth, Magellan Healthcare, and also Brandeis University (thank you, Marci McPhee), all of whom brought me in to conduct workshops or retreats in 2000 and early 2001. These offerings had titles like "The Quest for Presence: Time & the Transformation of Work," "Time & Intimacy: Finding Serenity in a Busy World," and "Time and the Soul's Journey." Positive reactions from many participants suggested my ideas had personal relevance.

Around that time, I sent a copy of *Time and Intimacy* to the then-editor of *Spirituality & Health* magazine, Stephen Kiesling. Steve was a key to everything that came next. Through several great conversations, he helped me to reimagine my early drafts of the Quest for Presence Inventory™ (QFPI™). Thanks to Steve for publishing "Navigating in Time" in his magazine in the Winter 2002 issue. I received some calls from readers of that article. One, in particular, was a bookstore owner who encouraged me to write a book.

I also continued to offer workshops, especially at the National Wellness Institute (NWI) in Stevens Point, Wisconsin. I also delivered a train-the-trainer workshop at NWI on "Time and Spiritual Health." Then, the Center for Substance Abuse Prevention (CSAP) at the Substance Abuse and Mental Health Services Administration (SAMHSA) provided further support. Because of a CSAP research grant, between 2002 and 2004 I was able to deliver "Time and Spiritual Health" to employees at small businesses in the Dallas-Fort Worth Metroplex as part of a randomized clinical trial. I especially want to thank Dr. Deborah Galvin, who helped me navigate the grant application and implementation process.

This research study made the concepts even more real. My colleagues (from the Recovery Resource Council in Fort Worth) and I taught "Time and Spiritual Health" to employees in diverse occupations, including car wash attendants, construction workers, engineers, employees in a manufacturing plant, school bus drivers, university administrators, teachers, and physical plant staff. When results from our research with these "everyday" people showed improvements in well-being, I knew these ideas were no longer just academic concepts. Thanks to Richard Sledz, Camille Patterson, Kelly Heath, Wyndy Wiitala and the whole team who helped to implement this study. Thanks to Shawn Reynolds for getting these research findings published.

The many conversations with dozens of these early colleagues and students laid the foundation for the next phase of this work. I am grateful to them and apologize for not mentioning them all. This next phase began with writing. The first draft of *Quest for Presence* was actually a single book. I asked Sandra Wendel (of Write On, Inc.), the editor for my previous book, *Raw Coping Power: From Stress to Thriving*, to start editing. Instead, Sandy suggested I first have a group of beta readers provide feedback. She recommended approaching individuals who were familiar with my work as well as others who did not know me.

This five-book Quest for Presence collection emerged as a result of the in-depth, honest, and very insightful feedback from twenty beta readers. Sandy received the feedback anonymously but separately shared the names of reviewers. I am grateful to Sandy for her ongoing guidance (then and now) and to each and every one of the reviewers: Art Wimberly, Briane Agostinelli, Cassie Menn, Cynthia Conigliaro, Gary Loper, Heather Sittler, Heidi Postupack, Janette Helm, Jaymee Spannring, Katharine Hunter, Kimberly Gray, Laura Anne Crowder, Michele Studer, Paul Feather, Rachel Kopke, Regina Novak, Rose Whitcomb, Sadie Liller, Sandy Kogut, and Teresa Przetocki. I also appreciate input from Faith Geiger, Rachael Baker, Janet DeLong and many others who I likely have forgotten. Oh, Wait! Special thanks to Kimberly Gray for always reminding me about the quantum "popping in."

These reviewers were given a list of almost 20 questions, providing a structure for their reactions to the book. Nonetheless, I was overwhelmed with the sheer amount and detail of feedback—almost 20,000 words and over 40 pages. My colleague Shelby Pittman combed through the data searching for common words and themes. Her analysis revealed that readers were excited about the content but overwhelmed by the complexity and depth of the ideas. Importantly, they wanted to retain all the key features of the book; for example, the spiritual message, the odes, the contemplations, and my own story. Many suggested that several books and a separate workbook would make the quest easier to digest. Shelby helped me take the next step to start restructuring the book.

At the same time, I had started teaching virtual courses of "The Quest for Presence." The students who took the class also helped me further refine ideas, and several contributed their QFPI™ profiles (see Book 3). These students included Anissa Amason, Briane Agostinelli, Laura Anne Crowder, Cynthia Conigliaro, Tracey Cox, Madge Cruse, Tyler Currier, Melanie DuPon, Shahinaz Elhennawi, Kristie Ellison, Brenda Fister, Kimberly Gray, Deborah Hamlin, Susan Hansen, Mark Head, Lucy Hoblitzelle, Kathleen Klug, Lindsay Levin, Michele

Mariscal, Jennifer Markley, Jocelyne Maurice, Wesley Miller, Renee Moy, Alan Porzio, Sazha Ramos, Desiree Reynolds, Sandy Salvo, John Shelton, Stephany Sherry, Andy Siegle, John Steakley, Michele Studer, Zac Tolbert, Melanie Weinberger, Art Wimberly, and Susan Yenzer. Thank you for your presence.

Throughout this process, I have been most grateful to those contributing a "treasure story" (see Book 1 and Book 5). This includes a number of people already mentioned, as well as Kathy Carlton, Sara Christopher (Acker), Michaela Conley, and John Weaver. Thank you for reminding me that the Treasures are real and true.

Repackaging a single document into multiple volumes and a workbook was daunting. I want to thank Shelby again for her help. Also, Aldrich Chan went through manuscripts, collated all the research references, and found the proper citations for the hundreds of research notes found at the back of every book. Both Shelby's and Aldrich's responsiveness to my requests was a tremendous aid that kept me going.

The final phase of this story was guided by my editors. First, thanks to Sue Hansen of Duck Sauce Life for her exquisite detail in meaningful developmental reviews. Sue's questions, along with her own personal insights, helped me to further clarify ideas in substantive rewrites. Candace Johnson took these edited drafts and, with great thoughtfulness, helped to refine final drafts. Thank you, Sue and Candace, for your patient and thorough work.

Special thanks go to others who helped with design: Gary Rosenberg (from The Book Couple) for beautiful interior design and book covers, Jeffrey McQuirk for his ideas and patience in rendering the images of the four Radiant Forces, and my dear friend Ellen McCown for her gentle spirit and suggestions for artwork.

At the start of this acknowledgment section, I refer readers to reading the books to find acknowledgments of people in my personal life. I also have to give special thanks to my friends Art Wimberly, Spencer Seidman, and Cynthia Conigliaro—each of whom spent many hours listening to me ramble on and on about my struggles as a writer on this quest of time. Their playful feedback helped me feel so much less alone during periods of dismay and doubt. Thanks, guys!

For Book 4 (*The Trajectories*) I had a lot of help from Aldrich Chan, Cameron Marbach, and Catherine Normand in preparing for and reviewing the Appendices. Special thanks to Catherine for her assistance with research on Day Crafting, conducting interviews, tabulating data, and designing the Day Crafting profiles. Also, Aldrich Chan and Mary Anne Shepard were invaluable in preparing all research references and much gratitude for Mary Anne's attention to detail and patience with references and research notes.

Finally, I could say that none of this would have been possible without the love, support, and kindest patience of my wife, Jan. The truth is, I could have pulled off some of it . . . maybe. However, I know it would not be anything approaching the rich tapestry that I hope readers see through so many words. My own ability to see this tapestry—of the preciousness of this life and my love of life—comes from Jan. She, more than anyone I have ever known, lightens me, gives me confidence, and so makes it possible for me to listen more and listen deeply. I am so grateful for her and our many years together.

About the Author

Joel Bennett, PhD, is president of Organizational Wellness & Learning Systems (OWLS), a consulting firm that specializes in evidence-based wellness and e-learning technologies to promote organizational health and employee well-being. Dr. Bennett first delivered stress management programming in 1985, and through the efforts of over 400 resilience facilitators and coaches who have been trained in OWLS' evidence-informed curriculum as well as consulting in South Africa, Italy, and Brazil, OWLS programs have since reached over 250,000 workers across the United States and internationally. OWLS has received over $6 million in National Institutes of Health funding for workplace well-being research, and their programs have been recognized as effective by independent bodies, including the US Surgeon General's office. See https://www.hhs.gov/surgeongeneral/index.html

OWLS consults on Integral Organizational Wellness™ approaches that combine leadership, champion, team, and peer-to-peer strategies: nudging the true culture of health. Joel is the author of 50 peer-reviewed research articles and chapters and has authored or coauthored five books, including *Heart-Centered Leadership* (with Susan Steinbrecher), *Raw Coping Power: From Stress to Thriving*, *Your Best Self at Work* (with Ben Dilla), and *Well-Being Champions: A Competency-Based Guidebook*.

Dr. Bennett has served in advisory and board roles for various organizations including Magellan Health; Aetna; the National Wellness Institute; It's Time Texas, Work Healthier Advisory Committee; the Academy of Management Division on Management and Spirituality; the Global Wellness Institute; the International Foundation of

Employee Benefits Plans; and the State of Texas Primary Prevention Planning Committee (Preventing Sexual Violence). In 2022, Joel received the William B. Baun Lifetime Achievement Award from the National Wellness Institute for his leadership and service to the field of wellness.

Joel lives in North Texas with Jan, his wife of twenty-eight years, and around the corner from his wonderful son, daughter-in-law, and grandchildren, who call him "Obi." He hopes that one day, he will become a Jedi Knight or something.